The Reference Shelf®

Celebrity Culture in the United States

Edited by Terence J. Fitzgerald

Editorial Advisor Paul McCaffrey

The Reference Shelf
Volume 80 • Number 1

The H.W. Wilson Company
New York • Dublin
2008

The Reference Shelf

The books in this series contain reprints of articles, excerpts from books, addresses on current issues, and studies of social trends in the United States and other countries. There are six separately bound numbers in each volume, all of which are usually published in the same calendar year. Numbers one through five are each devoted to a single subject, providing background information and discussion from various points of view and concluding with a subject index and comprehensive bibliography that lists books, pamphlets, and abstracts of additional articles on the subject. The final number of each volume is a collection of recent speeches, and it contains a cumulative speaker index. Books in the series may be purchased individually or on subscription.

Library of Congress has cataloged this serial title as follows:

Celebrity culture in the United States / edited by Terence J. Fitzgerald ; editorial advisor Paul McCaffrey.
    p. cm.—(The reference shelf ; v. 80, no. 1)
  ISBN 978-0-8242-1078-6 (alk. paper)
  1. United States—Civilization—1970– 2. Popular culture—United States. 3. Celebrities—United States. 4. Fame—Social aspects—United States. I. Fitzgerald, Terence J.
  E169.12.C39 2008
  973.92—dc22
                    2007049591

Cover: Bouncer preventing entrance to a celebrity event, Hill Street Studios, Blend Images, Hill Street Studios/Getty Images

Visit H.W. Wilson's Web site: www.hwwilson.com

Printed in the United States of America

Contents

Preface vii

I. The Cult of Celebrity 1

Editor's Introduction 3
1) From Barnum to "Bling:" The Changing Face of Celebrity Culture.
    Amy Henderson. *The Hedgehog Review*. 5
2) Celebrity Culture. Joseph Epstein. *The Hedgehog Review* 12
3) Before Lindsay or Paris, There Was Mrs. L_fle. Jessica Grose.
    The New York Times. 26
4) Our Celebrity Madness: A Reflection of Consumerism.
    Tirdad Derakhshani. *Philadelphia Inquirer*. 29
5) Seeing by Starlight. Carlin Flora. *Psychology Today*. 33
6) Not Exactly the Stuff of Legends. John Intini. *Maclean's* 40

II. Celebrity Activism and American Politics 43

Editor's Introduction 45
1) American Politics in the Age of Celebrity. Darrell M. West.
    The Hedgehog Review. 47
2) Jesse Ventura™ and the Brave New World of Politainer Politics. Ann Conley
    and David Schultz. *Journal of American & Comparative Cultures* 54
3) Victory for Arnold. Roger Simon. *U.S. News & World Report*. 73
4) Can Oprah Boost Her 'Favorite Guy'? Eugene Robinson.
    The Washington Post 79
5) Stage Left. Ed Leibowitz. *Los Angeles Magazine* 81
6) Celebrity and Politics. Andrew Kamons. *SAIS Review* 84
7) Foreign Policy Goes Glami. Daniel W. Drezner.
    The National Interest 87

III. The Price of Fame 95

Editor's Introduction 97
1) Falling Stars. Simon Dumenco. *New York* 99
2) Why Did We Watch? The Answer Isn't Pretty. Caryn James.
    The New York Times. 104
3) The Other Side of Fame. Mary Loftus. *Psychology Today* 107
4) Falling Stars: Will Lohan Be the Next Celebrity Flame-Out?
    Katherine Monk. *The Ottawa Citizen* 118

5) Right Time, Wrong Publicity. Caryn James. *The New York Times* 121
6) Being Bad: The Career Move. Guy Trebay. *The New York Times* 124
7) What Price, Fame? Greg Sevik. *Popular Music and Society* 128
8) Screen Idols: The Tragedy of Falling Stars. Reni Celeste.
    Journal of Popular Film and Television 133

IV. The Democratization of Celebrity 151

Editor's Introduction 153
1) Open-Source Celebrity: The Wisdom of the Audience.
    Jonathon Keats. *Wired Magazine* 155
2) Mirror, Mirror On the Web. Lakshmi Chaudhry. *The Nation*. 157
3) She's Famous (and So Can You). Guy Trebay. *The New York Times* 164

Bibliography 167
Books 169
Additional Periodical Articles with Abstracts 171

Index 181

Preface

Pop star Britney Spears had a bad year in 2007. Her aunt died in January, and she spent the next several months publicly engaged in what appeared to be a nervous breakdown. She had bouts of public intoxication, was photographed after raggedly shaving off her hair, and checked in and out of drug treatment centers. Then Spears lost custody of her children to her former husband, Kevin Federline, a B-list musical performer whom she divorced in July. So when it was announced that Spears would perform her new song "Gimme More" at the 2007 MTV Video Music Awards, the appearance was touted in the media as her "comeback" and her "return to music."

Unfortunately for Spears, television and music critics—not to mention the public at large—roundly panned her performance. They noted that her dancing was not as sharp or athletic as it once had been and that her lip-synching was out of time with the recorded music and lyrics. Most damning, however, was the attention lavished by the media on her paunch. Though not obese by any reasonable standard, Spears, who wore a tight outfit that exposed her belly, no longer sported the tight abdominal muscles that were once her trademark.

Shortly after this televised appearance and critical debacle, a 19-year-old fan named Chris Crocker posted a sob-filled video defense of Spears on the Web site YouTube. Images of Crocker weeping "leave Britney alone" became viral, spreading throughout the Internet in blogs, wikis, and email. And thus a formerly unknown fan became famous in his own right, generating press coverage that even established stars would envy and fielding offers for his own television program.

Why do we care so much about the famous? And since we clearly do care, why do we revel so much in celebrity downfall? This volume attempts to explore the heart of these questions and arrive at, if not answers, at least some greater understanding of both ourselves and this strange celebrity culture we have created.

Selections in the first chapter, "The Cult of Celebrity," consider the broader aspects of American celebrity culture: its roots, its current manifestations, the difference between then and now, and how that transformation was brought about. Articles in the second chapter, "Celebrity Activism and American Politics," explore the celebritization of politics and activism. Not only have performers become presidents and governors, but lifelong politicians have become celebrities in their own right. At the same time, celebrities have emerged, for better or worse, as the public conscience of the nation, with Angelina Jolie and others outdoing the politicians in drawing attention and offering solutions to global inequities. In the process, we are forced to examine whether the commingling of government and entertainment in fact cheapens both.

Free from the glare of the spotlight, a stalled career and a marriage in decline, with or without drugs and alcohol thrown into the mix, would pose a serious challenge to even the best among us. For such celebrities as Spears, these dilemmas must be dealt with in full view of the cameras. Consequently, every misstep, every sub-par performance, every umbrella-wielding tantrum is effectively taped, aired, and deconstructed by the public. Indeed, for the famous, every disgrace is a public one. The third chapter, "The Price of Fame," features articles that examine the considerable toll that celebrity exacts from star and fan alike.

Entries in the final section, "The Democratization of Celebrity," explore the effect the Internet and reality television have had on our conception of fame. Now that everyone—even Chris Crocker, armed only with his video recorder and heartfelt empathy for Spears—truly has a shot at their 15 minutes, what does it mean to be a celebrity and is it still so special or even desirable?

To the authors and publishers of the articles collected here, I would like to extend my thanks. To Paul McCaffrey, Rich Stein, Christopher Mari and Julia Weist, I owe my gratitude for shepherding this book through the various stages of production. To my wife, Patti, I owe everything for being the very embodiment of patience, fortitude, and love.

Terence J. Fitzgerald
February 2008

I. THE CULT OF CELEBRITY

Editor's Introduction

As the cultural historian Neal Gabler has noted, Daniel J. Boorstin once "defined a celebrity as someone who is known for being well known." Boorstin, who died in 2004, lived long enough to see his statement morph from quip into prophecy. Thanks largely to an entertainment industry and its accompanying press coverage, which grants extraordinary attention to people of otherwise average gifts, we now live in a society in which Paris Hilton can be famous simply for being famous. But haven't celebrities of this sort always existed? To a degree, yes.

European social castes made their nobility into a kind of celebrity class. They were the tastemakers and trendsetters of their day. Artists have also always achieved a level of fame, formerly for creating objects deemed beautiful and now for making their lives part of the story of their art.

But celebrity has developed its own particular flavor in the United States, a country whose residents ostensibly "hold these truths to be self-evident, that all men are created equal." As Americans, we believe that even the most common of commoners can achieve greatness. Therefore, should fame be different from any other endeavor, if celebrity is a measure of greatness?

Amy Henderson starts this collection off with a bang—or a "bling"—by tracking the evolution of the American concept of fame, from its early roots up through the modern era in "From Barnum to 'Bling': The Changing Face of Celebrity Culture." In so doing, she argues that the great showman and circus impresario P. T. Barnum is the creator of our current celebrity ethos.

In the subsequent piece, "Celebrity Culture," Joseph Epstein further refines our definition of celebrity and explores the relationship between the celebrity and the public. Central to that relationship is the public's sometimes ambivalent attitude. As Epstein notes, "the worshipping of celebrities by the public tends to be thin, and not uncommonly the worship is nicely admixed with loathing."

In today's celebrity culture, gossip magazines are ubiquitous—and perhaps as integral a component of the culture as the stars themselves. Moreover, as the Internet age has evolved, Web sites have emerged as a powerful means of disseminating celebrity gossip. While it is tempting to think of these publications as merely a product of the peculiar times in which we live, their antecedents go back centuries. As Jessica Grose demonstrates in the subsequent piece, "Before Lindsay or Paris, There Was Madame L_fle," periodicals reporting on the lives and scandals of the rich and famous have a long history.

Offering a critique of our celebrity obsession, Tirdad Derakhshani, in "Our Celebrity Madness: A Reflection of Consumerism," blames the emergence of consumer culture. According to Derakshani, "celebs are nothing more—or less—than products themselves. They not only embody the ideal consumer;

they also urge us to become commodities to survive in modern society." Carla Flora, in "Seeing By Starlight," sees similar forces at work, describing celebrities as "common currency in our socially fractured world."

Will Bart Simpson be this era's most enduring celebrity? John Intini rounds out this section by asking that simple question in his brief but provocative piece, "Not Exactly the Stuff of Legends." Think about it: Bart may be a scamp, but he's also a cartoon, and thus his celebrity is unlikely to be smeared by scandal.

From Barnum to "Bling"

The Changing Face of Celebrity Culture

By Amy Henderson
The Hedgehog Review, Spring 2005

Showman P.T. Barnum set the stage for modern celebrity culture by opening the curtain on mass entertainment in the mid-nineteenth century. He dazzled in an era before technology could "broadcast" performance—before the advent of the recording, radio, and motion picture industries; before the heyday of advertising; before the mass distribution of photography in rotogravure sections of the Sunday newspapers. Yet somehow he ignored these constraints and created such popular culture events as the establishment of the American Museum in New York in 1841, the introduction of "General Tom Thumb" shortly thereafter, the orchestration of Swedish songbird Jenny Lind's celebrated 1851–1852 American tour, the organization of "The Greatest Show on Earth" (a traveling circus/menagerie/museum) in 1871, and the creation ten years later, with James Bailey, of the Barnum & Bailey Circus. His American Museum on Broadway in particular showcased Barnum's love of humbug in such wildly diverse entertainments as "industrious fleas, automatons, jugglers, ventriloquists, living statuary, tableaux, gypsies, albinos, giants, dwarfs, models of Niagara, American Indians. . . ." "It was my monomania," he said in his autobiography, "to make the Museum the town wonder and town talk." And this he did with astonishing ingenuity: "my 'puffing' was more persistent, my posters more glaring, my pictures more exaggerated, my flags more patriotic." It worked brilliantly.[1]

The bravado Barnum used to create his wondrous celebrities, illusions, and spectacles injected ballyhoo into the rarified air of America's earlier devotion to Great Men on a Pedestal. Lacking millennia of history as a nation, Americans of the Revolutionary republic fashioned a mythic national character out of military heroes and eminent statesmen who embodied the ideals of virtue, self-reliance, and achievement.

This article was originally published in *The Hedgehog Review*, vol. 7, no. 1, Spring 2005. Reprinted with permission.

[1] Quoted in Neil Harris, *Humbug: The Art of PT Barnum* (Boston: Little, Brown, 1973) 40, 53–54.

[2] See Warren Susman, "'Personality' and the Making of Twentieth Century Culture," *Culture as History: The Transformation of American Society in the Twentieth Century* (New York: Pantheon, 1984) 271–85.

By mid-twentieth century, this heroic pedestal was claimed not by politicians and generals but by sports stars and movie legends—by "personality" rather than "character."[2] This shift, reflecting the cultural changes wrought by the communications revolution of the late nineteenth and early twentieth centuries, and by the rise of immigration and urbanization between the 1890s and 1920s, says a great deal about the nation's continuing need for self-definition, and about the culture that contributed to the search for it. In his groundbreaking book *The Image*, Daniel Boorstin described this metamorphosis as one from traditional "larger-than-life" heroes known for their achievement to "celebrity-personalities" recognized for their "well-knownness" in a society enamored of "pseudo-events."[3]

By the end of the twentieth century and the beginning of the twenty-first, the changing face of fame existed squarely at eye level, lacking any pretense of pedestal altogether: postmodern pseudo-celebrity blips flooded the airwaves with "reality television" and Americans eagerly clawed their way to fame as "Apprentices" and "American Idols." Yet flash and spectacle remain crucial components of "celebrity," as exemplified today by "bling bling"—the diamond-studded, showy rapper style that has recently won approval by the Oxford English Dictionary.[4]

From Revolutionary Hero to "American Adam"

Heroes of the Revolutionary era were invoked to give the nation a sense of historical legitimacy. If, as Milton wrote, "Fame is the spur that the clear spirit doth raise,"[5] then it was a spur to industry and virtue. Above all others, George Washington stood as the great embodiment of national virtue, the symbol of the nation's essential worthiness. Heroes of this era were gentlemen, scholars, and patriots—traditional representatives of such basic social institutions as the state, the military, and the church—and their lives served as examples.

Literary historian R. W. B. Lewis has written that the heroic image contrived between 1820 and 1860 was that of an "American Adam,"[6] a figure of innocence and promise who was, as Emerson defined him, "the simple genuine self against the whole world."[7] In an age optimistic about an indigenous culture-in-the-making, the nation's novelists, poets, essayists, critics, historians, and preachers all entered into the discourse with gusto, seeking to construct not only a national narrative, but to create that epic's protagonist. The

---

[3] Daniel Boorstin, The Image: A Guide to Pseudo-Events in America (New York: Atheneum, 1971) 57.

[4] See < www.mtv.comlnewslarticlesl1471629/20030430/bg.jhtml?headlines=true>.

[5] John Milton, "Lycidas," *The New Oxford Book of English Verse, 1250–1950* (New York Oxford University Press, 1972) 294.

[6] R. W. B. Lewis, *The American Adam* (Chicago: The University of Chicago Press, 1955) 1–10.

[7] Lewis vi.

Adamic hero, freed from the past and boasting such intrinsic characteristics as self-reliance, virtue, and achievement, would become the central figure in the quest for national legitimacy. James Fennimore Cooper notably invented Natty Bumppo, the selfless, stoic, and enduring hero who has been described as "timeless and sturdily innocent," and "the essential American soul."[8]

The conceptual distance separating Revolutionary heroes from their mid-nineteenth century counterparts was indiscernible. Core values remained, as Emerson demonstrated in extolling the democratic "central man" who was the source of all national vitality.[9] Elsewhere he depicted history in terms of "representative men"[10]—a sensibility that would not have been alien to earlier generations. It was only in the later nineteenth century, with the revolution in communications technology, the rise of a substantial monied class, and the emergence of a mass urban landscape, that the nation's heroic vision evolved into a new stage.

The Communications Revolution

The look of fame itself changed with what Daniel Boorstin has termed the "Graphic Revolution," the advent both of mechanical means of image reproduction and of the facility for mass diffusion of information. The emergence of photography and chromolithography in post–Civil War America led to an explosive growth in such mass publications as newspapers and magazines. The first truly mass urban newspapers appeared in the 1880s and were made possible by high-speed presses, the linotype, halftone photo reproduction, and the emergence of news-gathering organizations like the Associated Press—all of which made the daily newspaper the central supplier of national and world news. The circulation of daily papers increased 400% between 1870 and 1900, partly as a result of technology and partly because of rising literacy rates and the growth of leisure time.[11]

The new magazines like *McClure's* that appeared in the 1890s also played a role in enlarging the popular imagination, thereby redefining ideals of fame, success, and national heroism. At century's end America's most-admired figures were hero-inventors like Thomas Edison, Henry Ford, and Italian émigré Guglialmo Marconi. Financial wizards such as J. P. Morgan, Andrew Carnegie, and John D. Rockefeller (either "captains of industry" or "robber barons," depending on your perspective) were idolized for fighting their way to Darwinian peaks of capitalist success/excess.

---

[8] Lewis 3–4.

[9] E. O. Matthiessen, *American Renaissance: Art and Expression in the Age of Emerson and Whitman* (New York: Oxford University Press, 1941)

[10] Ralph Waldo Emerson, *Representative Men* (London: Dent, 1901).

[11] Boorstin 57 and passim.

Immigration, the Melting Pot, and the New Urban Landscape

But then the look of fame shifted again, turning full face in the twentieth century. The new era's heroes were activists who muckraked the old: figures such as Theodore Roosevelt rode the crest of change and attempted to change the cultural context, busting trusts and monopolies to leaven the social landscape while elevating the United States to a heightened role in the international order. Journalist William Allen White wrote in his autobiography that "that decade which climaxed in 1912 was a time of tremendous change in our national life. . . . The American people were melting down old heroes and recasting the mold in which heroes were made."[12] This sentiment was echoed in Israel Zangwill's hit 1908 play, *The Melting Pot*, which depicted America as "God's Crucible, the great Melting-Pot, where all the races of Europe are melting and reforming."[13]

Between 1890 and the 1920s, twenty-three million new immigrants arrived on America's shores. The "genteel tradition" that had been the core of America's mainstream culture dissolved in this new urban stew, replaced by a vernacular culture that rose from the streets. The sounds and rhythms of this new culture were captured best by the rising entertainment industry: indeed, the most successful performing art of the time was vaudeville—literally, the "voice of the city." Magazines and newspapers trumpeted the phenomenon: one article in the late 1880s proclaimed: "It is remarkable how much attention the stage and things pertaining to it are receiving nowadays from the magazines." Twenty years ago, it was argued, such a thing would have been thought "indecorous," but drama "now makes such a large part of the life of society that it has become a topic of conversation among all classes."[14] No longer "indecorous," entertainment had become decidedly mainstream. Advertising the entertainment at his Opera House, vaudeville impresario Tony Pastor assured his patrons that his "Temple of Amusement" was in fact "The Great Family Resort of the City where heads of families can bring their Ladies and children." Good order was observed at all times, and there were strict rules against "peanut feasts and boisterous applause."[15]

In the 1920s, cultural critic Gilbert Seldes rhapsodized about the "lively arts"—including jazz, musicals, radio, and motion pictures— that were creating an "American" culture to match the country's new immigrant, urban personality. Broadway flourished, and one of its leading lights, George Gershwin, composed staccato-paced, syncopated rhythms that helped define the Jazz Age. It was a highly

---

[12] William Allen White, *The Autobiography of William Allen White* (New York: Macmillan, 1946) 428.

[13] Israel Zangwill, *The Melting Pot: A Drama in Four Parts* (New York.-Macmillan, 1908) 33.

[14] See "Theatre Scrapbooks, 1877–1903," vol. 3: article "Concerning the Stage," c. 1890, University of Virginia Manuscript Room.

[15] Amy Henderson and Dwight Bowers, *Red, Hot & Blue: A Smithsonian Salute to American Musicals* (Washington: Smithsonian Press, 1996) 10.

visual culture as well. In 1915, poet Vachel Lindsay wrote of the "increasingly hieroglyphic civilization" that characterized the rise of American modernism.[16] Times Square and Broadway's "Great White Way" were blanketed by extravagant displays of signs and blinking lights that bespoke what one chronicler called "a staggering machine of desire."[17] And who would emerge as the dominant symbol of modernism? Media-generated "celebrities" whose popularity was achieved via the mass media of radio, recordings, and motion pictures.

The Emergence of "Celebrity"

"Celebrity" became a measure of success in a culture preoccupied with personality. In biographical articles that appeared in *The Saturday Evening Post* and *Colliers* from 1901 to 1914, 74% of the subjects came from traditional fields such as politics, business, and the professions. But from 1922 until 1941, over half came from the world of entertainment: sports figures like Babe Ruth and Joe Louis, movie stars like Gloria Swanson and Charlie Chaplin.[18] The machinery providing mass information in the broadcasting, recording, and film industries created a ravenous market for celebrity culture: media-generated fame became a raging—and lasting—popular vogue.

Celebrities were able to broach all cultural levels. Between 1906 and 1920, Metropolitan Opera stars Enrico Caruso and Geraldine Farrar were the company's most successful box office draws. But their popularity transcended Golden Horseshoe audiences, as newspapers and periodicals fanned their fame and enormously lucrative sales placed their recordings in millions of households. Farrar even went to Hollywood in 1915 to star in such Cecil B. DeMille "spectaculars" as a silent version of *Carmen*, and *Joan the Woman*.

Motion pictures helped make celebrity culture a national pastime. Though early "flickers" and back-alley lantern shows were considered slightly sleazy, by the teens movies had achieved a middle-class respectability. Whereas early film actors remained anonymous, the public began to lobby for its box office favorites, and by 1915 there were such authentic "stars" as Charlie Chaplin, Mary Pickford, and Douglas Fairbanks.

In the twenties and increasingly with the advent of "talkies," movie celebrities came to represent the visual quintessence of glamour. Stars such as Marlene Dietrich, Joan Crawford, and Greta Garbo glowed with glamour—draped in diamonds and wrapped in silk, feathers, and fur, they were silvered beings worshipped by

---

[16] Vachel Lindsay, quoted in Susman xxvi.

[17] Quoted in William Leach, "Brokers and the New Corporate Industrial Order," *Inventing Times Square: Commerce and Culture at the Crossroads of the World*, ed. William R. Taylor (New York: Russell Sage Foundation, 1991) 99.

[18] Leo Lowenthal, *Literature, Popular Culture, and Society* (Englewood Cliffs: Prentice-Hall, 1961) 110–14.

what Norma Desmond in *Sunset Boulevard* would call "all those lit-tle people out there in the dark." By the late 1920s, each of the major studios had its own portrait gallery where studio photogra-phers created a style of portraiture that crystallized stardom. Armed with banks of lights, large format cameras, retouching pen-cils, but above all an aesthetic of glamour, they coaxed celluloid icons from mere flesh and blood.

In the Depression, the American public responded exuberantly to this larger-than-life celebrity. Fan magazines like *Photoplay* docu-mented star activities (or at least the studio's version) with gushing stories about stars "at home"—what they ate, what their beauty secrets were, what pets they pampered, what cars they drove, what they wore. Fabric stores sold patterns of favorite star dresses for at-home seamstresses to copy, as in the phenomenally successful dress Adrian designed for Joan Crawford in the 1932 movie *Letty Lynton*: in addition to countless Butterick patterns of this puffed-sleeve, cinched waist dress, over 500,000 copies of the dress were sold at Macy's alone![19] And how many women peroxided their hair à la Har-low, or later adopted Veronica Lake's "peekaboo" look?

The Advent of the Broadcast Industry

The advent of the broadcast industry in the 1920s marked another quantum leap in the cultivation of celebrity culture. While the film industry expanded in response to popular demand and the recording industry enjoyed a 600% sales increase between 1933 and 1938, radio became an everyday medium for mass culture. A household presence, an average radio in 1934 cost about $35, and 60% of all American households had at least one set.[20] And unlike records, radio was live: entertainment and information were available at the touch of the dial. Radio stars like Rudy Vallee, Jack Benny, Molly Goldberg, and Burns and Allen became virtual members of the fam-ily.

While entertainers dominated the airwaves, broadcasting created political celebrities as well. Franklin D. Roosevelt's election in 1932 coincided with radio's own coming of age, and he proved himself a master of this ubiquitous medium. Of FDR's "fireside chats," a New York newspaper reporter noted that, "while painting a verbal pic-ture expansive enough for a museum mural, Roosevelt reduced it to the proportions of a miniature hanging cozily on the wall of a living room."[21]

Others thought that radio would "purify politics." In 1928 Missis-sippi Senator Pat Harrison waxed that "the venomous darts (of the demagogue) cannot pass through the air"—an optimism soon dis-

---

[19] Howard Gutner, *Gowns by Adrian: The MGM Years 1928–1941* (New York: Abrams, 2001) 120.

[20] Cited in Amy Henderson, *On the Air: Pioneers of American Broadcasting* (Washington: Smithsonian Press, 1988) 22.

[21] Henderson, *On the Air*, 186.

pelled by the likes of Father Charles E. Coughlin, who won an enormous following in the 1930s by using radio to spread an increasingly
proto-fascist brand of politics.[22]

In its early decades, television vastly expanded broadcasting's
impact: the Army-McCarthy hearings, political conventions, and the
1960 Kennedy-Nixon debates established television's center stage
significance. Radio and television—even before the advent of cable
and 24/7 coverage—had become the essential means for communi-
cating political messages.

Contemporary Celebrity Culture

Those two factors—cable and 24/7 coverage—have transformed
contemporary celebrity culture. Whereas earlier celebrity was
broadly encompassing, encouraging general agreement at least in
mainstream culture, contemporary celebrity is carefully niched,
appealing not to wide swaths of society but to minute slivers. The
consequences of this narrow-casting range from a fundamentally
decentralized and trivialized culture of special interests to a society
that is polarized on such national issues as red/blue politics and gay
rights.

Another consequence of contemporary celebrity harkens back to
the ballyhoo of Barnum and his gleeful use of illusion and spectacle
to make humbug out of "reality." Boorstin found contemporary
media-generated celebrity dependent on "pseudo-events," and
French sociologist Jean Baudrillard has argued that a culture dominated by "simulacra" is not capable of discriminating between reality and the illusion or simulation of reality. The popularity of reality
television where participants—regardless of talent—are convinced
of their own celebrity clearly continues the tradition of humbug.
Instead of Major Bowes' gong, Simon tells them they are pitiful, or
the Donald declaims, "You're fired!" Do they believe in their fame
fallibility? Of course not.

Contemporary celebrity is eons from an age when heroes were
placed on pedestals: today, rather than reverential and upward-
looking, the perspective is eye-to-eye—an immense psychological
sea change. The disposable culture spawned by today's 24/7 media
seems relentless, devouring anything in its path while leaving its
audience permanently unsated. But the show will always go on:
bling bling!

---

[22] Henderson, *On the Air*, 188.

Celebrity Culture

BY JOSEPH EPSTEIN
THE HEDGEHOG REVIEW, SPRING 2005

Perhaps the best way to begin is briefly to examine the words "celebrity" and "culture," each on its own first, and then to see if the two slide together and click, making a decent fit.

In *The Nature of Culture*, his book of 1952, the anthropologist Alfred Kroeber offered more than one hundred ways in which the word "culture" was then used. By now, more than fifty years later, the number of its uses has doubtless more than doubled. "The Culture of . . . ," like "The Death of . . . " and "The Politics of . . . ," has become a fairly common prefix for book and article titles, usually ones of extravagant intellectual pretensions, from Christopher Lasch's *The Culture of Narcissism* on down.[1]

The word "culture" no longer, I suspect, stands in most people's minds for that whole congeries of institutions, relations, kinship patterns, linguistic forms, and the rest for which the early anthropologists meant it to stand. Words, unlike good soldiers under the Austro-Hapsburg empire, don't remain in place and take commands. Instead they insist on being unruly, and slither and slide around, picking up all sorts of slippery and even goofy meanings. An icon, as we shall see, doesn't stay a small picture of a religious personage but usually turns out nowadays to be someone with spectacular grosses. "The language," as Flaubert once protested in his attempt to tell his mistress Louise Colet how much he loved her, "is inept."

Today, when we glibly refer to "the corporate culture," "the culture of poverty," "the culture of the intelligence community"—and "community" has, of course, become another of those hopelessly baggy-pants words so that one hears talk even of "the homeless community"—what I think we mean by "culture" is the general emotional atmosphere and institutional ethos surrounding the word to which "culture" is attached. In this newer context, culture also implies that the general atmosphere pervading any discrete aspect of life determines a great deal else. Thus, corporate culture is thought to breed self-protectiveness practiced at the Machiavellian level; the culture of poverty, hopelessness and despair; the culture of the intelligence community, viperishness; the culture of journalism, a

This article was originally published in *The Hedgehog Review*, vol. 7, no. 1, Spring 2005. Reprinted with permission.

[1] Alfred Kroeber, *The Nature of Culture* (Chicago: The University of Chicago Press, 1952); Christopher Lasch, *The Culture of Narcissism: American Life in an Age of Diminishing Expectations*, rev. ed. (New York: Norton, 1991).

short attention span; and so on. Or, to cite an everyday example I recently heard, "the culture of NASA has to be changed." The comedian Flip Wilson, after saying something outrageous, would use the refrain line, "the devil made me do it." So today, when spotting dreary or otherwise wretched behavior, people often say, "the culture made them do it."

As for "celebrity," the standard definition is no longer the dictionary one but rather closer to the one that Daniel Boorstin gave in his book *The Image: Or, What Happened to the American Dream*: "The celebrity," Boorstin wrote, "is a person who is well-known for his well-knownness," which is improved in its frequently misquoted form as "a celebrity is someone famous for being famous."[2] (The other well-known quotation on this subject is Andy Warhol's "in the future everyone will be world-famous for fifteen minutes," which is also frequently misquoted as "everyone will have his fifteen minutes of fame.")

To be sure, there are people well-known merely for being well-known: What the hell do a couple named Sid and Mercedes Bass do, except appear in bold-face in *The New York Times* "Sunday Styles" section and other such venues (as we now say) of equally shimmering insignificance, often standing next to Ahmet and Mica Ertegun, also wellknown for being well-known? Many moons ago, journalists used to refer to royalty as "face cards"; today celebrities are perhaps best thought of as bold-faces, for as such do their names often appear in the press.

But to say that a celebrity is someone well-known for being well-known, though clever enough, is not, I think, sufficient. The first semantic problem our fetching subject presents is the need for a distinction between celebrity and fame—a distinction more easily required than produced.

I suspect everyone has, or would rather make, his own. The distinction I prefer derives not from Aristotle, who didn't have to trouble with celebrities, but from the baseball player Ted Williams, of whom a sportswriter once said that he, Williams, wished to be famous but not a celebrity. What Ted Williams wanted to be famous for was his hitting. He wanted everyone who cared about baseball to know that he was—as he believed and may well have been—the greatest hitter who ever lived; what he didn't want to do was to take on any of the effort off the baseball field involved in making this known. As an active player, Williams gave no interviews, signed no baseballs or photographs, chose not to be obliging in any way to journalists or fans. A rebarbative character, not to mention a slightly menacing s.o.b., Williams, if you had asked him, would have said that it was enough that he was the last man to hit .400; he did it on the field, and therefore didn't have to sell himself off the field.

---

[2] Daniel Boorstin, *The Image: Or, What Happened to the American Dream* (New York: Atheneum, 1962).

As for his duty to his fans, he would have said, in the spirit of the alleged deathbed words of W. C. Fields, "on second thought, screw 'em," though in Williams's case, it would probably have been on first thought.

Whether Ted Williams was right or wrong to feel as he did is of less interest than the distinction his example provides, which suggests that fame is something one earns—through talent or achievement of one kind or another—while celebrity is something one cultivates or, possibly, has thrust upon one. The two are not, of course, entirely exclusive. One can be immensely talented and full of achievement and yet wish to broadcast one's fame further through the careful cultivation of celebrity; and one can have the thinnest of achievements and be less than immensely talented and yet be made to seem so through the mechanics and dynamics of celebrity-creation, in our day a whole mini- (or maybe not so mini-) industry of its own.

Or, yet again, one can become a celebrity with scarcely any pretense to talent or achievement whatsoever. Much modern celebrity seems the result of careful promotion or great good luck or something besides talent and achievement: Mr. Donald Trump, Ms. Paris Hilton, Mr. Regis Philbin, take a bow. The ultimate celebrity of our time may have been John F. Kennedy, Jr., notable only for being his parents' very handsome son—both his birth and good looks in any case beyond his control—and, alas, known for nothing else whatsoever now, except for the sad, dying-young, Adonis end to his life.

Fame, then, as I prefer to think of it, is based on true achievement; celebrity on broadcasting that achievement, or inventing something that, if not scrutinized too closely, might pass for achievement. Celebrity suggests ephemerality, while fame has a shot at reaching the happy shores of posterity.

There are, of course, divisions of fame to consider. Oliver Goldsmith, in his poem "The Deserted Villages," refers to "good fame," which implies that there is also a bad or false fame. Bad fame is sometimes thought to be fame in the present, or fame on earth, while good fame is that bestowed by posterity—those happy shores again. (Which doesn't eliminate the desire of most of us, at least nowadays, to have our fame here and hereafter, too.) Not false but wretched fame is covered by the word "infamy"—"Infamy, infamy, infamy," remarked the English wit Frank Muir, who had an attractive lisp, "they all have it in for me"—while the lower, or pejorative, order of celebrity is covered by the word "notoriety," also frequently misused to mean notable.

We know from Leo Braudy's magnificent book on the history of fame, *The Frenzy of Renown*, that the means of broadcasting fame have changed over the centuries: from having one's head engraved on coins, to purchasing statuary of oneself, to (for the really high rollers—Alexander the Great, the Caesar boys) naming cities or even months after oneself, to commissioning painted portraits, to writing books or having books written about one, and so on into our day of the publicity or press agent, the media blitz, and the public relations expert. One of the most successful of public-relations experts, Ben Sonnenberg, Sr., used to say that he saw it as his job to construct very high pedestals for very small men.

Which leads one to a very proper suspicion of celebrity. As George Orwell said about saints, so it seems to me sensible to say about celebrities: they should all be judged guilty until proven innocent. Guilty of what, precisely? I'd say of fraudulence (however minor); of inflating their brilliance, accomplishments, worth; of passing themselves off as something they aren't, or at least are not quite. If fraudulence is the crime, publicity is the means by which the caper has been brought off.

Celebrity, then, does indeed exist, but is the current heightened interest in the celebrated sufficient to form a culture—a culture of a kind worthy of study? Alfred Kroeber defines culture, in part, as embodying "values which may be formulated (overtly as mores) or felt (implicitly as in folkways) by the society carrying the culture, and which it is part of the business of the anthropologist to characterize and define."[3] What are the values of celebrity culture? They are the values, largely, of publicity. Did they spell one's name right? What was the size and composition of the audience? Did you check the receipts? Was the timing right? Publicity is concerned solely with effects and does not investigate causes or intrinsic value too closely. For example, a review of a book of mine called *Snobbery: The American Version* received what I thought was a muddled and too greatly mixed review in *The New York Times Book Review*. I remarked on my disappointment to the publicity man at my publisher's, who promptly told me not to worry: it was a full-page review, on page 11, right-hand side. That, he said, "is very good real estate," which was quite as important, perhaps more important, than the reviewer's actual words and final judgment. Better to be confusedly attacked on page 11, in other words, than extravagantly praised on page 27, left-hand side. Real estate, man, it's the name of the game.

We must have new names, Marcel Proust presciently noted—in fashion, in medicine, in art, there must always be new names. It's a very smart remark, and the fields Proust chose seem smart, too, at least for his time. (Now there must also be new names among movie stars and athletes and politicians.) Implicit in Proust's remark is the notion that if the names don't really exist, if the quality isn't there to sustain them, it doesn't matter; new names we shall have in any case. And every society somehow, more or less implicitly, contrives to supply them. I happen to think that we haven't had a major poet writing in English since perhaps the death of W. H. Auden, or, to lower the bar a little, Philip Larkin. But new names are put forth

---

[3] Alfred Kroeber, abstract of "Culture, Events, and Individuals," manuscript "not for publication," Supper-Conference for Anthropologists, Viking fund.

nevertheless—high among them has been that of Seamus Heaney—because, after all, what kind of a time could we be living in if we didn't have a major poet? And besides there are all those prizes that,

> Writers are supposed to be aristocrats of the spirit, not promoters, hustlers, salesmen for their own work.

year after year, must be given out, even if so many of the recipients don't seem quite worthy of them.

Considered as a culture, celebrity does have its institutions. We now have an elaborate celebrity-creating machinery well in place—all those short-attention-span television shows (*Entertainment Weekly, Hollywood Access [Excess?], Lifestyles of the Rich and Famous*); all those magazines (beginning with *People* and far from ending with *The National Enquirer*). We have high-priced celebrity-mongers—Barbara Walters, Diane Sawyer, Jay Leno, David Letterman, Oprah—who not only live off others' celebrity but also through their publicity-making power, confer it and have in time become very considerable celebrities each in his or her own right.

Without the taste for celebrity, they would have to close down whole sections of *The New York Times* and *The Washington Post* and the "Style" sections of every other newspaper in the country. Then there is the celebrity—usually movie star—magazine profile (in *Vanity Fair, Esquire, Gentlemen's Quarterly*; these are nowadays usually orchestrated by a press agent, with all touchy questions declared out-of-bounds) and the television talk show interview with a star, which is beyond parody. Well, *almost* beyond: Martin Short in his brilliant impersonation as talk-show host Jimmy Glick remarks to actor Kiefer Sutherland: "You're Canadian, aren't you? What's that all about?"

Despite all this, we still seem never to have enough celebrities, so we drag in so-called "It Girls" (Paris Hilton, Cindy Crawford, other supermodels), tired television hacks (Regis Philbin, Ed McMahon), back-achingly boring yet somehow sacrosanct news anchors (Walter Cronkite, Tom Brokaw). Toss in what I think of as the lower-class punditi, who await calls from various television news and chat shows to demonstrate their locked-in political views and meager expertise on network and cable stations alike: Pat Buchanan, Eleanor Clift, Mark Shields, Robert Novak, Michael Beschloss, and the rest. Ah, if only Lenny Bruce were alive today, he could do a scorchingly cruel bit about Dr. Joyce Brothers sitting by the phone wondering why Jerry Springer never calls.

Many of our current-day celebrities float upon "hype," which is really a publicist's gas used to pump up and set floating something that doesn't quite exist. Hype has also given us a new breakdown, or hierarchical categorization, of celebrities. Until twenty-five or so years ago great celebrities were called "stars," a term first used in the movies and entertainment and then taken up by sports, politics, and other fields. Stars proving a bit drab, "superstars" were called into play, this term beginning in sports but fairly quickly branching outward. Apparently too many superstars were about, so the trope was switched from astronomy to religion, and we now have "icons." All this takes Proust's original observation a step further: the need for new names to call the new names.

This new ranking—stars, superstars, icons—helps us believe that we live in interesting times. One of the things celebrities do for us is suggest that in their lives they are fulfilling our fantasies. Modern celebrities, along with their fame, tend to be wealthy or, if not themselves beautiful, able to acquire beautiful lovers. "So long as man remains free," Dostoyevsky writes in the Grand Inquisitor section of *The Brothers Karamazov*, "he strives for nothing so incessantly and painfully as to find someone to worship."[4] Are contemporary celebrities the best thing on offer as living gods for us to worship? If so, this is not good news.

But the worshipping of celebrities by the public tends to be thin, and not uncommonly the worship is nicely admixed with loathing. We also, after all, at least partially, like to see celebrities as frail. Cary Grant once warned the then-young director Peter Bogdanovich, who was at the time living with Cybil Sheppard: "Will you stop telling people you're happy? Will you stop telling them you're in love?" When Bogdanovic asked why, Cary Grant answered, "Because they're not happy and they're not in love. . . . Let me tell you something, Peter, people do not like beautiful people."[5]

Grant's assertion is borne out by our grocery press, *The National Enquirer*, *The Star*, *The Globe*, and other variants of the English gutter press. All these tabloids could as easily travel under the generic title of *The National Schadenfreude*, for more than half the stories they contain come under the category of "See How the Mighty Have Fallen": Oh, my, I see where that bright young television sit-com star, on a drug binge again, had to be taken to a hospital in an ambulance! To think that the handsome movie star has been cheating on his wife all these years—snakes loose in the Garden of Eden, evidently! Did you note that the powerful senator's drinking has caused him to embarrass himself on any number of public occasions? Dear me, the outwardly successful Hollywood couple turn out to have had a child who died of anorexia! Who'd've thought?

How pleasing to learn that our own simpler, less moneyed and glamour-laden lives are, in the end, much to be preferred to those of these frightfully beautiful and powerful people, whose vast publicity has diverted us for so long and whose fall proves even more divert-

---

[4] Fyodor Dostoevsky, *The Brothers Karamazov*, trans. Constance Garnett (New York: Norton, 1976) 234.

[5] See Gavin Esler, "Peter Bogdanovich—Hollywood Survivor," interview, BBC News, <http://news.bbc. co.uk/1/hi/programmes/hardtalk/4149215.stm>.

[6] Thomas McGuane, "Ice," *The New Yorker* (24 January 2005): 78–83.

ing now. In a recent short story called "Ice" in *The New Yorker*, Thomas McGuane writes: "As would become a lifelong habit for most of us, we longed to witness spectacular achievement and mortifying failure. Neither of these things, we were discreetly certain, would ever come to us; we would instead be granted the frictionless lives of the meek."[6]

Along with trying to avoid falling victim to schadenfreude, celebrities have to be careful to regulate the amount of publicity they allow to cluster around them. And not celebrities alone. Edith Wharton, having published too many stories and essays in a great single rush in various magazines during a concentrated period, feared, as she put it, the danger of becoming "a magazine bore." Celebrities, in the same way, are in danger of becoming publicity bores, though few among them seem to sense it. Because of improperly rationed publicity, along with a substantial helping of self-importance, the comedian Bill Cosby will never again be funny. The actress Elizabeth McGovern said of Sean Penn that he "is brilliant, *brilliant* at being the kind of reluctant celebrity."[7] At the level of high culture, Saul Bellow used to work this bit quite well on the literary front, making every interview (and there have been hundreds of them) feel as if it were given only with the greatest reluctance, if not under actual duress. Others are brilliant at regulating their publicity. Johnny Carson was very clever about carefully husbanding his celebrity, choosing not to come out of retirement, until exactly the right time or when the perfect occasion presented itself. It apparently never did. Given the universally generous obituary tributes he received, dying now looks, for him, to have been an excellent career move.

Close readers will have noticed above that I referred to "the actress Elizabeth McGovern" and felt no need to write anything before or after the name Sean Penn. True celebrities need nothing said of them in apposition, fore or aft. The greatest celebrities are those who don't even require their full names mentioned: Marilyn, Winston, Johnny, Liz, Liza, Oprah, Michael (could be Jordan or Jackson—context usually clears this up fairly quickly), Kobe, Martha (Stewart, not Washington), Britney, Shaq, JLo, Frank (Sinatra, not Perdue), O. J., and, with the quickest recognition and shortest name of all—trumpets here, please—W.

One has the impression that being a celebrity was easier at any earlier time than it is now, when celebrity-creating institutions, from paparazzi to gutter-press exposé to television talk-shows, weren't as intense, as full-court press, as they are today. In the *Times Literary Supplement*, a reviewer of a biography of Margot Fonteyn noted that she "was a star from a more respectful age of celebrity, when keeping one's distance was still possible."[8] My own

---

[7] Manohla Dargis, "The Authorized Sean Penn," *The New York Times Book Review* (23 January 2005): 7.

[8] Zoë Anderson, "She Was Groomed to Conquer," *Times Literary Supplement* (21 January 2005): 18.

candidate for the perfect celebrity in the twentieth century would be Noel Coward, a man in whom talent combined with elegance to give off the glow of glamour—and also a man who would have known how to fend off anyone wishing to investigate his private life. Today, instead of elegant celebrities, we have celebrity criminal trials: Michael Jackson, Kobe Bryant, Martha Stewart, Robert Blake, Winona Ryder, and O. J. Simpson. Schadenfreude rides again.

A received opinion about America in the early twenty-first century is that our culture values only two things: money and celebrity. Whether or not this is true, vast quantities of money, we know, will buy celebrity. The very rich—John D. Rockefeller, et alia— used to pay press agents to keep their names out of the papers. But today one of the things money buys is a place at the table beside the celebrated, with the celebrities generally delighted to accommodate, there to share some of the glaring light. An example is Mort Zuckerman, who made an early fortune in real estate, has bought magazines and newspapers, and is now himself among the punditi, offering his largely unexceptional political views on *The McLaughlin Group* and other television chat shows. Whether or not celebrity in and of itself constitutes a culture, it has certainly penetrated and permeated much of American (and I suspect English) culture generally.

> A received opinion about America in the early twenty-first century is that our culture values only two things: money and celebrity.

Such has been the reach of celebrity culture in our time that it has long ago entered into academic life. The celebrity professor has been on the scene for more than three decades. As long ago as 1962, in fact, I recall hearing that Oscar Cargill, in those days a name of some note in the English Department of NYU, had tried to lure the then-young Robert Brustein, a professor of theater and the drama critic for *The New Republic*, away from Columbia. Cargill had said to Brustein, "I'm not going to bullshit you, Bob, we're looking for a star, and you're it." Brustein apparently wasn't looking to be placed in a new constellation, and remained at Columbia, at least for a while longer, before moving on to Yale and thence to Harvard.

The academic star, who is really the academic celebrity, is now a fairly common figure in what the world, that ignorant ninny, reckons the Great American Universities. Richard Rorty is such a star; so is Henry Louis Gates, Jr. (who as "Skip" even has some nickname celebrity recognition); and, at a slightly lower level, there are Marjorie Garber, Eve Sedgwick, Stanley Fish, and perhaps now Stephen Greenblatt. Stanley Fish doesn't even seem to mind that much of his celebrity is owed to his being portrayed in novels by David Lodge as an indefatigable, grubby little operator (though Lodge claims to admire Fish's happy vulgarity). Professors Garber and Sedgwick seem to have acquired their celebrity through the *outreisme* of the topics they've chosen to write about.

By measure of pure celebrity, Cornel West is, at the moment, the star of all academic stars, a man called by *Newsweek* "an eloquent prophet with attitude." (A bit difficult, I think, to imagine *Newsweek* or any other publication writing something similar of Lionel Trilling, Walter Jackson Bate, Marjorie Hope Nicolson, or John Hope Franklin.) He records rap CDs and appears at benefits with movie stars and famous athletes. When the president of Harvard spoke critically to West about his work not constituting serious scholarship (as if that had anything to do with anything), it made front-page news in *The New York Times*. West left, as we now know, and was instantly welcomed by Princeton. If West had been a few kilowatts more the celebrity than he is, he might have been able to arrange for the firing of the president of the university, the way certain superstars in the National Basketball Association—Magic Johnson, Isaiah Thomas, Larry Bird, Michael Jordan—were able, if it pleased them, to have their coaches fired.

Pure scholarship, sheer power of intelligence glowing brightly in the classroom, is distinctly not what makes an academic celebrity or, if you prefer, superstar. What makes an academic celebrity, for the most part, is exposure, which is ultimately publicity. Exposure can mean appearing in the right extra-academic magazines or journals: *The New York Review of Books*, *The London Review of Books*, *The Atlantic Monthly*; *Harper's* and *The New Republic* possibly qualify, as do occasional cameo performances on the op-ed pages of *The New York Times* or *The Washington Post*. Having one's face pop up on the right television and radio programs—PBS and NPR certainly, and enough of the right kinds of appearances on C-Span— does not hurt. A commercially successful, much discussed book represents good exposure. So does strong public alignment with the correct political causes.

Harvey Mansfield, the neo-conservative political philosopher at Harvard, is a secondary academic celebrity of sorts, but not much in demand; Shelby Steele, a black professor of English who has been critical of various aspects of African-American politics, was always overlooked during the days when universities knocked themselves out to get black professors. Both men have been judged politically incorrect. The "renowned feminist" (in the words of princeton-info.com) Elaine Showalter wrote television reviews for *People*, but it didn't help: a bit too vulgar, I suspect. Nor did the fact (also learned from princetoninfo.com) that she has been called "Camille Paglia with balls," which is itself a thought one doesn't wish to contemplate overlong. The underlying and over-arching point is, to become an academic celebrity you have to promote yourself outside the academy, but in careful and subtle ways.

One might once have assumed that the culture of celebrity was chiefly about show business and the outer edges of the arts, occasionally touching on the academy (there cannot be more than twenty or so academic superstars). But it has also much altered intellectual life generally. The past ten years or so have seen the advent of the "public intellectual." I have always felt uncomfortable with that adjective "public," which, when first I saw it, I thought drained away much of the traditional meaning of intellectual. The root sense of an intellectual, I believe, is someone who is excited by and lives off and in ideas. An intellectual has traditionally been a person unaffiliated, which is to say someone unbeholden to anything but the power of his or her ideas. Intellectuals used to freelance, until fifty or so years ago, when jobs in the universities and in journalism began to open up to some among them. (Philip Rahv, the editor of *Partisan Review*, and Irving Howe, the editor of *Dissent*, broke the barrier when, without doctorates, they were accepted into the English Department at Brandeis University.) *Time* magazine used to be a safe if usually unhappy harbor for intellectuals with alimony problems or a taste for the expensive life.

Far from being devoted to ideas for their own sake, the intellectual equivalent of art for art's sake—and let us not pause to ask what art's sake is—the so-called public intellectual is usually someone who comments on what is in the news, in the hope of affecting policy, or events, or opinion in line with his own political position, or orientation. He isn't necessarily an intellectual at all, but merely someone who has read a few books, mastered a style, a jargon, and a maven's tone, and has a clearly demarcated political line.

But even when the public intellectual isn't purely tied to the news, or isn't thoroughly political, what he or she really is, or ought to be called, is a "publicity intellectual." In Richard A. Posner's interesting book, *Public Intellectuals*, intellectuals are ranked by the number of media mentions they or their work have garnered, which, if I am correct about publicity being at the heart of the enterprise of the public intellectual, may be crude but is not foolish.[9] Not knowledge, it turns out, but publicity is power.

The most celebrated intellectuals of our day have been those most skillful at gaining publicity for their writing and their pronouncements. Take, as a case very much in point, Susan Sontag. When Susan Sontag died at the end of last year, her obituary was front page news in *The New York Times*, and on the inside of the paper, it ran to a full page with five photographs, most of them carefully posed—a variety, it does not seem unfair to call it, of intellectual cheesecake. Will the current prime ministers of England or France receive equal space or pictorial coverage? Unlikely, I think. Why did Ms. Sontag, who was, let it be said, in many ways the pure type of the old intellectual—unattached to any institution, earning her living (apart from MacArthur Foundation and other grants) entirely from her ideas as she put them in writing—why, it seems worth asking in the context of the subject of celebrity, did she attract the attention she did?

---

[9] Richard Posner, *Public Intellectuals: A Study of Decline* (Cambridge, MA: Harvard University Press, 2002).

I don't believe Susan Sontag's celebrity finally had much to do with the power or cogency of her ideas. Her most noteworthy idea was not so much an idea at all but a description of a style, a kind of reverse or anti-style, that went by the name of Camp and that was gay in its impulse. Might it have been her politics? Yes, I think politics had a lot to do with it, even though when she expressed herself on political subjects, she frequently got things mightily askew: During the Vietnam War she said that "the white race is the cancer of human history."[10] As late as the 1980s, much too late for anyone in the know, she called Communism "Fascism with a friendly face" (what do you suppose she found so friendly about it?). To cheer up the besieged people of Sarajevo, she brought them a production of Samuel Beckett's *Waiting for Godot*. She announced in *The New Yorker* that the killing of 3,000 innocent people on 9/11 was an act that America had brought on itself.[11] As for the writing that originally brought her celebrity, she later came to apologize for *Against Interpretation*, her most influential single book. I do not know any people who claim to have derived keen pleasure from her fiction. If all this is roughly so, why, then, do you suppose that Susan Sontag was easily the single most celebrated—the greatest celebrity—intellectual of our time?

With Cynthia Ozick's face and body, with Camille Paglia's face and body, yes, even with my stunning face and body, I don't think Ms. Sontag would quite have achieved the same celebrity. I think, that is, that her attractiveness as a young woman had a great deal to do with the extent of her celebrity; and she and her publisher took that (early) physical attractiveness all the way out. From reading Carl Rollyson and Lisa Paddock's biography *Susan Sontag: The Making of an Icon*, one gets a sense of how carefully and relentlessly she was promoted, especially by her publisher, Roger Straus.[12] I do not mean to say that Sontag was unintelligent, or talentless, but Straus, by having her always dramatically photographed, by sending angry letters to the editors of journals where she was ill-reviewed, by bringing out her books with the most careful accompanying orchestration, promoted this often difficult and unrewarding writer into something close to a household name with a face that was ready, so to say, to be Warholed. That Sontag spent her last years with Annie Leibowitz, herself the most successful magazine photographer of our day, seems somehow the most natural thing in the world. Even in the realm of the intellect, celebrities are not born but made, usually very carefully—as was, I think, Susan Sontag.

---

[10] Susan Sontag "What's Happening in America," *The Partisan Review* (Winter 1967): 57.

[11] Susan Sontag, "The Talk of the Town: Comment: Tuesday, and After," *The New Yorker* (24 September 2001): 32.

[12] Carl Rollyson and Lisa Paddock, *Susan Sontag: The Making of an Icon* (New York: Norton, 2000).

One of the richest themes in Leo Braudy's *The Frenzy of Renown* is that of the fame and celebrity of artists and, above all, writers. To sketch in a few bare strokes the richly complex story Braudy tells, writers went from serving power (in Rome) to serving God (in early Christendom) to serving patrons (in the eighteenth century) to serving themselves, with a careful eye cocked toward both the public and posterity (under Romanticism), to serving mammon, to a state of interesting confusion, which is where we are today, with celebrity affecting contemporary literature in what strikes me as a more and more significant way.

Writers are supposed to be aristocrats of the spirit, not promoters, hustlers, salesmen for their own work. Securing a larger audience for their work was not thought to be their problem. "Fit audience, though few," in John Milton's phrase, was all right, so long as the few were the most artistically alert, or aesthetically fit, few. Picture, I ask you, Lord Byron, Count Tolstoy, Charles Baudelaire at a lectern at Barnes & Noble, C-Span camera turned on, flogging (wonderful word!) their own books. Impossible!

Some superior writers have been very careful caretakers of their careers. In a letter to one of his philosophy professors at Harvard, T. S. Eliot wrote that there were two ways to achieve literary celebrity in London: one was to appear often in a variety of publications; the other to appear seldom but always to make certain to dazzle when one did.[13] Eliot, of course, chose the latter, and it worked smashingly. But he was still counting on gaining his reputation through his actual writing. Now good work alone doesn't quite seem to make it; the publicity catapults need to be hauled into place, the walls of indifference stormed. Some writers have been able to steer shy from publicity altogether: Thomas Pynchon for one, J. D. Salinger for another (if he is actually still writing or yet considers himself a writer). But actively seeking publicity was thought for a writer, somehow, vulgar—at least it did when I began publishing.

Edmund Wilson, the great American literary critic, used to answer requests with a postcard that read:

> Edmund Wilson regrets that it is impossible for him to: Read manuscripts, Write articles or books to order, Make statements for publicity purposes, Do any kind of editorial work, Judge literary contests, Give interviews, Conduct educational courses, Deliver lectures, Give talks or make speeches, Take part in writers' congresses, Answer questionnaires, Contribute or take part in symposiums or "panels" of any kind, Contribute manuscripts for sale, Donate copies of his books to Libraries, Autograph books for strangers, Allow his name to be used on letterheads, Supply personal information about himself, Supply photographs of himself, Supply opinions on literary or other subjects.

---

[13] T. S. Eliot, *Letters of T. S. Eliot*, Vol. 1: 1898–1922, ed. Valerie Eliot (New York: Harcourt, 1989).

A fairly impressive list, I'd say. I have long admired Edmund Wilson for his range of intellectual interests and his work habits. When I was a young man, he supplied the model for me of how a literary man ought to carry himself. One of the things I personally find most impressive about his list is that everything Edmund Wilson clearly states he will not do, Joseph Epstein has now done, and more than once, and, like the young woman in the Häagen-Dazs commercial sitting on her couch with an empty carton of ice cream, I will do them all again.

I tell myself that I do these various things in the effort to acquire more readers. After all, one of the reasons I write, apart from pleasure in working out the aesthetic problems and moral questions presented by my subjects and in my stories, is to find the best readers. I also want to sell books, to make a few shekels, to please my publisher, to continue to be published in the future in a proper way. Having a high threshold for praise, I also don't in the least mind meeting strangers who tell me that they take some delight in my writing. But, more than all this, I have now come to think that writing away quietly, producing (the hope is) solid work, isn't any longer quite sufficient in a culture dominated by the boisterous spirit of celebrity. In an increasingly noisy cultural scene, with many voices and media competing for attention, one feels—perhaps incorrectly but nonetheless insistently—the need to make one's own small stir, however pathetic. So, on occasion, I have gone about tooting my own little paper horn, doing book tours, submitting to the comically pompous self-importance of interviews, and doing so many of the other things that Edmund Wilson didn't think twice about refusing to do.

"You're slightly famous, aren't you, Grandpa?" my then eight-year-old granddaughter once said to me. "I am slightly famous, Annabelle," I replied, "except no one knows who I am." This hasn't changed much over the years. But of course seeking celebrity in our culture is a mug's game, one you cannot hope to win. The only large, lumpy kind of big-time celebrity available, outside movie celebrity, is to be had through appearing fairly regularly on television. I once had the merest inkling of this fame when, walking along one sunny morning in downtown Baltimore, a red Mazda convertible screeched to a halt, the driver lowered his window, pointed a long finger at me, hesitated, and finally, the shock of recognition lighting up his face, yelled, "C-Span!"

I was recently asked, through e-mail, to write a short piece for a high price for a volume about the city of Chicago. When I agreed to do it, the editor of the volume, who is (I take it) young, told me how very pleased she was to have me among the volume's contributors. But she did have just one request. Before making things final, she wondered if she might see a sample of my writing. More than forty years in the business, I thought, echoing the character played by Zero Mostel in *The Producers*, and I'm still wearing the celebrity equivalent of a cardboard belt.

"Every time I think I am famous," Virgil Thomson said, "I have only to go out into the world."[14] So it is, and so ought it probably to remain for writers, musicians, and visual artists who prefer to consider themselves, to put it as pretentiously as possible, *sérieux*. The comedian Richard Pryor once said that he would consider himself famous when people recognized him, as they recognized Bob Hope and Muhammed Ali, by his captionless caricature. That is certainly one clear criterion for celebrity. But the best criterion I've yet come across holds that you are celebrated, indeed famous, only when a crazy person imagines he is you. I especially like the fact that the penetrating and prolific author of this remark happens to go by the name of Anonymous.

---

[14] Virgil Thomson, *Virgil Thomson* (New York: Da Capo, 1977).

Before Lindsay or Paris, There Was Mrs. L_fle

By Jessica Grose
The New York Times, September 2, 2007

Quick: Name the once-gorgeous superstar who's been savaged in the press for destroying her good looks, wasting her fortune and ruining her reputation with her "excessive indulgence in love, liquor, lust and laudanum."

Nope, it's not that self-destructive moppet on the cover of Us Weekly or that tearful television interviewee bawling to Diane Sawyer. It's Mrs. B_dd_y, the fallen British society maven whose shocking indiscretions were the subject of a scandalous 1780 publication that was widely distributed among London's upper and working classes.

Apparently, Mrs. B_dd_y, whose sordid affairs were preserved in a pamphlet called "Characters of the Present Most Celebrated Courtesans Exposed, With a Variety of Secret Anecdotes Never Before Published," faced stiff competition for the title of 18th-century England's most debauched socialite.

In a 1772 issue of The Town and Country Magazine, or, Universal Repository of Knowledge, Instruction and Entertainment, the years-long affair between the married Mrs. L_fle and the dashing Lord H___n was chronicled in minute detail, from their initial meeting to the consummation of their love, complete with background information on their friends, spouses and social standing and a finely drawn bust of the comely L_fle gazing adoringly on a dapper H___n.

Then there was Mrs. H_tt_n, a wealthy young heiress and gold digger who was attacked in the pages of "Courtesans" for her "unbounded inclination to the acquisition of money."

While we think of our present-day fascination with the bed-hopping antics of the wealthy and famous as a modern obsession, the musty, oft-thumbed pages of centuries-old publications like The Spectator, "Courtesans," and Town and Country tell a different story.

Hundreds of years before there were glossy celebrity magazines to chronicle the failed marriages and furtive poolside seductions of the attractive and well-born, British society of the 1700s had already given us the fundamental elements of contemporary tabloid culture: an emerging industry of publications dedicated to covering bad celebrity behavior, and an abundance of notorious personalities who were committing it and blabbing about it later—not to mention an increasingly literate readership that was enthralled with it.

"The idea of gossip and scandal and celebrity culture that we have today was really coming into being in 18th-century London," said Sophie Gee, the author of the new novel "The Scandal of the Season." "It was a moment when a fascination with celebrity coincided with a number of very great writers wanting to write about celebrity."

Ms. Gee, 33, a Sydney-born academic and an assistant professor of English at Princeton, isn't usually found among the stacks at Firestone Library searching for 300-year-old bits of slanderous social ammunition. But such gossip was all but unavoidable as she researched "The Scandal of the Season," a fictionalized account of the true story behind Alexander Pope's 1712 poem, "The Rape of the Lock."

When Pope composed his satirical epic, he was shining a spotlight on a suspected affair between the British aristocrats Arabella Fermor and Lord Robert Petre, two mainstays of the London party scene. (The intrigue became common knowledge when Petre publicly cut off a lock of Fermor's hair.) In doing so, Pope provided the template for today's gossip writers: a middle-class striver who hung on the fringes of patrician circles, privy to upper-class dirt while maintaining his ironic distance.

"Pope quickly got himself a rep for his willingness to launch unsparing attacks on people who offended him," Ms. Gee said, "and so it became a big deal for the aristocracy to have him on their side."

British readers did not have to rely solely on epic poetry to satisfy their appetite for gossip. The Spectator, considered the most sophisticated publication of 18th-century London, meted out weekly coverage of politics, literature and art—along with a healthy dollop of social scandal—on a single tightly packed page.

"The Spectator discussed new habits people were falling into, and it prided itself on giving these habits new names," Ms. Gee explained as she carefully paged through a well-preserved compilation of Spectator back issues. "It would describe the kind of elaborate headdress people had started wearing to the opera, and then mock someone for wearing the wrong kind of wig."

With its erudite celebrity dish and insider's tone, The Spectator was aimed at middle-class readers who used it as a cheat sheet to ingratiate themselves into high society, as well as upper-class types eager to make sure they knew all the latest dirt on their contemporaries. And like its modern-day counterparts, the publication's most frequent targets were also its most reliable informants: women of power who loved to spread rumors about their frenemies and foes. "There was a competition among upper-class women about who had the best gossip," Ms. Gee said. "They were fantastically catty and loved to see their contemporaries fall."

At the other end of the spectrum, pamphlets like "Characters of the Present Most Celebrated Courtesans" were intended for a working-class audience—scullery maids and serving wenches who would have picked it up at lending libraries—though the gentry enjoyed it as a guilty pleasure, too.

Printed on much cheaper paper than The Spectator, these pamphlets trafficked exclusively in the tales of highborn women who had disgraced themselves in public, ensnaring readers with lurid titles like "The History of Betty Bolaine, the Canterbury Miser," and crude drawings of dissipated women in various stages of physical ruin—the etched equivalents of a bleary-eyed Lindsay Lohan mug shot.

Like today's celebrity weeklies, "Courtesans" feigned concern and moral acuity (see OK!'s recent description of a Britney Spears meltdown as "heartbreaking") while reveling in the scandal. Of a Mrs. H_tt_n, "Courtesans" says, "She is expensive in dress, extravagant in the indulgence of her palate, violently addicted to wine and strong liquors which she often drinks to excess, not infrequently to intoxication." It then reminds its readers that good conduct is "a perfect security to all indelicate or fornicative consequences."

The authors of "Courtesans" attempted to mask the identities of its subjects by leaving out letters in their surnames, but just as in a Page Six blind item, part of the sport for readers was filling in the blanks. The copy of "Courtesans" at Firestone Library reveals Mrs. H_tt_n to be Mrs. Hutton: an in-the-know reader had penciled in the missing letters.

Though "Courtesans" has long since gone out of print, the 18th-century Spectator endures: it evolved into the modern-day British society magazine Tatler (the publication's original name when it was first published in 1709), with much of its roguish sensibility still intact.

"There was always an element of mischief and irony," said Geordie Greig, Tatler's editor. "We're known as the magazine that bites the hand that feeds it."

But if the centuries-old exploits of women long since forgotten have been preserved in academic research and contemporary novels, does that mean that future generations will be reading about the antics of Paris, Lindsay and Britney for hundreds of years to come?

"Though nothing is more ephemeral than fame," Ms. Gee said, "I can't imagine that we're going to forget about Paris Hilton and Lindsay Lohan anytime soon."

Our Celebrity Madness

A Reflection of Consumerism

BY TIRDAD DERAKHSHANI
PHILADELPHIA INQUIRER, AUGUST 19, 2007

We've become junkies—craving more and more news about a growing cadre of celebrities ranging from accomplished artists to do-nothing heiresses and know-nothing reality-show stars.

Most critics treat our celebrity madness as if it were just a public nuisance, one we could cure by modifying our habits: Debate world hunger at the watercooler instead of Britney Spears' parental skills.

But we should take the big questions far more seriously. Why are celebs so . . . *everywhere* today? And what function does celeb culture play in *our* culture?

Our obsession with celebrity is not some aberration, but an intrinsic aspect of the central economic, social and political force in Western life: consumerism.

Celebrity culture reflects consumerism by flattening distinctions: If all cultural products—from video games to poems, from roller sneakers to religious beliefs—are reduced to commodities, then the only thing that matters is buying and selling. A Rembrandt and a *Lil' Abner* comic strip are basically the same as long as they entertain me or make me a profit.

Celeb culture has helped bring about the commodification of human life.

I Want! I Want!

A famous William Blake engraving shows a boy who has just begun to climb a long ladder extended to the moon. "I Want! I Want!" he says.

Consumerism cultivates a similar form of desire—the desire to consume more and more goods and services, with the hope that someday we'll reach ultimate satisfaction.

We never will, of course. We will always remain wanting, because what we want in the end—what consumers are implicitly taught to want—is not things, but social distinction. A Jaguar is as much a class symbol as it is a car. Same for an Ivy League education, or the taste for European art flicks, or a knowledge of fine wines, or . . . the game has no end.

"Consumerism isn't just about spending money: It's about reconstituting our conceptions of self, our self-worth and self-identity," said Ellis Cashmore, author of *Celebrity Culture*, *The Black Culture Industry* and *Beckham*.

Cashmore, who teaches at Staffordshire University in England, argues that celebrity culture has "actually changed the relationship we have . . . with each other, to the point where we actually live vicariously through mediated figures—[Princess] Diana being the most resplendent example."

If Blake's moon represents where we want to be, the stars surrounding it are . . . well, the *stars*—the celebrities who (we are led to believe) are already there. Celebrites invoke in us—and also literally *embody* for us—the same endless, ever-growing anxious desire that governs our relation with consumer goods.

Your Life or Your Money!

Celebrities fulfill three symbolic functions:

- They are models of behavior—the ultimate sellers. They sell us things. And because of the intimacy and kinship we feel for them, they humanize the process.

- They are ideal consumers, always buying more. Luxurious lifestyles make celebs symbols for consumption itself.

- They themselves are commodities. As consumer goods whose lives are laid out for us to enjoy, celebs are (nothing but?) objects to be bought and sold—and eventually discarded.

Models of Personality

Every word you hear from celebs is a sales pitch. They are either hawking goods in an official capacity as brand representatives, or recommending objects and memes we ought to check out. The way they do this is such a part of their public personas that it's almost impossible to see it as a form of marketing.

Consider last year, when two couples—Angelina Jolie/Brad Pitt and Tom Cruise/Katie Holmes—played hide-and-seek with frenzied media over their respective relationships. While staging romantic moments, or waxing poetic about love on talk shows, each happened to have major films to sell. Perfectly natural.

As the ultimate sellers, celebs are the ultimate "models of personality": They show us how others (the folks who make what the celebs are selling) want us to be.

The role of celebs is similar to that once played by priests, rulers and military heroes who offered us ideal personality types.

David Schmid of the University at Buffalo says celebrities now fulfill that function by offering us "models of selfhood . . . at a time when our society has been through a massive shift" that has left us feeling "dislocated and rootless."

What are celebs selling? Cultural productions—the songs, movies and TV shows of everyday life—that millions of us use, in various ways, to define who we are. Many people say such things "aren't important"—then go out and buy that gansta-rap CD, that *World of Warcraft* video game, that Homer Simpson or Ché Guevara or Garth Brooks or *Fantasia* or Frédéric Bastiat or Joris-Karl Huysmans or

> Celebs are nothing more—or less—than products themselves.

Rage Against the Machine T-shirt—all of which might as well be spiritual bumper stickers. We use art, politics and even religion the same way. In each case, celebs are there, modeling how to be.

The Ultimate Consumers

Celebs not only sell us products. They also embody the American Dream—as reconfigured by consumer society. They are the ultimate consumers who, Cashmore said, "have become walking advertisements for a new type of society in which every human need has been satisfied."

For Cashmore, celebs embody the promise that everyone can transform themselves from nothing into autonomous, self-created individuals—by consuming product, whether it be lipstick or a three-month Buddhist retreat in the Himalayas.

Salesman, Sell Thyself

Third and last, celebs are nothing more—or less—than products themselves. They not only embody the ideal consumer; they also urge us to become commodities to survive in modern society. Look at online dating sites that demand each person market him or herself as an ideal mate. Look at the offstage mom; the careers office at the local high school that gives after-school seminars in "selling your-self"; the hungry audience gestures on YouTube; spam spam spam; the triumph of unapologetic self-marketing. Celebs sell, they consume, they are what they sell—and they teach us to follow suit.

The Death of Celebrity?

The massive rise in celebrity-related chatter over the last five years has included an expansion of the definition of "celebrity" itself: There's no way Richard Hatch, winner of the first *Survivor*, would be considered a celeb 10 years ago.

As media have shifted and expanded to cable, satellite, handheld devices, and Web services such as blogs and Webcasts, there's been more demand for content—for faces to love or mock.

"There has been a democratization of media coverage and fame access," said Schmid, who sees shows such as *American Idol* as an "experiment in American democracy" since they (at least seemingly) open the door to fame to more and more people.

It seems Andy Warhol's prophecy—15 minutes of fame for each one of us—has come true.

But ironically, if everyone can be a celeb, then that radical difference that once marked celebs off will be gone: Celebrity will die.

Seeing by Starlight

By Carlin Flora
Psychology Today, July/August 2004

A couple of years ago, Britney Spears and her entourage swept through my boss's office. As she sashayed past, I blushed and stammered and leaned over my desk to shake her hand. She looked right into my eyes and smiled her pageant smile, and I confess, I felt dizzy. I immediately rang up friends to report my celebrity encounter, saying: "She had on a gorgeous, floor-length white fur coat! Her skin was blotchy!" I've never been much of a Britney fan, so why the contact high? Why should I care? For that matter, why should any of us?

Celebrities are fascinating because they live in a parallel universe—one that looks and feels just like ours yet is light-years beyond our reach. Stars cry to Diane Sawyer about their problems—failed marriages, hardscrabble upbringings, bad career decisions—and we can relate. The paparazzi catch them in wet hair and a stained T-shirt, and we're thrilled. They're ordinary folks, just like us. And yet . . .

Stars live in another world entirely, one that makes our lives seem woefully dull by comparison. The teary chat with Diane quickly turns to the subject of a recent $10 million film fee and honorary United Nations ambassadorship. The magazines that specialize in gotcha snapshots of schleppy-looking celebs also feature Cameron Diaz wrapped in a $15,000 couture gown and glowing with youth, money and star power. We're left hanging—and we want more.

It's easy to blame the media for this cognitive whiplash. But the real celebrity spinmeister is our own mind, which tricks us into believing the stars are our lovers and our social intimates. Celebrity culture plays to all of our innate tendencies: We're built to view anyone we recognize as an acquaintance ripe for gossip or for romance, hence our powerful interest in Anna Kournikova's sex life. Since catching sight of a beautiful face bathes the brain in pleasing chemicals, George Clooney's killer smile is impossible to ignore.

But when celebrities are both our intimate daily companions and as distant as the heavens above, it's hard to know just how to think of them. Reality TV further confuses the picture by transforming ordinary folk into bold-faced names without warning. Even celebrities themselves are not immune to celebrity watching: Magazines print pictures of Demi Moore and "Bachelorette" Trista Rehn reading the very same gossip magazines that stalk them. "Most pushers are users, don't you think?" says top Hollywood publicist Michael Levine. "And, by the way, it's not the worst thing in the world to do." Celebrities tap into powerful motivational systems designed to foster romantic love and to urge us to find a mate. Stars summon our most human yearnings: to love, admire, copy and, of course, to gossip and to jeer. It's only natural that we get pulled into their gravitational field.

Exclusive: Fan's Brain Transformed *by* Celebrity Power!

John Lennon infuriated the faithful when he said the Beatles were more popular than Jesus, but he wasn't the first to suggest that celebrity culture was taking the place of religion. With its myths, its rituals (the red carpet walk, the Super Bowl ring, the hand prints outside Grauman's Chinese Theater) and its ability to immortalize, it fills a similar cultural niche. In a secular society our need for ritualized idol worship can be displaced onto stars, speculates psychologist James Houran, formerly of the Southern Illinois University School of Medicine and now director of psychological studies for True Beginnings dating service. Nonreligious people tend to be more interested in celebrity culture, he's found, and Houran speculates that for them, celebrity fills some of the same roles the church fills for believers, like the desire to admire the powerful and the drive to fit into a community of people with shared values. Leo Braudy, author of *The Frenzy of Renown: Fame and its History*, suggests that celebrities are more like Christian calendar saints than like spiritual authorities (Tiger Woods, patron saint of arriviste golfers; or Jimmy Carter, protector of down-home liberal farmers?). "Celebrities have their aura—a debased version of charisma" that stems from their all-powerful captivating presence, Braudy says.

Much like spiritual guidance, celebrity-watching can be inspiring, or at least help us muster the will to tackle our own problems. "Celebrities motivate us to make it," says Helen Fisher, an anthropologist at Rutgers University in New Jersey. Oprah Winfrey suffered through poverty, sexual abuse and racial discrimination to become the wealthiest woman in media. Lance Armstrong survived advanced testicular cancer and went on to win the Tour de France five times. Star-watching can also simply point the way to a grander, more dramatic way of living, publicist Levine says. "We live lives more dedicated to safety or quiet desperation, and we transcend this by connecting with bigger lives—those of the stars," he says. "We're afraid to eat that fatty muffin, but Ozzy Osborne isn't."

Don't I Know You?!

Celebrities are also common currency in our socially fractured world. Depressed college coeds and laid-off factory workers both spend hours watching Anna Nicole Smith on late night television; Mexican villagers trade theories with hometown friends about who killed rapper Tupac Shakur; and Liberian and German business-men critique David Beckham's plays before hammering out deals. My friend Britney Spears was, in fact, last year's top international Internet search.

In our global village, the best targets for gossip are the faces we all know. We are born to dish dirt, evolutionary psychologists agree; it's the most efficient way to navigate society and to determine who is trustworthy. They also point out that when our brains evolved, any-body with a familiar face was an "in-group" member, a person whose alliances and enmities were important to keep track of.

Things have changed somewhat since life in the Pleistocene era, but our neural hardwiring hasn't, so on some deeper level, we may think NBC's *Friends* really are our friends. Many of us have had the celebrity-sighting mishap of mistaking a minor star—a local weath-erman, say, or a bit-part soap opera actor—for an acquaintance or former schoolmate. Braudy's favorite example of this mistake: In one episode of the cartoon show *King of the Hill*, a character meets former Texas Governor Ann Richards. "You probably know me," he says. "I've seen you on TV." That's also why we don't get bored by star gossip, says Bonnie Fuller, editorial director of American Media, which publishes *Star* and *The Enquirer*: "That would be like getting bored with information about family and friends!"

The brain simply doesn't realize that it's being fooled by TV and movies, says sociologist Satoshi Kanazawa, lecturer at the London School of Economics. "Hundreds of thousands of years ago, it was impossible for someone not to know you if you knew them. And if they didn't kill you, they were probably your friend." Kanazawa's research has shown that this feeling of friendship has other reper-cussions: People who watch more TV are more satisfied with their friendships, just as if they had more friends and socialized more fre-quently. Another study found that teens who keep up to date on celebrity gossip are popular, with strong social networks—the inter-est in pop culture indicates a healthy drive for independence from parents.

The penchant for gossiping about the stars also plays into our spe-cies' obsession with status. Humans naturally copy techniques from high-status individuals, says Francisco Gil-White, professor of psy-chology at University of Pennsylvania. It's an attempt to get the same rewards, whether that's "attention, favors, gifts, [or] laudatory exclamations." Stars get all kinds of perks and pampering: Sarah Jessica Parker was allowed to keep each of her *Sex in the City* char-acter's extravagant getups; Halle Berry borrowed a $3 million dia-mond ring to wear to the Oscars. Understandably, we look to get in on the game.

The impulse to copy is behind the popularity of celebrity maga-zines, says Fuller. Regular women can see what the stars are wear-ing, often with tips on how to buy cheap knockoffs of their outfits. Taken to extremes—which television is only too happy to do—the urge to copy produces spectacles like the MTV reality show *I Want a*

Famous Face. By dint of extensive plastic surgery, ordinary people are made to look more like their famous heroes. In one episode, two gangly 20-year-old twin brothers are molded into Brad Pitt look-alikes. The brothers want to be stars, and they've decided that looking more like Pitt is the fastest road to fame. No wonder makeover shows are so popular, points out Joshua Gamson, an associate professor of sociology at the University of San Francisco. These shows offer drab nobodies a double whammy: simultaneous beauty and celebrity.

The most fascinating measure of status is, of course, sex. "We want to know who is mating with whom," says Douglas Kenrick, professor of psychology at Arizona State University. He speculates that we look to stars to evaluate our own sexual behavior and ethics, and mistake them unconsciously for members of our prospective mating pool.

Given this me-too drive to imitate and adore, why are celebrity flame-outs and meltdowns so fascinating? Even though we love to hear about the lavish rewards of fame—remember *Lifestyles of the Rich and Famous?*—we're quick to judge when stars behave too outrageously or live too extravagantly. We suspect some stars are enjoying society's highest rewards without really de serving them, says University of Liverpool anthropologist Robin Dunbar, so we monitor their behavior. "We need to keep an eye on the great-and-the-good because they create a sense of community for us, but also because we need to make sure that they are holding to their side of the bargain."

Diva Alert: Beauty Isn't Everything (Being Nice Helps!)

The beauty bias is well-known. We all pay more attention to good-looking people. Kenrick's eye-tracking research has shown that both men and women spend more time looking at beautiful women than at less attractive women. Babies as young as 8-months-old will stare at an attractive female face of any race longer than they will at an average-looking or unattractive female face. Certain human traits are universally recognized as beautiful: symmetry, regularity in the shape and size of the features, smooth skin, big eyes and thick lips, and an hourglass figure that indicates fertility. Men interpret these features as evidence of health and reproductive fitness. Women's responses are more complex, says psychologist and Harvard Medical School instructor Nancy Etcoff, author of *Survival of the Prettiest*. Women stare at beautiful female faces out of aesthetic appreciation, to look for potential tips—and because a beautiful woman could be a rival worth monitoring.

It's not surprising that gorgeous people wind up famous. What's less obvious is that famous people often wind up gorgeous: The more we see a certain face, the more our brain likes it, whether or not it's actually beautiful. Thanks to what is known as "the exposure effect," says James Bailey, a psychologist at George Washington University, the pleasurable biological cascade that is set off when we see a certain celebrity "begins to wear a neurochemical groove," making her image easier for our brains to process. It begins to explain why Jennifer Aniston—not exactly a classic cover girl—was again named one of *People* magazine's 50 "most beautiful" in the world this year.

On the flip side, celebrity overload—let's call it the J.Lo effect—can leave us all thoroughly sick of even the most beautiful celeb. With the constant deluge of celebrity coverage, says Etcoff, "they at first become more appealing because they are familiar, but then the ubiquity becomes tedious. That is why the stars who reign the longest—Madonna is the best example—are always changing their appearance." Every time Madonna reconfigures her look, she resets our responses back to when her face was recognizable but still surprising.

Just as in pageants, personality plays a part in the beauty contest, too. State University of New York at Binghamton psychology professors Kevin Kniffin and David Sloan Wilson have found that people's perceptions of physical appeal are strongly influenced by familiarity and likability. "Almost all of the beauty research is based on subjects looking at strangers in photos or computer-generated images—but we don't live in a world of strangers!" Kniffin points out.

In one of Kniffin's experiments, students worked on an archeological dig together toward a shared goal. Those who were deemed cooperative and likable were rated as more attractive after the project was finished than they were at the outset. Conversely, students who were not as hardworking were rated as less attractive after the chore was done.

Kniffin believes this same mechanism is at work in our feelings toward celebrities, who rank somewhere between strangers and intimates. Athletes are an obvious example: Team spirit gives even ugly guys a boost. NBA great Wilt Chamberlain might have been a bit goofy-looking, but his astonishing abilities to propel his team to victory meant that he was a hero, surrounded with adoring—and amorous—fans.

Kniffin points to William Hung, the talent-free and homely also-ran on the contest show *American Idol*, as evidence of his theory at work. In part because of his enthusiasm and his good-natured willingness to put up with ridicule, Hung became a bigger star after he was kicked off the show: His album, *Inspiration*, sold more than 37,000 copies in its first week. "William doesn't display the traits of universal attractiveness, but people who have seen the show would probably rate him as more attractive because of nonphysical traits of likabllity and courage. He's even received some marriage proposals." Kniffin's theory also explains why models are less compelling objects of fascination than actresses or pop stars. They're beautiful, but they're enigmatic: We rarely get any sense of their personalities.

Saved from Oblivion!

What's the result of our simultaneous yearning to be more like celebrities and our desire to be wowed by their unattainable perfection? We've been watching it for the past decade. Reality television is an express train to fame, unpredictably turning nobodies into somebodies. Reality TV now gives us the ability to get inside the star factory and watch the transition to fame in real time.

"The appeal of reality stars is that they were possibly once just like you, sitting on the couch watching a reality TV program, until they leaped to celebrity," says Andy Denhart, blogger and reality TV junkie. "With the number of reality shows out there, it's inexcusable to not be famous if you want to be!" In the past, ambitious young men who idolized a famous actor might take acting lessons or learn to dance. Now, they get plastic surgery and learn to tell their life stories for the camera. In fact, says editor Fuller, the newly minted stars of reality TV are better at the celebrity game than many of the movie and television stars: "They are more accessible, more cooperative. They enjoy publicity. They will open up and offer insight, often more than a 'traditional' celeb, because they want the attention, whereas an actress might have ambivalent feelings about fame and how it is tied in with her 'craft.'"

At the same time, shows like *The Simple Life* and *The Newlyweds* (and amateur videotapes like Paris Hilton's) let us gawk at the silly things that stars do in the privacy of their own home. As a result, the distance between celebrity stratosphere and living room couch dwindles even further.

Yet there's still something about that magic dust. A celebrity sighting is not just about seeing a star, author Braudy points out, but is about being *seen by* a star: "There is a sense that celebrities are more real than we are; people feel more real in the presence of a celebrity." It wasn't just that I saw Britney, it was that Britney saw *me*.

The Stalker in All of Us

How Harmless Stargazing Turns Hazardous

We like to think that we're nothing like star stalkers, but former Southern Illinois University School of Medicine psychologist James Houran and his colleagues have found that the interest in celebrities runs on a continuum, from *Entertainment Tonight* regulars all the way to John Hinckley.

The team has devised a Celebrity Attitude Scale to measure the span. On the innocuous end of the scale are people who join fan clubs or buy lousy records out of loyalty—about one in five of us fit this category, according to the teams' 600-person survey. And these fans aren't lonely singles at home with their cats. "These people are outgoing and believe people should have close relationships with others," says Houran. "For some reason [they don't] feel a part of their social milieu." Adoring celebrities is normal for children and adolescents, Houran notes, since they are still figuring out their own identities.

The next stage of celebrity fascination, Intense-Personal, involves feelings that are a little stronger—and stranger. "I consider my favorite celebrity to be my soul mate," people in this category assert. About 1 percent of those in the survey are true celebrity worshippers, who agree that "if I were lucky enough to meet my favorite celebrity and he/she asked me to do something illegal as a favor, I would probably do it." These intense fans probably get sucked in when their lives go off the rails for other reasons, the team theorizes.

Houran's studies indicate that the most deeply obsessed also show signs of erotomania, the delusion of having a love affair with an unattainable or uninterested person. Helen Fisher, the Rutgers University anthropologist who studies courtship and attraction, speculates that celebrity obsession is a form of romantic love. Romance is associated with lower levels of the neurochemical serotonin, breeding the obsessive and addictive behavior characteristic of both love affairs and the compulsion to buy *Us Weekly*. Star worshippers, though, are bound to be disappointed, she points out: "It won't last forever, because the love can't be returned."

Not Exactly the Stuff of Legends?

By John Intini
Maclean's, February 7, 2005

Johnny Carson's death makes you wonder about the current state of celebrity. In 50 years, who among today's stars will be remembered as a legend after they die? Scanning magazine covers or watching entertainment news offers little help narrowing the field. That's because earning notoriety from reality TV or a high-profile court case doesn't count towards greatness. Being remembered for your jokes is cool. Being remembered as a joke-not so cool.

Many people fascinated by the rich and famous these days love scandal and gossip. The trashier the better. And sadly, this preference for a good celebrity train wreck (i.e. daily coverage of Lindsay Lohan's late-night partying) puts less emphasis on real talent. Celebrities have become easily disposable, making it rare for anyone to survive long enough in the machine to achieve a career worthy of legendary status-Madonna and U2 are two exceptions. Of course, killing yourself in your prime is one way to speed up the process, but thankfully few resort to Kurt Cobain's messy and selfish way of immortalizing genius.

Another problem is that few celebrities know when to step out of the spotlight-a key to generating your own legend, and something Carson understood. Many tarnish their careers by hanging on too long, accepting any roles available. That's right, Robert De Niro-I'm talking to you.

Then there are those high-profile celebs who seem destined for greatness but simply self-destruct. Nobody has done famous to infamous better than Michael Jackson. The King of Pop could easily have gone down in history as one of the greatest, even if he'd stopped making music after *Thriller* and gone into hiding at the Neverland Ranch. But he didn't. And thanks to his courtroom troubles, the tune *Billie Jean* is not the first thing that comes to mind when you think about Wacko Jacko.

The world of sports has also been tainted in the last few years-making the development of new living legends all the more difficult. Sure, there have been a fair share of greats—from Michael Jordan to Wayne Gretzky to Joe Montana—but labour strikes, lockouts and doping have taken a toll on fans. Take Barry Bonds, for instance. He's possibly the greatest home run hitter in baseball history, but the fact he took performance-enhancing drugs will, at least in the minds of purists, put an asterisk next to his name in Cooperstown. Hank Aaron, they'll say, didn't need steroids to hit 755 dingers.

So, although it may sound strange, it's conceivable that in 2055 the most memorable celebrity from present-day film, TV, music and sports could end up being Bart Simpson. Think about it. He's made people laugh for 18 years, never had a scandal threaten his career, and will live on forever in syndication. And since he never ages, he'll even be around to star in his own biopic.

II. CELEBRITY ACTIVISM AND AMERICAN POLITICS

Editor's Introduction

Celebrity and politics have long made strange bedfellows. However, given the performative nature of politics, perhaps their coupling is not so odd. After all, Ronald Reagan parlayed a successful acting career into an even more successful political one that culminated with two terms in the White House. Indeed, the on-screen personas of former Minnesota Governor Jesse Ventura and current California Governor Arnold Schwarzenegger are only slightly larger than their political profiles. And who wouldn't want *The Love Boat*'s friendly purser Burl "Gopher" Smith, played by Fred Grandy, representing them in Congress, as Grandy did for the people of Iowa from 1987 to 1995?

Contrary to the popular belief that the mingling between Washington, D.C., and Hollywood is a recent phenomenon, political activism among entertainers has a much longer history. In World War II, for example, Hollywood produced public service messages urging the populace to help the war effort by rationing materials and buying bonds. Despite such overt support for the American cause, however, by 1947 Hollywood had become a prime target of the federal government's inquiry into Communist Party membership in the United States.

Throughout the ensuing decade, during the so-called "Red Scare," actors, writers, and directors were paraded before the House Committee on Un-American Activities to swear their allegiance to the United States and to inform on colleagues who may or may not have been members of the Communist Party. Those who were outed or suspected were placed on a blacklist and barred from employment in the industry. This blacklist would remain in effect until 1960. Given this uncomfortable common history, it is little wonder that entertainers have since engaged in activism and, along the way, have introduced their own brand of hype to the political process.

This chapter begins with "American Politics in the Age of Celebrity," in which Darrell M. West describes "what factors have contributed to the blurring of the lines between politics and entertainment, how politicians mimic celebrities (and vice versa), what the age of celebrity reveals about our culture, and what risks a celebrity culture faces."

Citing the 2000 election of the former professional wrestler Jesse "The Body" Ventura as governor of Minnesota, Ann Conley and David Schultz explore the emergence in recent years of the "politainer," a celebrity-politician hybrid, in "Jesse Ventura™ and the Brave New World of Politainer Politics." Many of the themes discussed by Conley and Schultz are further illuminated in the next article, "Victory for Arnold," in which Roger Simon describes Arnold Schwarzenegger, the ultimate politainer, and his triumphant run for governor of California.

In terms of influence, few celebrities in American life can match Oprah Winfrey. Through her afternoon talk show, Winfrey has forged a singular bond with the American public. Indeed, by selecting a novel for her book club, Winfrey can turn an obscure text into a bestseller overnight. Recently Winfrey has exerted her influence in presidential politics, endorsing and campaigning for Illinois Senator Barack Obama. As Eugene Robinson notes in "Can Oprah Boost Her 'Favorite Guy?'" celebrity endorsements rarely pay dividends for a candidate, but Oprah's may prove an exception to the rule.

Of the many stereotypes in American politics, few have the resonance of the so-called "Hollywood liberal." In "Stage Left," Ed Leibowitz profiles the political works of one "Hollywood liberal," the actor Tim Robbins, whose opposition to the war in Iraq and advocacy of various progressive causes has drawn the wrath of many conservative commentators.

In the subsequent piece, "Celebrity and Politics," Andrew Kamons analyzes how the expanding cult of celebrity has enabled those with little experience to access political power not simply as advocates, but as policymakers. Despite the knee-jerk negativity that celebrity politicians tend to evoke, Kamons concludes, it is hard to quibble with what activists such as Angelina Jolie and U2's Bono have achieved for the plight of refugees and Third World debt reform, respectively. Rounding out this section is "Foreign Policy Goes Glam," in which Daniel Drezner further explores the impact of celebrities on foreign policy.

American Politics in the Age of Celebrity

By Darrell M. West
The Hedgehog Review, Spring 2005

It is the Age of Celebrity in the United States. Movie stars run for elective office and win. Politicians play fictional characters on television shows. Rock stars raise money for political parties. Musicians, athletes, and artists speak out on issues of hunger, stem cell research, and foreign policy. While this is not the first time celebrities have sought elective office or spoken out on questions of public policy, there are a number of factors in the contemporary period that have accentuated celebrity politics and given it a far greater prominence. The culture has changed in ways that glorify fame and fortune.[1] The news industry has become highly competitive. Media reporters need good copy, and few sources provide better copy than actors, athletes, and entertainers. The fact that politics has become very expensive places a premium on those who can convince others to give money.[2]

In this essay, I describe what factors have contributed to the blurring of the lines between politics and entertainment, how politicians mimic celebrities (and vice versa), what the age of celebrity reveals about our culture, and what risks a celebrity culture faces. In important respects, the contemporary period has undergone crucial changes, sometimes to the detriment of society as a whole. In particular, at a time when the press plays closer attention to celebrities speaking out on complex policy subjects than to experts with detailed knowledge, there is a danger that politics will be drained of substance, and serious deliberation and discourse will be diminished. If politics becomes an entertainment show based on performance skills, society loses its capacity for nuance, compromise, and deliberation.

Blurring the Lines Between Politics and Entertainment

Celebrity politics is not a new phenomenon. In the eighteenth and nineteenth centuries, it was common in the United States for famous families and former military generals to use their prominence as an asset to gain elective office. Many of our leading presi-

---

This article was originally published in *The Hedgehog Review*, vol. 7, no. 1, Spring 2005. Reprinted with permission.

[1] Leo Braudy, *The Frenzy of Renown: Fame and Its History* (New Yor:k Vintage, 1986).

[2] David Canon, *Actors, Athletes, and Astronauts* (Chicago: The University of Chicago Press, 1990).

dents were famous for their exploits on the military field, including George Washington, Andrew Jackson, William Henry Harrison, and Ulysses S. Grant, whose military fame led them to high office.[3] Other historical leaders were legacy politicians who came from celebrated families such as the Roosevelts, Adams, and Harrisons. These three families produced six presidents (Theodore and Franklin Roosevelt, John and John Quincy Adams, and William Henry and Benjamin Harrison). When Blair Lee was elected governor of Maryland in the 1970s, he was the 21st member of his extended family to hold political office since 1647. According to Stephen Hess, 700 families account for "1,700 of the 10,000 men and women who have been elected to the federal legislature since 1774."[4]

Throughout American history, celebrated writers and non-politicos have spoken out on issues of the day. Mark Twain's political satire and quips twitted many a prominent public figure. Ernest Hemingway was involved in a number of foreign and domestic controversies of his era. Charles Lindbergh gained fame as the first pilot to fly solo, nonstop across the Atlantic. He then used this prominence to lead America's isolationist movement in the 1930s and 1940s.

Several trends over the past few decades, however, have contributed to a celebrity culture that is far more pronounced and politically important than in earlier epochs.[5]

Fundamental shifts in media have blurred the lines between politics and entertainment. With the rise of new technologies such as cable television, talk radio, and the Internet, the news business has become very competitive and more likely to focus on gossip and prominent personalities. Tabloid shows such as Access Hollywood, which attract millions of viewers, glorify celebrities and provide a "behind-the-scenes" look at the entertainment industry, with reporters staking out "star" parties and nightclubs and reporting on who is in attendance. The old "establishment" press that kept rumors of President John F. Kennedy's marital infidelities out of the newspapers has been replaced by a news media that specializes in reporting on the private lives of politicians and Hollywood stars. Individuals who have drinking problems or drug habits, or gamble too much, are likely to find themselves in today's news.[6] Reporters are now more likely to focus on human features than detailed substance. According to William Winter, who was one of America's first television news broadcasters in 1950, the modern era is a time when news broadcasts are "increasingly shallow and trivial."[7] Competition in

---

[3] Darrell M. West and John Orman, *Celebrity Politics* (Englewood Cliffs: Prentice Hall, 2003).

[4] Stephen Hess, "Political Dynasties: An American Tradition" (27 February 2000): <www.tompaine,com>.

[5] Ronald Brownstein, *The Power and the Glitter: The Hollywood-Washington Connection* (New York: Pantheon, 1990).

[6] Larry Sabato, Mark Stempel, and Robert Lichter, *Peep Show: Media and Politics in an Age of Scandal* (Lanham: Rowman & Littlefield, 2000).

American politics centers around who can reduce complex messages down to understandable, nine-second (or, more recently, five-second) sound bytes.[8]

The growing cost of American campaigns has also contributed to the emergence of celebrity politics. Needing money to finance television ads and get-out-the-vote drives, politicians have become fundraising machines. Senators in large states must raise $5,000 a day every day of their six-year term in order to have enough money for their re-election efforts. Without large amounts of money, candidates cannot run television ads or mobilize likely voters. This need for cash forces politicians into alliances with athletes, actors, and artists who can headline fundraising events. In order to guarantee a large turnout at a fundraising party, it has become common to feature comedians, singers, and other celebrities who can attract a large crowd. In the 2004 presidential election, Bruce Springsteen gave a series of concerts to raise money to defeat President George W. Bush, and other Hollywood celebrities such as actors Sean Penn, Mike Farrell, and Linda Ronstadt spoke out against the Iraq War. With their strong support in "red" states, Republicans relied on country singers, and individuals such as Garth Brooks lent their names to the cause of electing Republicans across the country.

The intertwining of politics and entertainment has blurred the lines between these two fields. The old days when entertainers and politicians led more or less separate existences has been replaced with a system that regularly brings members of each club into close contact with the other side.

How Politicians Mimic Celebrities (and Vice Versa)

In today's world, politicians need celebrities and celebrities need politicians—each possesses attributes that the other requires. From the standpoint of politicians, celebrities are a way to reach voters jaded by political cynicism. In the 1950s, two-thirds of Americans trusted the government in Washington to do what is right.[9] Presidents had high moral authority, and citizens had confidence in the ethics and morality of their leaders. However, following scandals in Vietnam and Watergate, economic stagflation, and controversies over Iran-Contra and Monica Lewinsky, the public became far less trusting. They are no longer confident about political leaders and are less likely to trust their motives. When asked whether they trust the government in Washington to do what is right, two-thirds express mistrust.[10] Citizens feel that politicians are in it for them-

---

[7] Quoted in Ron Miller, "TV News: Increasingly Shallow, Trivial," *Bridgeport Post* (17 May 1990): D8.

[8] Kiku Adatto, *Picture Perfect: The Art and Artifice of Public Image Making* (New York: Basic, 1993).

[9] Paul Abramson, *Political Attitudes in America* (San Francisco: Freeman, 1983).

[10] Warren Miller and Santa Traugott, *American National Election Studies Data Sourcebook* (Cambridge, MA. Harvard University Press, 1989).

selves and that they serve special interests. A citizenry that trusts its politicians to tell it the truth has been replaced by a public that is highly skeptical about motives and intentions. In this situation, it is difficult for politicians to raise money and build public support; they simply do not have the credibility necessary for political persuasion. They need to associate themselves with people who have higher credibility than they themselves do—people, in other words, from outside the political realm who are considered more trustworthy and less partisan, and who have high credibility with the general public.

Politicians love to draw on athletes, musicians, and actors because they come from outside the political world. In many cases, celebrities are seen as white knights, not tainted by past partisan scandals or political dealings, who can clean up the political establishment and bring new ideas to public policymaking. Plus, they are seen as too rich to be bought. Their fame attracts press coverage and campaign contributors. Journalists crowd their press conferences and strain to hear everything they say about issues of foreign and domestic policy. Even though they lack detailed knowledge on these issues, they have a platform that allows them to participate in civic discourse.

These were central assets in Arnold Schwarzenegger's campaign for governor of California, and his election demonstrates why celebrities are effective in running for office and speaking out on public affairs. Seeking office at a time when three-quarters of state voters thought California was headed in the wrong direction and when the incumbent governor, Gray Davis, had a job approval rating hovering around twenty percent, the Hollywood actor campaigned for change and reform, and said that, having spent most of his life outside the political world, he was better equipped than career politicians to bring about necessary changes.[11]

Politicians form alliances with celebrities and use them to raise money, attract media attention, and persuade recalcitrant voters, but celebrities also need politicians. In today's rapidly changing world, celebrities feel pressure to keep their names in the news, and it is a long time between movies or concert tours. Having a charitable or political cause is one way to keep one's name before the public and gets one a spot on talk and entertainment shows. While celebrities generally prefer non-controversial causes such as more money for children living in poverty or breast cancer research, increasingly entertainment figures are taking stances on controversial subjects, such as the Iraq War and election campaigns.

There used to be concern about celebrities' images getting tangled up in political controversies. Dating back to Jane Fonda's opposition to the Vietnam War and the resulting political backlash among vet-

[11] John Wildermuth, "Voters Show Uncommon Interest in Recall," *San Francisco Chronicle* (21 August 2003): A13.

erans upset with her visit to Hanoi, celebrities have worried that too much political involvement could damage their careers. However, in recent years, the large number of entertainers taking active political positions suggests that there is far less concern about negative fallout than would have been the case a few decades ago. There is safety in numbers: as long as many celebrities are politically active, there is far less danger that any one of them will suffer a debilitating backlash from his or her political activities. The activism of some encourages activism by other celebrities.

What the Age of Celebrity Says About Us

The Age of Celebrity is a cultural lens that reveals what Americans value, for it is clear that celebrityhood is as much about us as it is about prominent people. Celebrity culture is not something that is being inflicted on an unwilling public. Rather, it is a development that people watch and willingly participate in. Tabloid newspapers have a large circulation: *The National Enquirer* sells around 2.3 million copies every week, and *Star* magazine has a circulation of 1.7 million. Television shows devoted to gossip about the famous do well. An average of 3.5 million viewers watches the syndicated television show *Inside Edition*, and the E! Entertainment network attracts several million viewers to its shows about Hollywood figures.[12] Celebrities dominate the list of personalities that people would like to meet. A national survey of teenagers found they would most like to meet musicians, followed by athletes and actors—politicians were well down the list.

Not only are people fascinated with famous individuals and their personal lives, they want to be on television themselves. Indeed, their quest for fame is so strong they are willing to eat rats or betray loved ones to achieve stardom. Note the popularity of "reality-based" television shows. The final episode of the first season of *Survivor* earned ratings that were second only to the Super Bowl. The popularity of this genre led pollsters to ask a national sample what they would be willing to allow a reality show to film them doing. The most popular results were 31 percent for being in their pajamas, 29 percent for kissing, 26 percent for crying, 25 percent for having an argument with someone, 16 percent for being drunk, 10 percent for eating a rat or insect, 8 percent for being naked, and 5 percent for having sex.[13] This "democratization" of fame, first described by Leo Braudy many years ago, allows people of ordinary means and talent to become "temporary" celebrities.[14]

Based on these trends, it is clear that the cult of personality resonates with many Americans and is alive and well in society at large. Viewers love to hear tidbits about celebrity lives, even what these

---

[12] *Ulrich's International Periodicals Directory* (New York Bowker, 2000).

[13] CNN/Time Poll conducted June 14–15, 2000. Reported at <www.pollingreport.com>.

[14] See Braudy's *The Frenzy of Renown*.

individuals think about political issues of the day. America is a voyeuristic society that values news and information about prominent people as well as ordinary people who have fleeting moments of fame.

The Risks of Celebrity Politics

America's celebrity politics makes for an entertaining show. It is interesting to see a former wrestler such as Jesse Ventura win the governorship of a major state or Schwarzenegger win the California gubernatorial election. Hillary Clinton's campaign for Senate attracted considerable interest, as did the campaigns of various "third-generation" Kennedys from around the country.[15] But there is more at stake than merely entertainment in the rise of celebrity culture, particularly in the political arena.

At one level, this celebrity regime might be beneficial to our culture and to our political system. Celebrities could bring new ideas to the process. Unlike conventional politicians, celebrities do not have to serve a long apprenticeship before they run for major offices. In a world where entangling alliances are the rule, these individuals are as close to free agents as one can find. This freedom might allow them to challenge the conventional wisdom, adopt unpopular stances, and expand the range of ideas represented in our national dialogue. Since they are not conventional politicians and are not limited to mainstream coalitions based on Left or Right, they have a greater potential to innovate than career politicians.

But in other respects, a system based on celebrityhood raises a host of problems. Our fascination with celebrities raises the risk that there will be more superficiality and less substance in our political process. Celebrities have contributed to the circus atmosphere that has arisen in American politics; increasingly, politics has become a matter of public performance. Politicians get judged more by their ability to deliver crisp sound bytes than by their substantive knowledge. With journalists interested in celebrity quotes and good copy, experts with detailed knowledge about public policy are more likely to become marginalized. It is easier to go to the famous and get their opinion than to seek out voices of less prominent people who may actually know more.

National surveys document that more than ten percent of Americans get information about politics from late-night entertainment shows such as *The Tonight Show* or *Letterman*. And for those under the age of thirty years old, that figure rises to nearly half.[16] As the network news has emphasized entertainment features and lifestyle

---

[15] Darrell M. West, *Patrick Kennedy: The Rise to Power* (Englewood Cliffs: Prentice Hall, 2000).

[16] Paul Brownfield, "Iowa, New Hampshire . . .'Tonight Show'?" *Los Angeles Times* (11 February 2000): 1.

stories at the expense of hard news, more and more Americans are turning to entertainment shows such as *The Daily Show with Jon Stewart* for political commentary.

Both democracy and culture depend on deliberation, participation, and engagement. But what we have now is a system where star-power is weighted more heavily than traditional political skills, such as bargaining, compromise, and experience. Conventional politicians are being replaced by famous, media-savvy fundraisers. The quality of civic deliberation is becoming trivialized. The gossip quotient has increased, and politics has become a 24-hour entertainment spectacle. With attention spans for important stories dropping precipitously, the system rewards celebrity politicians with famous names. Unless these individuals provide citizens with proper information, it short-circuits our system of governance. Without quality information, voters cannot make informed choices about their futures.

American politics has never placed a strong emphasis on substance. Compared to other Western democracies, fewer people vote at election time, and many appear not to be very informed about their decisions. As celebrity politics takes root, there is the long-term danger that citizens will become even less knowledgeable about policy choices, and they may become content to watch and be entertained. But elections are a key device by which representative democracy takes place. Citizens must feel engaged in the process, must be able to think about their options, and must feel they have a stake in the important decisions that get made. Without serious deliberation and discourse, politics becomes mere entertainment. Without experience and knowledge, society may lose its ability to confront pressing problems and resolve social conflict.

Jesse Ventura™ and the Brave New World of Politainer Politics

By Ann Conley and David Schultz
Journal of American & Comparative Cultures, Fall 2000

The example of celebrity-turned-politician Jesse Ventura is but one clear indication of how the media, politics, and popular culture are becoming increasingly intertwined in our lives, and in the lives of politicians. Here, an individual named James Janos rose to fame as a popular, cult-like, outlandish personality in the televised world of wrestling with the assumed persona Jesse Ventura. From there, he appeared in several films popular with teenagers and college students; then he moved on to be a controversial host of several AM radio talk shows in Minnesota. As a host, he was known for his brash, hard-talking, "take no prisoners" views that often criticized the political establishment. Jesse carried that persona over into his surprise run for governor, using it as a way to distinguish himself from the political establishment and to demonstrate that, if elected, he would be a different kind of governor.

And elected he was. Using his media image in televised debates, and even in commercials that featured "Jesse Ventura action figures," Jesse Ventura did shock the world. Since his election he has become an international celebrity, merging his role as governor with that of professional wrestler into a unique figure in American politics.

Since taking office, Ventura has continued to capitalize on his fame, selling his action figures and other merchandise bearing his name and returning to the wrestling ring to referee a 1999 World Wrestling Federation "Summer Slam" event. The media popular culture icon's personality and his role as governor have become indistinguishable.

What Jesse Ventura has taught us all, besides the level of his marketing genius, is the incredible potential to reach the public (read: voters) through entertainment venues. Jesse's power and value as a politician come not just from his use of a particular venue. Because Jesse is a politician who is also an entertainer, he has become what other politicians, thus far, will never be—a politainer.

This article explains what it means to be a politainer, why the time is right for the politainer in our society, and what the implications of politainment are.

Emergence of the Politainer

Jesse Ventura emerged from a long line of predecessors who are celebrities (actors, newscasters, and athletes) turned politicians: Ronald Reagan, Sonny Bono, Clint Eastwood, Jack Kemp, Bill Bradley, and Fred Grandy (Love Boat's "Gopher"), to name just a few. While following in the footsteps of such notable politicians who have traded in their celebrity for political power, Jesse is forging his own distinct political pathae—one that others are sure to follow. He takes the trend of entertainer turned politician one step further because he is more than just a celebrity turned politician; he is simultaneously an entertainer and a politician; he is, in other words, a politainer.

Jesse's path has been marked by many firsts for an American politician: action figures modeled after his television persona; a not for-profit company ("Ventura for Minnesota, Inc.") that sells official, licensed Jesse Ventura paraphernalia, along with a trademarked name; a tell-all autobiography published in his first few months as Governor of Minnesota; a second book published (and aggressively promoted and publicized) just over a year later; an appearance on the soap opera *The Young and the Restless*; an appearance as the referee in a World Wrestling Federation match; and a weekly Minnesota radio show. His meteoric rise into the statewide, and now the national, political scene has been incredibly instructive for those who follow and study politics.

It is from Jesse's colorful activities that we can deduce the characteristics of a politainer. A politainer is simultaneously an entertainer and a politician; his persona is a fiction; his persona is a commodity; and he uses multi-media venues (many of which are entertainment outlets) and sophisticated mass-marketing techniques to distribute "message," and/or to market himself as a politician and as an entertainer.

Simultaneously an Entertainer and a Politician

A politainer has a dual career: he uses his entertainment career to benefit his political career, and he uses his political career to benefit his entertainment career. Jesse Ventura's autobiography, *I Ain't Got Time to Bleed*, his appearances on the late night shows (Jay Leno and David Letterman), a controversial interview in *Playboy*, and the sale of Jesse Ventura action figures might not have occurred had he never run for governor. Likewise, it would have been impossible for Jesse to become governor without the celebrity status that accompanied his role as Jesse Ventura, the wrestler. He capitalized on his entertainer status, ran for governor as a publicity stunt, and, much to his and everyone's surprise, was elected.

Entertainment Persona Is a Fiction, Yet We Elect the Persona Rather than the Person

Minnesota's current governor was born James Janos, not Jesse Ventura; yet Minnesotans elected Jesse Ventura™, a man with a trademarked name fashioned after a coastal California city and a persona fashioned as an over-the-top wrestler. Ventura the wrestler/governor beats up "special interest man"; he sells officially-licensed bumper stickers that say "My governor can beat up your governor"; and he refereed a World Wrestling Federation wrestling match. For Jesse Ventura the wrestler/governor, politics has become the crucible in which he continues to forge his persona as the tough-talking renegade wrestler. Where James Janos ends and Jesse Ventura begins, or where the entertainer or governor begins and ends, is not clear, but there is no doubt that the Jesse Ventura persona is a fiction—a fiction that he sold to the public and upon which he has built his political base. The public has always made a distinction between the public and private sides of politicians' personalities and lives. For a politainer, the public/private tension is far less relevant than the tension between fiction and non-fiction.

Indeed, the public allows a politainer to get away with behavior that falls within expected parameters of that particular politainer's entertainment persona. Since Jesse has always been over-the-top, people allow and even expect him to be consistent with that persona, even if his behavior is very different from what we might expect from an ordinary politician. He can be blunt, use coarse and vulgar language, and refer to his critics as "gutless cowards," and the public views each instance as simply another example of the Governor telling it like it is. Ventura is examined not through the lens normally used to evaluate elected officials, but instead through the magnifying glass normally used on movie stars and celebrities. Such a standard is less critical and introspective, and tolerant of the latest foibles so long as they entertain and amuse us. And just like in an all-star wrestling match, the public suspends its beliefs in order to participate in the myth and fiction of Jesse "The Body" Ventura, the wrestler in the governor's office. He is the Postmodern version of the Horatio Alger story: anyone can grow up and become famous, and the television viewer vicariously participates in the story. In its desire to be entertained, the public is willing to leave its critical faculties at the door and accept behavior from the politainer that it would not accept from another elected official.

Entertainment Persona Is a Commodity

The last two to three decades of the twentieth century are distinguishable from any others in their increasingly widespread and rampant *consumerism*. It is in this context that our culture (with the help of marketers and our mass media) has broken new ground in its ability to commodify almost anything. While the political world has never been immune to the influence of the marketplace, one can argue that the politainer becomes a commodity like Coke or Snicker's bars. Jesse's use of a trademarked name, his enforcement of his rights, his precluding others from capitalizing on his fame, and all the accompanying paraphernalia reinforce this fact (Caple). In fact, in an August, 1999 news conference, he refused to rule out any future product endorsements (Ragsdale A1).

Use of Multi-Media Venues and Marketing Techniques to Distribute "Message" and/or to Market Himself as a Politician and as an Entertainer

Politicians throughout U.S. history have made use of the media in their campaigns and during their terms of office. Political campaigns have continually adapted to the media and marketing practices of their times. In his book, *Adcult USA*, James Twitchell cites the "defining event of political maneuvering" in advertising as the 1952 election campaign of Dwight Eisenhower. A man named Rossier Reeves masterminded a highly successful campaign called "Eisenhower Answers America," in which Eisenhower answered on television a series of questions generated by Reeves but asked on camera by average citizens. Decades later, "Reagan did exactly what Rossier Reeves was attempting to do for Eisenhower. He traded intellectual content for emotional appeal" (Twitchell 121-22). John F. Kennedy, too, innovatively used television. Common wisdom has it that it was Kennedy's appearance on the first televised presidential debate with Nixon that helped him win the election. Kennedy's superb television presence contrasted so greatly with Richard Nixon's lack of presence that some say it cost Nixon the election. Bill Clinton, too, pushed his use of the media farther than any previous president when he went on MTV, and when he played the saxophone on Arsenio Hall's TV show. He and his wife Hillary have periodically used morning and prime time interview shows (e.g., the *Barbara Walters Specials* and *The Today Show*) to get particular messages out.

Finally, during the 2000 presidential race, Jay Leno and David Letterman hosted candidates John McCain, George W. Bush, and Al Gore. David Letterman even employed a long-running stunt, Campaign 2000, in a successful effort to hype ratings by enticing New York Senate candidate Hillary Clinton to appear on his show. For Letterman the purpose was clear: better ratings. But for the candidates, the free exposure was invaluable, and the result was a faint effort at emulating Ventura's success in bridging the politics and entertainment gap. In fact, Ms. Clinton, who used "Hillary!" as her slogan (reminiscent of other first-name-only celebrities such as Madonna and Cher), seemed poised to make a bid for public office using her first name much like a brand name for a product. "But Hillary! New and improved!" Overall, the trend toward celebrity news (Hess 28) dovetails with the emergence of celebrity politicians. Clearly there is historical precedent for politicians' use of the media.

What is different about a politainer's use of the media is the degree to which it is done. What the politainer represents is the complete saturation of politics by media and marketing.

Politainer's Postmodern Roots

The politainer is a creature of Postmodern culture. Postmodern society is characterized by:

1. the increasing heterogeneity or diversity of the public;
2. relativism (a core challenge to our cohesion as a culture in the Postmodern world is the relativism of values in the absence of shared foundational assumptions);
3. the blurring of the line between public and private life (improvements in technology, advancements in information processing, and flexible job structures allow us to do work anywhere and anytime, which leads to the blending of our work and private lives);
4. a multiplicity of roles (a denizen of the Postmodern world can be overwhelmed by the number of competing roles that she fulfills at any given moment; even more difficult is the task of trying to prioritize these multiple roles [Cooper 36–40]); and
5. consumerism and the commodification of knowledge.

In the United States, we are chronically inundated with what James Twitchell calls "commercial speech" (16), the language of advertising. Behind that language is the powerful, and frequently unchallenged, assumption that money will buy happiness, and that by consuming enough of the right products, we will eventually achieve personal satisfaction. Additionally, Jean-Francois Lyotard's criticism of Modernity implies that we must now recognize the new information society of the computer and the changing role of knowledge and knowing in the Postmodern world (3–6). Knowledge is not a ground, but a commodity for exchange and power. It is transmutable and its commodification reveals its nonpermanent nature. Lyotard thus proposes that this change in knowledge undermines Modernity and its belief in a fixed epistemological center. Knowledge is a commodity no different from any other, and it can be exchanged or changed on the market for any other thing. Knowledge has been reified, implying that it can be manipulated to suit the needs of the market . . . or the electorate.

Postmodernism challenges the traditional foundational basis of knowledge characteristic of Modernity, seeing in its place a more subject-orientated theory of truth that contests the clear boundaries demarcated by a rational-scientific conception of the world. According to Richard Rorty, a sense of commonness or agreement on what truth and knowledge are lies at the heart of the epistemological foundationalism of Modernity. Rorty believes that this foundationalism is either false or illusionary, since we do not really have access to some Archimedean epistemological point—because such a point does not exist (316). Kantian epistemological categories are not universal, but historical, and they are the product of individual cultures and psychologies. Knowledge is not universal but particular, more like perspectives or ideologies than anything else.

Rorty's point is that the confrontational (or subject/object) model of knowledge is an inadequate model of cognition. Rorty also denies that epistemology is an adequate ground for politics. In rejecting the notion that a fixed reality exists out there (or, for Kant, in the objective categories of the mind), Rorty rejects the belief in a fixed terra firma upon which one can build a permanent base of knowledge. This rejection leads to a denial of an epistemological center for politics. There is no one political truth or authority for political propositions, but many. One cannot assert that any natural laws validate universal truths of politics or prove that a political doctrine is the only correct one. Instead, there are many ways to view political questions, and all of us have the right to adjudicate them.

Rorty thus dismisses as failed the confrontation theory of knowledge. With that rejection, the epistemological ground of Modernity is gone and the entire project of Modernity is moribund. Rorty argues that we should instead view knowledge as conversational (163, 389–93) and dispense with the belief in a cognitive center. We should look to knowing as being plural and diverse (316). What we know, or what knowledge is (if we can even continue to use that term), is determined in some conventional conversational mode of unity being produced out of the many localized understandings or meanings found in the diversity of social practices (178, 361). There is no social or political center of truth. Claims to truth, or verifications of truth propositions, reside not in appeals of correspondence to some object, or in appeal to some political authority. Truth resides in how we can justify or persuade others to accept our beliefs (141).

Similarly, Paul Feyerabend also attacks the totalizing force of science as a paradigm for politics in Modernity (106–07). Modern science, as the paradigm for modern politics, has thus supported an elitist notion of politics that claims there are experts in scientific and political matters. This means that there are correct political truths and technical experts, who, when employing the correct tools, can find these truths and scientifically run the state and the polity. Scientific rationality and politics discourages the role of opinion in politics in the same way Plato discouraged doxa. Only a few really know, and are entitled to participate. Modern scientific politics, then, is antidemocratic and non-participatory, and enjoys its privileged status through its protection by the state. For Feyerabend, science has become the new state religion.

In medieval times, Christianity was the legitimizing force of monarchial power. Now, it is science justifying the modern state. While Christianity supported kings, kings supported Christianity. Similarly, science supports, and is supported by, the modern state. Feyerabend thus divorces science from politics. This presents Postmodern culture with a choice—either a foundationless politics or a politics searching for a new ground—that is filled by linking politics to entertainment.

Postmodern life is marked by shifting and uncertain identities, assumptions, and values. At the same time, Postmodern culture is saturated by the influence of commerce and consumerism. Despite our great diversity in the United States, we are tied together by our shared identity as marketplace consumers. It is the relative strength of our shared marketplace values and the relative weakness of other potentially competing value systems that makes Postmodern society particularly vulnerable to the influence of consumerism. Our shared materialism fills a cultural need for commonality. The common experience of shopping at Wal-Mart, eating at McDonald's, or watching television serves more to tie people together than anything else. The equality of Postmodern life is the shared experience of being consumers.

Postmodernism is the backdrop against which a number of inter-related trends play out: the deepening of the relationship between entertainment and advertising, the convergence of entertainment and the news media, and the convergence of politics and entertainment—all of which create the crucible in which a politainer is created.

Entertainment is obviously a common thread running throughout the trends mentioned above. A key ingredient of Postmodern culture is that people have a fundamental need to be entertained—to engage in the suspension of beliefs, the escapism, the imaginative process, the archetypal struggles (e.g., good vs. evil), and the emotional stimulation that are part of being entertained. It is from this need that the "entertainment imperative" arises in the advertising, news, and political arenas (McAllister 43).

The relationship between entertainment and advertising has been provocatively analyzed by James Twitchell, who coined the term "Adcult" as a way of capturing the degree that advertising has become the central institution in American society. In his thumbnail sketch of the advertising industry, he makes the link between advertising and entertainment: "The business of advertising is essentially the business of trafficking in audiences. After an audience has been gathered, its attention is rented to an agent who inserts a message from a sponsor. The audience pays attention because it is traded something in return, namely, entertainment" (5).

Twitchell highlights six characteristics of Adcult that demonstrate its cultural influence and importance. According to Twitchell, Adcult is:

- *Ubiquitous.* Advertising is everywhere.

- *Anonymous.* It is extremely difficult to determine authorship in advertising.

- *Symbiotic.* "Adcult shares the energy of other social organisms. The something with which it lives is on the surface entertainment and below the surface deep concerns of the specific culture." Advertisement merges with other cultural trends, like music. By viewing MTV videos, for example, one sees "how the colonizing power of commercial speech can quickly consume discrete forms and make them one."

- *Syncretic.* "Adcult layers itself on top of other cultures." It builds on what has come before, like the Burger King commercial that has two diapered babies chatting as in *Look Who's Talking*. Twitchell likens this self-referential aspect of Adcult to religious ceremonies.

- *Profane.* Advertising must excite and shock to get the consumers' attention.

- *Magical.* Twitchell contends that he is "hardly the first to recognize that advertising is the gospel of redemption in the fallen world of capitalism, that advertising has become the vulgate of the secular belief in the redemption of commerce. In a most profound sense advertising and religion are part of the same meaning-making process: they occur at the margin of human concern about the world around us, and each attempts to breach the gap between us and objects by providing a systemic understanding. Whereas the Great Chain of Being organized the world of our ancestors, the marketplace of objects does it for us. They both promise redemption: one through faith, the other through purchase. But how are order and salvation affected? By magical thinking, pure and simple." (16–30)

The concept of magic needs more exploration because, while it is the most surprising of the characteristics described above, it is also the most profound. We are so immersed in advertising that it is easy to miss the degree to which it promises us magical transformations, both big and small, from our current state of being. Through advertising we might come to believe that we can stop the aging process with the right skin cream or hair coloring; or we might become convinced that by purchasing the right make-up or beer, we could be more attractive to the opposite sex.

On one level, this kind of magical transformation is entertaining. On another, this type of advertisement goes far beyond entertainment, speaking to some of our deepest hopes (e.g., defeating loneliness) and fears (e.g., rejection or death). Twitchell contends that it is the conversation that advertising carries on with these deeper issues in our lives that puts it on a par with religion.

Twitchell goes on to draw parallels between the ancient gods (Zeus, Hera, Jupiter, etc.) and the commercial "gods" of today: The Jolly Green Giant, the Michelin Man, and Aunt Jemima, among others. The difference between modern and ancient gods is that modern gods "now reside in manufactured products and that, although earlier gods were invoked by fasting, prayer, rituals, and penance, the promise of purchase calls forth their modern ilk" (30). Through magic, disposable goods become "long-lasting charms." Through magic, a pitcher of Kool-Aid smiles and Dow Cleanser develops scrubbing bubbles that talk (30). Later, this article will return to the religious significance of advertising and will address how this point is relevant to the role of the politainer.

Matthew McAllister speaks more specifically about the tactics of what he calls "new advertising," which include cross-promotion, sponsorship, and place-based advertising. These three tactics have a particular salience when it comes to understanding the milieu from which a politainer emerges.

The first tactic, cross-promotion, is an increasingly-used practice in which companies pool their economic and symbolic resources to create joint advertising. McAllister believes that "cross-promotion increases the symbolic power of one product by using it as a referent system for another product" (250). This practice is further enhanced when database marketing is used to help the marketer precisely deduce what referent systems a consumer does or doesn't like.

Jesse Ventura's press conference regarding his foray back into the wrestling ring as a referee for a World Wrestling Federation (WWF) match could be viewed as cross-promotion—Jesse and the WWF received mutual benefit from Ventura's appearance. Jesse's symbolic power enhanced the WWF's and the WWF's symbolic power enhanced Jesse's (in the eyes of some, at least). Similarly, the sale of Jesse dolls by Ventura's political campaign reinforced the similar sale of the dolls by his nonprofit corporation Ventura for Minnesota, Inc.

A second tactic is sponsorship, a practice that McAllister defined as "an act of corporate giving to some activity—sometimes for-profit, sometimes not—in an attempt to capitalize on the philanthropic ethos of patronage as well as the promotional functions of advertising" (178). This tactic is not new, but it is provocative when viewed in the context of politics. In the next section of this article, we will discuss the ethical implications of a politainer with corporate sponsorship.

A third tactic is place-based advertising, which is a form of advertising that places advertising at the location or destination in which a particular audience is found. Advertising along the walls of an ice arena during a hockey game is one example. As McAllister states, "[p]lace-based advertising is not simply an ad-supported medium in a social place; it is also the use of the place (the school, the doctor' office) as a way to increase the credibility of the advertising message" (250).

All of these—cross-promotion, sponsorship, and place-based advertising—are practices that could be used by a politainer, and all create specific ethical concerns for politainers and the public. These will be discussed in the next section of this essay.

The world of advertising has had an enormous impact on the institutions surrounding it. The news media/journalism is one of the institutions that have fallen under the spell of the advertising industry's twin values of entertainment and profit. The result is infotainment, the merging of entertainment and journalism. Bill Kovach and Tom Rosenstiel lament the demise of journalistic integrity at the altar of profit and entertainment. They believe that we are living in an era of "post-O.J. media" in which "the cultures of entertainment, infotainment, argument, analysis, tabloid, and mainstream press not only work side by side but intermingle and merge" (4).

Put another way, ours is a "Mixed Media Culture" in which the "classic function of journalism to sort out a true and reliable account of the day's events is being undermined" (5). Kovach and Rosenstiel conclude that news programming is driven by, among many other things, the twenty-four hour news cycle, a fascination with a polarized story, and a desire to find "the 'big story' that will temporarily reassemble the now-fragmented [read: Postmodern] mass audience" (5). Ironically, the Mixed Media Culture weakens the press's ability to "serve as a cohesive cultural force, and weakens the public's tether to a true account of the news" (4-5). Under corporate control, news has simply become another form of entertainment (Schultz, "Cultural" 19–21).

News producers unfortunately are unable to afford, or keep up with, the information demands of round-the-clock news coverage. According to Kovach and Rosenstiel, channels do not adequately invest in reporting infrastructure. Short-staffed and in need of programming that will capture audiences' attention, news producers have been pushed into the "journalism of assertion" (8). The journalism of assertion has the feel of a talk show; it is populated with pundits who do not gather the news as much as they comment and speculate on it; and it entertains by engaging in polarized argumentation (1–9). News producers are falling sway to the same "entertainment imperative" that mobilizes the advertising industry.

Infotainment emerges from a milieu defined by consumerism and mass marketing. Taking its cue from the advertising industry, the news industry is becoming the infotainment industry, migrating ever closer toward the world of the entertaining, the unsubstantiated, the titillating, and the fictional. Aping a television commercial that opened with the line "I'm not a doctor, but I play one on television," infotainment takes as its slogan, "I'm not a real politician, but I play one on television."

Thus we have Jesse Ventura, who embodies all of the above in a parallel are in politics. What we observe in Jesse is the convergence of entertainment and politics to meet the demands of a populace that is cynical about most politicians, that wants to be entertained, and that is willing to suspend their beliefs to do so.

The Implications of Politainment

As politics merges with entertainment, entertainment becomes a doorway through which politics (and, by extension, governance) immerses itself in the vocabulary and behavior of mass marketing. What are the ethical implications of this trend for politicians and for democracy?

In light of the trends toward Adcult and infotainment, there are several emerging ethical concerns for the politainer, for his audience (the public), and for the institution of democracy.

For the politainer, the previous discussion about Adcult begs the question of whether a politainer is more vulnerable to individual corruption and conflicts of interest. Dennis Thompson defines individual corruption as private gain from public office (29). This is an ongoing concern for any politician, but a politainer has even more opportunity for conflicts of interest because she has a dual career in both the political and the entertainment fields. How can the public (or the politainer) determine which hat she is wearing? When is she acting in the interest of her entertainment career, and when is she acting on behalf of her political career? When might either or both careers conflict with her duty to act in the best interest of the people she was elected to represent? When it comes to having a multiplicity of roles, the politainer is surely a Postmodern phenomenon!

Furthermore, the politainer's entertainment career, with its immersion in Adcult and mass media, makes the politainer particularly susceptible to conflicts of interest. As described earlier, the advertising industry employs the tactics of cross-promotion, sponsorship, and place-based advertising. If we apply these advertising tactics to a politainer like Jesse Ventura^{TM}—who is, for all practical purposes, a marketable commodity—then it is logical to assume that he influences and is influenced by the advertising process. Indeed, the politainer in this situation is vulnerable to undue influence in the advertising process.

If, for example, Jesse Ventura were the recipient of corporate sponsorship from a nuclear power company or an entertainment event in which he was participating or that he was hosting, would Jesse be more inclined to sign a piece of legislation that would permit it to expand its storage of nuclear waste? Jesse Ventura says that he is not beholden to special interests—but what kind of influence would a lucrative sponsorship deal have on his decision-making? This same line of thinking would hold true for other advertising deals like endorsements and cross-promotion. Jesse Ventura^{TM} cannot separate his interests, those of his sponsor, and those of the public, because he and his governorship are simply products of the corporate infotainment culture, lacking distinct identities. Louis XIV once remarked, "L'état c'est moi," demonstrating an incapacity to distinguish himself from France. Perhaps Jesse Ventura^{TM}, who exclaimed in a *Playboy* interview that it was "good to be the king" (Sweeney, "Governor"), should have as his slogan either "L'march-andise c'est moi" or "L'idole c'est moi."

In the case of Jesse Ventura, as with all politainers, a dynamic that complicates this issue is his apparently deep philosophical grounding in what Terry Cooper identifies as the "spirit of western individualism" (114). Cooper contends that Americans place a high value on respecting an individual's right to protect his self-interest.

Small (554), in his survey of the problem of conflict of interest in American government, has produced findings that support the conclusion that this tendency has been on the increase in modern society. He writes, "Increasingly, then, in the late Twentieth Century it becomes more and more difficult to separate the simplistic, completely personal interest from the public interest. Because these interests are overlapping and no longer separable, older norms of right and wrong, desirable or undesirable are inadequate" (554). He concludes that it is "part of the human condition" to seek money and power from public sources for the sake of private gain. (Cooper 116)

This trend does not bode well for those who believe elected office is a form of public service. Jesse Ventura™ justifies his pursuit of private gain by claiming that he is doing it in his off hours, and that if one bans outside gain, then only rich professional politicians can run for office. In short, the politainer sets a standard of conduct clearly lower than we set for traditional politicians and government officials, and the public—rather, we consumers—seem to accept this behavior much in the same way that we accept other celebrities pursuing commercial ventures. In fact, since first being elected governor, Ventura has been subject to numerous criticisms of his behavior as violating generally-applicable codes of ethics (Sweeney, "Top Ethics").

Some suggest that using government or the public sphere for private purposes can be viewed as one way in which our "commons" are being exploited. "Conflict of interest, therefore, is an insidiously difficult problem[. . .]. Citizens in public administrative positions have special access to the governmental commons that most ordinary citizens do not. This access presents unusual opportunities and, therefore, temptations to exploit governmental resources for personal gain" (Cooper 117). The emergence of the politainer, as embodied by Jesse Ventura, is a signal that this individualistic ideology is indeed winning out over a concern for the common good. Jesse's own mantra of "personal responsibility" echoes this very trend.

Another ethical question that arises in this context of mass marketing and politics relates to whether a politainer devalues the public office he holds by selling himself as a commodity. In his critique of new advertising, Matthew McAllister points out that advertising practices "devalue original institutions" (250). For example, when a school participates in place-based advertising, it is "no longer a place where advertising does not influence," and therefore it is a little less special. When Jesse Ventura™, the Governor of Minnesota, becomes a *de facto* advertisement for the World Wrestling Federation through cross-promotion, he not only loses some of his authority as Minnesota's highest official in state office, but he also breaks down a wall that has traditionally kept commercialism out of the role of a serving public official. Perhaps this is not a terribly compelling argument in an era where a large segment of the population already has little regard for public office and believes that all politicians are corrupt. It is, however, noteworthy that Ventura the politainer has made an unprecedented move by allowing the office of governor to be commercialized.

Unfortunately, there are no clear answers to concerns about conflicts of interest and undue influence. There is not a great deal of political will to legislate restrictions on the actions of politainers. The public seems indifferent so long as the politainer entertains, and other legislators, either fearful of public wrath or hopeful that they too can profit from the bounty, steer away from acting. Indeed, public vigilance may be the most important remedy for potential conflicts of interest on the part of the politainer.

Ironically, even though a politainer is more susceptible to conflicts of interest, she is less likely to be scrutinized for it by the public. As the first section of this article pointed out, the public has different expectations for a politainer's behavior than it does for the behavior of an ordinary politician. We allow greater flexibility in how a politainer behaves, which might mean that we are more accepting of her conflicts of interest. Additionally, the relationship between the politainer and the public is one of audience to entertainer. This means that the audience's (the public's) critical faculties have been suspended—that, again, creates a situation in which the politainer is subject to less oversight by the public. As with a movie star or other celebrity, foibles and personal failings are part of the entertainment and attraction. Finally, Ventura often claims he is "just kidding" when he makes remarks which would damage other politicians, and the public seems to accept this as an apology.

Politainment raises ethical concerns for the public as well. These concerns could be viewed as questions of access. The politainer presents both opportunities and challenges to public participation in the democratic process.

What is clear from Jesse Ventura's campaign is the degree to which he mobilized previously unmobilized voters. Because of significant media access, and through the use of sophisticated marketing strategies, politainers like Jesse Ventura now have unprecedented access to multiple markets—i.e., markets that vary by race, ethnicity, socioeconomic status, and gender. That is good news for the "23 million American adults [who] are functionally illiterate and therefore are almost entirely beyond the reach of print media" (Graber 203). Mass media marketing through entertainment venues present incredible possibilities for reaching out to alienated or disenfranchised groups.

One might argue that, because of whom he mobilized, Jesse Ventura's victory is something of a Jacksonian "common man" revolution. One essayist in *Harper's Magazine* described the following scene at the Ventura victory party on election night:

> The betting windows are closed but the Ascot Lounge to the right of the escalators is open, and Ventura's supporters wait three deep for a chance to take full advantage. I try to move past them for a closer look but get cut off by a train of manly men who are using their 16-ounce Leinenkugel's as wedges against the crowd. All four of them are wearing army jackets, camouflage pants, and hunting boots. The only thing missing, so I hope, are the guns.
>
> I drop into their slipstream and ride it into the party, a fat, sweaty weisswurst of baseball hats, Twins sweatshirts, and high-school letter jackets in a makeshift staging area surrounded by television crews, whose lights fence in the dense crowd like a cattle pen. Thick of neck and stout of heart, Ventura's supporters are bleaching under the hot lights, but none of them seem to care. Next to me on the fringe, a ratty Vikings parka encases a man in his thirties. A thin layer of foam coats his mustache, and his brow is knit in drunken concentration as he tries to decide between the whiskey in his left hand and the beer in his right.
>
> All white and all worked up, the crowd near the stage builds up a stadium chant of "Packers suck! Packers suck!" which inexplicably segues into "Bikers suck! Bikers suck!" I look around and see one such biker walking out of the Ascot Lounge carrying a big beer and a paper plate with a pyramid of cocktail franks. Flipping his long black hair, he angrily surveys the pit. For a moment I think he's going to throw down his snack and put up his fists, but he only smiles and struts into the room, holding his beer high above his head like a torch. (Cass 65)

To what degree we might have heard the elite utter parallel sentiments about Andrew Jackson's supporters in the 1800s? However, despite the classist overtones in this passage, it is clear that Jesse Ventura's candidacy excited and mobilized an unusual group of voters. If it is true that Jesse is reaching disenfranchised voters, are we not one step closer to achieving a goal of full citizen participation in government? Perhaps yes, but is this an informed citizenry coming together to articulate the public good, or is merely another form of Nielsen rating or consumer choice of a brand name product? Or is it simply swapping votes for entertainment? Are elections simply People's Choice Awards? And do we have real political debate and discourse, or a brave new form of Huxleyian hypnopaedia that lulls us into McWorld (Barber 1–3)?

In addition, human communication researchers have discovered that "individuals who consume a lot of media, particularly television, are more knowledgeable about politics and other social issues" (Emmers-Sommer and Allen 490). If this is true, then a politainer's use of multiple media venues might provide a greater opportunity for a broader number of people to engage in our democratic process.

Along with opportunities come challenges. A politainer's increased level of access to the public certainly has a bright side. It also has a dark side. Increased access to and engagement of the public through advertising and entertainment venues creates the potential to manipulate who gets access to political information. It also has the potential to fictionalize the political process. Politainment is Orwellian in a doublethink or Newspeak sense: Politicians merge two arenas not previously combined—politics and entertainment— where fiction is reality, and where the message does not ask citizens to render careful political judgments, but instead asks for blind acceptance of the product being sold.

Indeed, a positive interpretation of the access argument assumes a free market of consumer choice in media venues. Ideally, demand determines what venues are available, and as our population becomes more diverse, so does the variety of media available to meet the population's needs. But perhaps the opposite is true. Perhaps the consumer does not choose the media, but, rather, the media choose the consumer.

Matthew McAllister contends that advertising-based media seeks out the demographic groups that have the money to buy the advertised products. He paraphrases the thinking of C. E. Baker: "[A]udiences who are not 'demogenic' are ignored or seriously underrepresented by advertising-supported media. Those who are poor, elderly or live in rural areas have less media options designed to appeal to them than those who are rich, young and urban[. .]. Advertising is much more likely to subsidize, with advertising revenue, media aimed at the upper-class than media aimed at the poor" (46).

In addition, McAllister says that media create and alter program content in order to gain audiences and to make these audiences more receptive to certain ads. Conversely, programming that makes audiences less receptive to certain advertising is less desirable to advertisers and therefore more difficult to maintain. Obviously, "advertising has an ideological effect upon media content. Advertising's economic presence significantly influences the view of the world that the media present, a view embedded in and influenced by social power and social relations" (47).

Clearly, this dynamic has implications for access to information. In the past, one might have argued that even though advertisers have a great deal of control over certain media venues, at least the news media could still be relied upon to protect some level of democratic public discourse. Bill Kovach and Tom Rosenstiel contend that "the news culture still shapes the lines of the political playing field and the context in which citizens define meaning for political events" (3). What the infotainment trend shows us, however, is the degree to which the news media have joined advertisers in turning public discourse into commercial speech. Advertising-based media, including the news media, are manufacturing and limiting the political debate.

Following the same logic, one might speculate that the politainer, with his vulnerability to advertisers and entertainment media, might engage in the same process of limiting public debate in order to please advertisers. The politainer is symbolic of how commercial speech has now permeated the political arena. All political speech is now commercial, and vice versa, challenging yet another barrier within First Amendment free speech jurisprudence that seeks to distinguish the two

There is yet another problem with the optimistic view that the methods of a politainer might improve the political process. The same researchers who proposed that media can be educative also showed that there is a problem with "impressionable" individuals whose "learning and beliefs are influenced by fictional media" (Emmers-Sommer and Allen 491). For example, viewers of Oliver Stone's *JFK* are more likely to accept as truth his and James Garrison's view of the Kennedy assassination than that of the Warren Commission (Kelly and Elliot 191). These researchers might have made a case study of the thirty-seven percent of the Minnesota electorate who voted for the fictional candidate, Jesse Ventura™. They are prime examples of the impressionable individuals who feel that they "know" Jesse Ventura through his character in the wrestling ring.

If we concur with the assertions made about the deep and pervasive influence of Adcult, then it is likely that to some degree, we are *all* impressionable. We are all, to varying degrees, well-conditioned congregants in the church of the marketplace in America; so much so that we are willing to believe in the magic that advertising offers us. With the convergence of politics and entertainment, and the concomitant influence of advertising on politics, one can foresee a future in which our notion of an educated electorate deliberating about candidates and public policy has been swept away. In its place is a populace that favors fictionalized candidates who not only entertain, but promise magic—such as simultaneously cutting taxes, raising military spending, and balancing the budget, all without smoke and mirrors!

One result of the merger of politics and entertainment is that the impression people now have of public officials is framed more by jokes and less by their stances on the issues. Thus, in the 2000 presidential race, George Bush was seen as an intellectual lightweight and a frat boy and Al Gore depicted as wooden. And because candidates were treated more like movie stars, politics is now thought of as entertainment, campaigning is like acting, and politicians are like actors. All this clearly leads to a loss of substance in politics and a degeneration into politainment.

In an essay reviewing five pieces of anti-utopian literature from the early twentieth century, Christopher Dornan comments on the prescience of the authors in their assessment of where our society would be at the end of this century. In our market-induced predilection for the world of fantasy and fiction, we are moving closer to this anti-utopian vision than we ever anticipated: "So as the 20th century draws to a close, its signature futurist motif is one of escaping reality into a media-maintained imaginary dimension where all fantasies are possible, all desires can be fulfilled. As the Microsoft ad put it, 'Where do you want to go today?' The very question presumes that the answer is elsewhere: somewhere more interesting than here and now" (Dornan 129).

Perhaps we are destined for a dual reality in which our hoped-for future is "Adtopia," the world of magic and wish fulfillment, and the reality an anti-utopia in which commercial speech passes for public discourse and advertisers control public discourse and thereby control political decisions (Twitchell 39). Dornan asks the question, "Who could have imagined that the media would come to usurp political authority, buffeting a political process and decision-making in the chaotic turbulence of perception?" (129)

Conclusion

Jesse Ventura™ did shock the world with his election, but the real shock is perhaps more Orwellian in what it bodes for politics. Perhaps Jesse Ventura™ is just the first of a new wave of politainers who will come to dominate politics in the twenty-first century. He is the culmination of many forces. As *The Wall Street Journal* proclaimed, "America is reaching the climax of a generation-long trend: the melding of entertainment and politics into a hybrid, all-purpose celebrity culture"—where, according to Frank Mankiewicz, a political consultant, "We're talking about seeing politics as an extension of popular culture" (Seib). Candidates for public office need not be real candidates or politicians; instead, it is enough, as with Warren Beatty, to have played one in a movie (*Bulworth*). Or, reality can mirror fiction, which mirrors reality, as in the movie *Wag the Dog*, which told the tale of a United States president starting a war to distract the public away from a sex scandal in which he was entwined. In 1998, as impeachment was bearing down on President Clinton because of allegations that he lied about an affair he had with White House intern Monica Lewinsky, he announced that he would begin bombing Iraq. Almost immediately, the public and the press stated this was simply "wagging the dog," using this phrase to describe what they assumed to be the real motives Clinton had in this military action.

Is the future of politics in the twenty-first century really so bleak? Perhaps not. But we can be sure that there will be many more politainers to come. Future candidates for office may not come from state houses and the halls of Congress, but from television shows such as T*he West Wing*, movie houses, and sports arenas. The power of Adcult and the shaping influence of infotainment almost require it. Politics, like the news, will become yet another entertainment medium through which products are sold—including the politicians/ politainers themselves. We are sure to see more Bob Doles selling Viagra, Mario Cuomos selling Doritos, and Jesse Venturas™ selling World Wrestling Federations, with little regard for whether the politician is currently in office. And, as for the public, as long as we are entertained—we simply will not mind.

Works Cited

Barber, Benjamin R. *Jihad Vs. McWorld: How Globalism and Tribalism Are Reshaping the World.* New York: Ballantine, 1996.

Beatty, Warren, dir. and writer. *Bulworth.* Perf. Warren Beatty, Hallie Berry. Twentieth Century Fox, 1998.

Caple, Jim. "Ventura Won't Let Others Cash in on his Cachet." *St. Paul Pioneer Press* 24 Dec. 1998: A1.

Cass, Dennis. "An Action Figure for All Seasons." *Harper's Magazine* Feb. 1999: 65.

Cooper, Terry L. *The Responsible Administrator.* San Francisco: Jossey-Bass, 1998.

Dornan, Christopher. "Peering Forward: The Conduct of the News Media is Part of a Fretful Arc of Apprehension That Spans the Twentieth Century." *Media Studies Journal* 13:2 (1999): 120-29.

Emmers-Sommer, Tara, and M. Allen. "Surveying the Effect of Media Effects." *Human Communication Research* 25:4 (1999): 478-98.

Feyerabend, Paul. *Farewell to Reason.* London: Verso, 1987.

Graber, Doris A. *Mass Media and American Politics.* Washington, DC: Congressional Quarterly, Inc., 1993.

Hess, Stephen. "Federalism & News: Media to Government: Drop Dead." *Brookings Review* Winter 2000: 28-31.

Kelly, Jim, and Bill Eliott. "Synthetic History and Subjective Reality: The Impact of Oliver Stone's Movie JFK." *It's Show Time! Media, Politics, and Popular Culture.* Ed. David Schultz. New York: Peter Lang, 2000. 171-96.

Kovach, Bill, and Tom Rosenstiel. *Warp Speed: America in the Age of Mixed Media.* New York: The Century Foundation Press, 1999.

Lyotard, Jean-Francois. *The Postmodern Condition: A Report on Knowledge.* Minneapolis: U of Minnesota P, 1984.

McAllister, Matthew. *The Commercialization of American Culture.* Thousand Oaks, CA: Sage Publications, 1996.

Ragsdale, Jim. "Ventura Lambastes His Critics on Radio." *St. Paul Pioneer Press* 21 Aug. 1999: A1.

Rorty, Richard. *Philosophy and the Mirror of Nature.* Princeton: Princeton UP, 1980.

Schultz, David. "The Cultural Contradictions of the American Media." *It's Show Time! Media, Politics, and Popular Culture.* Ed. David Schultz. New York: Peter Lang, 2000. 13-28.

Schultz, David. "Kenny Meets George Washington or 'Come on Down, Your 15 Minutes of Fame Are Now!" *It's Show Time! Media, Politics, and Popular Culture.* Ed. David Schultz. New York: Peter Lang, 2000. xi-xiv.

Seib, Gerald F. "Live From Hollywood, It's American Politics with Warren Beatty." *The Wall Street Journal* 14 Sept. 1999: A1.

Small, J. "Political Ethics: A View of the Leadership." *American Behavioral Scientist* 19 (1976): 543-66.

Sweeney, Patrick. "Governor Bares All (Opinions) in Playboy." *St. Paul Pioneer Press* 30 Sept. 1999: A1.

Sweeney, Patrick. "Top Ethics Official's Memo Says Ventura Ventures Violated State Statutes." *St. Paul Pioneer Press* 10 Sept. 1999: A1.

Thompson, Dennis F. *Ethics in Congress: From Individual to Institutional Corruption.* Washington, DC: The Brookings Institution, 1995.

Twitchell, James B. *Adcult USA.* New York: Columbia UP, 1996.

Wag the Dog. Dir. Barry Levinson. Perf. Dustin Hoffman, Robert DeNiro, Anne Heche, Denis Leary. New Line, 1997.

Victory for Arnold

By Roger Simon
U.S. News & World Report, October 20, 2003

On the morning of October 7, an earthquake measuring 3.6 rattled Southern California. By that evening, however, the entire state had been shaken up. The second tremor came in the form of Arnold Schwarzenegger, the Austrian-born bodybuilder and high-body-count actor, who had been a professional politician for exactly 62 days but had now beaten an incumbent governor with nearly 30 years of political experience.

Through California's bizarre recall law, which allows citizens to dump officeholders for any (or no) reason, Schwarzenegger had surfed a tsunami of voter anger all the way to the governor's chair in Sacramento, which he will assume in mid-November. Some 31 times in the past, California voters had tried to get rid of their governors—they tried to jettison Ronald Reagan three times—but this was the first time they had ever succeeded.

Why this time?

And while the media immediately used the Schwarzenegger victory as an excuse to commit sociology, does his victory really mark a national trend with wider implications? Or was it the result of the coming together of three strands unlikely to be found outside California: an incumbent unsuited to the demands of modern campaigning; a recall law that does not demand misfeasance, malfeasance, or nonfeasance to be proved against the incumbent; and a method of election that allowed the "pro-choice," pro-gun-safety, pro-gay-rights Schwarzenegger to avoid a Republican primary that he might well have lost to a more conservative candidate?

The bland incumbent, Gray Davis, thought he knew why he was facing defeat. "I never underestimate an actor who is a celebrity," Davis said on the eve of the election. "This is California; celebrities are a big deal here." Though Californians like to pretend they are blase about entertainers, they have elected a number of them to high office, ranging from Reagan to Sonny Bono. And Schwarzenegger, a Republican, did generate hoopla without precedent: On election night he attracted nearly 100 TV crews from 14 countries, far more than even a president of the United States usually gets.

Up Close

The very excitement generated by a superstar candidate not only helped Schwarzenegger during the campaign but helped doom his opponent: Davis had managed to win statewide office five times because he didn't really have to go out and campaign. California is so vast physically, and media interest, especially TV interest, has been so low in recent years that candidates campaign largely via TV commercials. At this, Davis did well. But the explosion of interest caused by Schwarzenegger forced the candidates to go out and do actual campaign events in front of real people so television would have something to broadcast. Millions were spent on TV commercials by the campaigns, but voters wanted to watch the campaign on their nightly news shows, too. Schwarzenegger proved adept at providing good sound bites: He kept his speeches to just a few minutes, he avoided specifics, and he presented a message of optimism and hope. In desperation, Davis held a series of town meetings, but this did not help much. Often arrogant and always defensive, Davis reminded voters why they disliked him.

But though Schwarzenegger used his celebrity status effectively—a born showman, he knows there is little difference between entertainment and politics—his campaign gurus told him early on that just being a celebrity would not be enough to win: There are 1.3 million more Democrats than Republicans in California, and not a single Republican currently holds statewide office.

So Schwarzenegger needed something more, and that something, which has been taken seriously by politicians ever since the term-limit movement of the 1990s, was empowering the angry. It was perfect for California, where voters were not just angry but in a white-hot fury. And that fury had been directed at Davis ever since the electricity blackouts of 2000 and 2001, which resulted in higher utility bills, and the collapse of the California economy, which created multibillion-dollar budget deficits that threaten state programs and—most enraging of all—led to a tripling of the car tax, which caused vehicle license fees to jump from about $70 to $210 for the average passenger car. But this also created a problem for Schwarzenegger. The very financial crisis in which California now found itself argued for a steady and experienced hand on the tiller. When people thought of Schwarzenegger they thought of *Pumping Iron* or the Terminator. They did not think financial expert.

"Our most difficult task was getting people to see Arnold as a plausible governor in difficult times," a top aide to Schwarzenegger told *U.S. News.* "I mean here was a guy with no political experience. He had just come off a movie. And he wanted to go from Terminator 3 to governor in 60 days."

In the beginning, the campaign struggled. After his surprise announcement on the *Tonight Show with Jay Leno* and making a dumb joke about bikini waxing that trivialized his own candidacy, Schwarzenegger dropped from public sight. The reason: His campaign barely existed. There was little staff and even less planning. Further, knowledge about issues had to be "downloaded" into Schwarzenegger's head, in the words of one aide. He was bright and a quick study, the aide said, but he had not spent half his life in state government as Davis had.

But Schwarzenegger was frustrated with the slow pace of his campaign. He has a keen sense of how to please an audience, and he knew the people wanted to see him. More important, he wanted to see them. He wanted the big trappings of a major campaign—the buses, the planes, the motorcades—and most of all he wanted what he would soon get: the screaming crowds, the adoration, the frenzy. "The feeling like Kennedy had, you know, to speak to maybe 50,000 people at one time and having them cheer," he reportedly said years ago, "or like Hitler in the Nuremberg stadium. And have all those people scream at you and just being in total agreement with whatever you say." (Schwarzenegger said during the campaign he couldn't remember if he made this statement, but he denied ever admiring Hitler.)

Schwarzenegger's staff was as frustrated as he was. "By the time we have this figured out, the campaign will be over," one depressed staffer complained to *U.S. News* at the beginning of the campaign. But things improved: Schwarzenegger's wife, Maria Shriver, a network journalist and a Kennedy, who was used to big-time politicking, took a major role in campaign planning and immediately saw the need to hire experienced politicos. "There was no campaign, no apparatus when I came on board," one top aide says. "It was like building a battleship while you are swimming in the ocean."

Further, the campaign had no real theme. Don Sipple, an expert on campaign commercials and message strategy, was brought in, and the first thing he did was to try to tap into voter anger by changing the Schwarzenegger campaign into a movement. Schwarzenegger campaign signs—and they sprang up everywhere—never asked citizens to "vote for" Schwarzenegger. They always asked them to "join" him. "This was about voter discontent," Sipple says. "The public sees politics as a game, a game that benefits only the political ruling class. That is what their discontent is about. Our campaign was about creating a movement for change. 'Join Arnold' was our brand. We wanted people to join a movement, and that resonated."

Blink Test

Sipple was not overly worried about Schwarzenegger's lack of political experience. Sipple had once worked for another first-time candidate running for governor, a man whose intellectual prowess had been called into question and who was facing a canny and experienced incumbent. That candidate was George W. Bush; he was running for governor of Texas in 1994, and he did quite well. He also had an odd ability that Sipple liked: a low blink count. Bush was so good at this that he could look into a camera for an entire 30-second commercial and not blink once. Schwarzenegger could do the same thing. "Blinking is weak!" Sipple said with a laugh.

Even the Schwarzenegger campaign theme song, played relentlessly at each stop, fit into the "brand." It was the 1984 Twisted Sister hit "We're Not Gonna Take It," one refrain of which is: "We'll fight the powers that be, just don't pick our destiny." Then, less than a week before Election Day, disaster struck: *The Los Angeles Times* began printing in chilling detail accusations by women that Schwarzenegger had groped and improperly touched them. The number of accusers eventually rose to 15, and Schwarzenegger, who had just begun a four-day bus trip—exactly the kind of big-time campaign event he had wanted—was forced to apologize to any woman he had "offended."

Schwarzenegger's poll numbers dipped, and the campaign was clearly worried. Women are 52 percent of likely voters in California, and the ability to grope women with impunity was not the kind of empowerment that the campaign was selling. But Schwarzenegger did have powerful friends, who helped minimize the impact. Leno said in one of his nightly monologues: "You've got Arnold, who groped a few women, or Davis, who screwed the whole state."

Then Davis handed Schwarzenegger an unexpected boost. At first, Davis refused to comment on the accusations against Schwarzenegger. But he soon went into attack mode, bringing the accusations up again and again and suggesting that Schwarzenegger might face criminal prosecution. Almost immediately, Schwarzenegger's poll numbers improved. People had been reminded of what they didn't like about Davis: his negativity. "When Davis embraced the scandal stories, our numbers shot up," Sipple says.

In the end, it was a blowout: Voters turned Davis out of office by a vote of 55 percent to 45 percent and elected Schwarzenegger over his nearest competitor by a vote of 49 percent to 32 percent. And Sipple is one of those who believe that the election sends a national message. "It puts the political establishment on notice," he says. "It says, 'Get your act together or you are next.'" Top Schwarzenegger campaign aide Rob Stutzman agrees. "Definitely, career politicians have got to take pause from this whether they are Democrats or Republicans," he says. "People now feel empowered. They feel things can change."

While Schwarzenegger's victory means that the nation's four most populous states—California, Texas, New York, and Florida—all have Republican governors, politically speaking there may be less to this than meets the eye, especially for President Bush, who faces re-election in 2004. It is always nice to have as many governors on your side as possible when running for president, but in 2000 there were Republican governors in Pennsylvania, Michigan, and Illinois, and Bush lost all three states. And even in Florida, where the Republican governor was his brother, he won only by a razor-thin margin that had to be established by the Supreme Court. The political reality is that Bush will have a very tough time winning either California or New York in 2004, and while Texas is virtually a sure thing, Florida is not.

If Schwarzenegger's victory is indeed a sign of a genuine angry-voter movement, it is a movement that can cut both ways: Democrats lose today, but Republicans can lose tomorrow. "This recall was about the frustration so many people are feeling," Democratic presidential hopeful Howard Dean says. "Voters in California directed their frustration with the country's direction on their incumbent governor. Come next November, that anger might be directed at a different incumbent—in the White House."

Kevin Starr, a professor of California history at the University of Southern California and the state's librarian, says, "We have learned the lesson that the public is a sleeping giant. Sometimes the public is asleep at the switch. But when things began to go wrong [in California], they concentrated and rose up."

It is unlikely, however, that officeholders in other states have much to fear. California's law is nearly unique. In Minnesota, for instance, the recall of a governor requires the state's Supreme Court to find evidence of wrongdoing. "In California there doesn't have to be malfeasance, there is no due process, and you don't have to have any cause," Starr says. "Colorado is the only other state with a similar law."

Fuzzy Math

Will they rise up again in California? And next time will they rise up to recall Governor Schwarzenegger? He faces huge problems: The state has a deficit of as much as $8 billion, which will immediately grow to $12 billion if Schwarzenegger succeeds in rescinding the vehicle-tax increase. By law, the budget must be balanced. But Schwarzenegger has sworn he will not raise taxes, and the California legislature, both houses of which are controlled by Democrats, is not going to be eager to let him cut programs. So how will Schwarzenegger do it? "I don't know the answer to that," Duf Sundheim, the Republican state chairman, says. "And anybody who says he does is lying."

So if Schwarzenegger does not have any greater success than Davis, could he be recalled by angry Democrats? "I would be very surprised if there is any talk of a recall," says Stutzman. "The Democrats are whipped in this state. We expected big protests at our rallies and it didn't happen. We expected a big union get-out-the-vote effort and it didn't happen. Schwarzenegger has received a mandate and the Democrats know it." Starr agrees that any immediate talk of another recall is unlikely. "It would look terribly shabby," he says. "It is very hard to have a recall without a deep-seated grievance."

Whatever happens, it's likely to be a bumpy ride for Schwarzenegger. Which is why on election night, Don Sipple called Maria Shriver and said: "Maria, the good news is that you won. But, Maria, the bad news is that you won."

Sipple believes, however, that Schwarzenegger will not accept failure because he now has attained his lifetime goal and will let nothing sully it. "Governor of California is the highest job he can achieve given his citizenship," Sipple says.

Maybe. Republican Sen. Orrin Hatch of Utah has already introduced a resolution to amend the Constitution to allow foreign-born citizens who have lived here for 20 years to ascend to the White House. "If Arnold Schwarzenegger turns out to be the greatest governor of California, which I hope he will, if he turns out to be a tremendous leader and he proves to everybody in this country that he's totally dedicated to this country as an American, we would be wrong not to give him that opportunity," Hatch says.

President Schwarzenegger? It might sound funny now, but so did Governor Schwarzenegger a few months ago. And as Schwarzenegger likes to say in both his movies and his speeches: "I'll be back!"

Can Oprah Boost Her 'Favorite Guy'?

By Eugene Robinson
The Washington Post, November 27, 2007

The conventional wisdom says that celebrity endorsements don't mean much in politics. But the conventional wisdom also says that enormously long, difficult novels published more than a century ago don't suddenly become bestsellers. Now we're about to see whether the "Oprah effect" can do for Barack Obama what it did for Leo Tolstoy.

The Obama campaign's announcement yesterday that Oprah Winfrey will barnstorm the early-primary states with the candidate she has called "my favorite guy" was big news in Iowa, New Hampshire and South Carolina. Theoretically, the active support of a popular talk-show host shouldn't have much impact on Obama's prospects one way or the other. But we're talking Oprah here.

The Pew Research Center polled on the subject in September, shortly after Winfrey hosted a star-studded fundraiser that netted an estimated $3 million for Obama's campaign. According to the Pew survey, 15 percent of Americans said that Winfrey's endorsement would make them more likely to vote for Obama, 15 percent said less likely and 69 percent said it would make no difference to them.

But 60 percent of respondents predicted that Winfrey's support would help Obama's candidacy, against only 3 percent who said it would hurt. And among Democrats—who, after all, are the voters who count at this point—23 percent said they would be more likely to vote for Obama because of Winfrey's support, while just 13 percent said they'd be less likely to vote for him.

The Pew survey found that Winfrey's endorsement also gives Obama a boost among women (17 percent more likely to vote for him, 12 percent less likely) and African Americans (28 percent more likely, 16 percent less likely)—groups now leaning toward front-runner Hillary Clinton.

No one expects Winfrey's appearances with Obama next month to have the astonishing impact of Oprah's Book Club, which has made Winfrey—already one of the most powerful individuals in the entertainment industry—one of the most powerful individuals in book publishing. Perhaps the best example of the "Oprah effect" came three years ago when she picked Tolstoy's "Anna Karenina" as a monthly selection, and the epic shot to the top of the bestseller list.

It's easier to persuade people to buy a book, even a book as daunting as "Anna Karenina," than to persuade them to vote for a presidential candidate. Still . . . we're talking Oprah here.

Winfrey occupies a unique place in American culture; her show offers a blend of self-empowerment, spirituality and consumerism—"Oprah's Favorite Things"—that enthralls millions of viewers every day. Two years ago, sellout crowds filled arenas and convention centers around the nation when she staged a series of motivational events. Famously protective of the Oprah brand, she has steered clear of electoral politics—until now.

In an interview with the Hollywood Reporter, Winfrey said she will not use her "platform" on Obama's behalf—meaning her show and her eponymous magazine—but instead will speak for him with her "personal voice."

Why? "Because I felt it was the right thing to do. And you know, I weighed that: What is the cost to me for doing it? Am I going to lose viewers? I made the decision that I have the right to do it as an American citizen. . . . I know him well enough to believe in his moral authority. And that is the number one reason why I am supporting him."

Timing is everything, in entertainment as well as politics. Winfrey's upcoming campaign appearances with Obama will come less than a month before the nominating caucuses in Iowa, where a recent Post-ABC News poll showed Obama with a slim lead. Winfrey's support might not make any difference. But if I were running for president, I'd rather have her with me than against me.

Asked by the Hollywood Reporter whether she had any doubts—not specifically about politics but about herself, about life, about anything—Winfrey gave this answer:

"No, I don't have any doubts. I really don't. Because I live in a very spiritual space—not a religious space, but I live in a spiritual space where I understand the connection that we all have with each other. It's not just rhetoric for me. I really do understand the common denominator in the human experience."

If anyone else were to say such a thing, it would sound like nothing but a bunch of New Age newspeak. When Oprah Winfrey says it, you can't escape the nagging feeling that she knows something the rest of us don't.

Stage Left

By Ed Leibowitz
Los Angeles Magazine, March 2006

At six feet four inches, it's a short hop off the stage and a couple of strides before Tim Robbins—the tallest actor to ever win an Oscar— reaches a front-row seat at the Kirk Douglas Theater in Culver City, where he's been rehearsing a one night benefit performance for a homeless services agency and the Actors' Gang. This evening's show is culled from first-person narratives of abuse victims, addicts, and the mentally ill. Don Cheadle, Eva Mendes, Alfre Woodard, Marisa Tomei, and Morgan Freeman will soon be joining him to dramatize the life stories of society's shunned and neglected because, Robbins says, "I asked them."

Even now, at 47, there's something not fully grown about Robbins. The actor's convex brow, pug nose, soft, puffy cheeks, and indefinite chin—together they give the impression of so much child's modeling clay perched at the summit of a giant's frame. In his best performances, he's been the master sculptor of that face. His breakthrough came in 1988, as pitching prospect "Nuke" LaLoosh in *Bull Durham*—a dim-witted, half-formed freak of nature butting heads with Kevin Costner. Then came the postal worker haunted by his Vietnam service in *Jacob's Ladder*, *The Player*'s smarmy studio executive, and *Arlington Road*'s right-wing terrorist next door. Most memorably Robbins has played accused murderers: Andy the battered but resilient banker who escapes prison for a Mexican beach in *The Shawshank Redemption*, and Dave, pushing middle age and wasting away from the kidnapping and molestation he suffered as a boy in *Mystic River*. In both roles, Robbins's baby face betrays innocence, pain, and inscrutability—and a wariness that says since no one's going to understand, why bother?

It's the same wariness that causes the cleft between Robbins's blue eyes to deepen as a reporter switches on a tape recorder, the same depressingly familiar conclusion that once the conversation shifts to politics, as it inevitably will, he'll be misread. "I don't think it's happenstance," he says. "People have kind of gotten the message that if you do cross that line from a progressive perspective, there will be negative things said about you. The neoconservatives understand the influence that anyone with access to the media has, not echoing their philosophy."

Since the first Gulf War, Robbins has declared himself an enemy combatant, not against U.S. servicemen, whom he makes clear he supports, but against the federal government that sent them onto the field and rewards the extremely wealthy—a class to which he belongs. It's a war he's waged on television and radio, on the streets and in cautionary films he's written and directed. *Bob Roberts*, his 1992 debut as an auteur, was a satire about a folksinging right-wing Senate candidate. He cowrote and performed 13 original ballads and barnstormers for the film that were canny perversions of early Dylan. Still, he never released a soundtrack album because, he says, "I just didn't want to hear those songs played out of context." Three years later Robbins directed his partner, Susan Sarandon, to a Best Actress Oscar for her starring role in *Dead Man Walking*, as a nun trying to stave off the execution of a convicted killer.

In *Embedded*, last year's straight-to-DVD release, he melded Rush Limbaugh, Karl Rove, and Condoleezza Rice into grotesque puppet masters bungling the invasion of an oil-rich state called Gomorrah while reporters toadied up and ordinary soldiers suffered, killed, and died. The film began as a play produced by the Actors' Gang, the L.A. experimental theater troupe Robbins cofounded right out of the UCLA drama school, and to which he returned as artistic director in 2001 after a four-year hiatus.

This month, again under his direction, the Gang is debuting a new adaptation of George Orwell's *1984* that he also plans to make into a movie. "The book has played for the last 46 years, sometimes as an allegory and sometimes as a warning," Robbins says. "This particular production plays as a mirror image of what's going on. "We remember the greatest hits—'Big Brother is watching you.' It's the details that are fascinating to me—what Orwell has to say about governments and how they control people and the idea that language must be co-opted in order to control the discussion and the debate. All of these things are relevant now."

In the early '80s, when his activism didn't ripple much beyond his circle of friends, when he was getting modest press at best as the phallus-wielding lead in the Gang's production of Alfred Jarry's *Ubu the King*, and when Hollywood was hiring him for roles like Larry "Mother" Tucker in *Fraternity Vacation*, he could never have assembled the cast of fellow Academy Award winners and nominees he's put together for tonight's benefit; nor could he have channeled his dissent into feature film.

For the past 15 years, though, Robbins's experience as of Hollywood's most vocal progressives has hardly read like a cautionary tale against speaking one's mind. "After my activism in 1991, with the first Gulf War," he says, "I had one of the best years—or couple of years—in my career. *Bob Roberts*, *The Player*, *The Shawshank Redemption*, and *The Hudsucker Proxy* all came out then." During the lead-up to the Iraq War, Robbins was prominent among the millions who marched through London in protest. "After that," he says, "I did *Mystic River* and won an Oscar."

Robbins has hurt or shamed his opponents more than himself. Two years ago Dale Petroskey, the president of the Baseball Hall of Fame, canceled a 15th-anniversary celebration of Bull Durham because, he explained, two of the costars—Sarandon and Robbins— had imperiled U.S. troops in Iraq with their words. Within a week Petroskey issued a public apology and Robbins was not only chiding him but also warning against a broader attack on free speech before the National Press Club.

"People love to generalize and attempt to marginalize who you are," he says, joining his fellow movie stars in the theater's court-yard under the cool night sky for a triple macchiato from Starbucks. So are there any last misconceptions he'd like to clear up? "Yeah," he says, grinning. "I actually have a much better time than people think."

Celebrity and Politics

By Andrew Kamons
SAIS Review, Winter/Spring 2007

A politician's ability to take advantage of innovations in media has long been central to his or her electoral success. It's been nearly fifty years since JFK demonstrated that in the age of television, a close shave and an effective antiperspirant could be as important to a presidential election as bold leadership and a robust foreign policy strategy. Yet as innovations in the media continue to blur the line between celebrity and politician, politicians must not only keep abreast of the latest media technology, they must also be wary of those celebrities eager to supplant them in their leadership roles.

The link between celebrity and activism is well established. There is a natural transition from being a spokesperson for someone else's product—a practice almost as old as that of hawking goods themselves—to speaking up for one's own causes or interests. Traditional politicians have moved beyond the staid celebrity endorsement to more creative uses of their famous friends. When British Prime Minister Tony Blair is photographed listening attentively to Bono and Bob Geldof talk about debt relief, he's not just selling the idea that celebrities support his views, but rather that he himself is willing to entertain their opinions and to heed their counsel.[1]

Whether it is Bill Clinton playing the saxophone on the Tonight Show or President George W. Bush poised mid-deck in his flight suit, our leaders clearly recognize that behaving like celebrities can translate into public approval. But why settle for politicians who attempt to emulate celebrities when one can have the celebrities themselves? The growing cult of celebrity has enabled those with limited political experience to rise higher within the political sphere, not only as activists, but also as policymakers. The trends suggest that celebrity can serve as a proxy for political accomplishment.

Critics contend that while celebrities may succeed in engaging with the public, they rarely do so without diluting the message they are trying to convey. Celebrity endorsements succeed in large part because they apply a veneer of attractiveness to whatever policy or cause they support. Unfortunately, celebrities often prove reluctant to wrestle with ambiguities and quick to gloss over the very distinctions that give a position importance. It's hard to argue against those who seek to reduce the toll of AIDS in the developing world, but when it comes to decisions over sex education, access to medications, or resource allocation, the issue is far from clear-cut.[2]

Celebrity politicians often run as populist outsiders who can reach across the aisles and who can draw disaffected voters into the political process. As such, they succeed best where party systems are poorly entrenched and barriers to outside entry are low. In Minnesota, former actor and political pundit Jesse Ventura won the gubernatorial race due in large part to lax restrictions on late voter registration that allowed him to capitalize on a last minute swing in momentum by attracting unregistered voters to the polls.[3] Where the party system is weak and politics personalized, celebrity often carries more weight. The runner up in Liberia's election last year was George Weah, a political novice known principally for his success as a professional soccer player in Europe. Despite having a modest academic record and spending most of his adult life outside the country, he achieved a plurality of votes in the first ballot, and lost by a slim margin in the runoff election.[4]

One of the strongest critiques of celebrity politicians is that they in fact short-circuit the democratic process by winning on personal appeal instead of sound policies. Darrell West and John Orman argue, "Celebrity politics accentuates many of the elements in our society that drain substance out of the political process and substitutes trivial and nonsubstantive forms of entertainment. [This] endangers the ability of ordinary citizens to hold leaders accountable for their policymaking decisions."[5] Unlike other populist outsiders, celebrities rarely offset this failing with their reformist credentials. That celebrities are not proponents of the policies favored by the people they represent is a criticism that could also be applied to any number of successful politicians whose entrée to the field came from family connections, inside maneuvering, or other more nefarious activities than good looks and charisma. Yet the celebrity appears somehow more despicable than these other archetypes because the asset being traded upon is so transparent, and the very strength of their public persona raises awkward questions about the nature of democracy that are not so easy to brush aside.

Still, despite the knee-jerk negativity that celebrity politicians tend to engender, it is hard to argue with what activists like Angelina Jolie and U2's Bono have accomplished for their pet issues. On behalf of UNHCR, Jolie has publicized the plight of the refugees more effectively than any prior government efforts while Bono has been arguably the most decisive factor in reframing the global debate on third world debt reform. Whether those same star qualities translate as well to the world of policy making remains to be seen. But it certainly seems as if we're going to find out.

Notes

1. Richards, Steve. "How Blair and Brown Turned the Power of Rock Star Politics to Their Advantage." *The Independent* (London), July 5, 2005, Comment, 25.

2. Street, John. "Celebrity Politicians: Political Representation and Popular Culture." *British Journal of Politics and International Relations* 6 (2004): 443.

3. Disch, Lisa "Minnesota and the 'Populism' of Political Opposition," *Theory & Event* 3 (1999).

4. Donnelly, John. "Pressure Builds on Liberia's Pioneer; 'Iron Lady' Tries to Restore Nation." *The Boston Globe*, May 14, 2006, Third Edition, Al.

5. West, Darrell M., and John M. Orman. *Celebrity Politics*. Upper Saddle River: Prentice Hall, 2003, 113.

Foreign Policy Goes Glam

By Daniel W. Drezner
The National Interest, November/December 2007

Who would you rather sit next to at your next Council on Foreign Relations roundtable: Henry Kissinger or Angelina Jolie? This is a question that citizens of the white-collared foreign-policy establishment thought they'd never be asked. The massive attention paid to Paris Hilton's prison ordeal, Lindsay Lohan's shame spiral and anything Britney Spears has done, said or exposed has distracted pop-culture mavens from celebrities that were making nobler headlines.

Increasingly, celebrities are taking an active interest in world politics. When media maven Tina Brown attends a Council on Foreign Relations session, you know something fundamental has changed in the relationship between the world of celebrity and world politics. What's even stranger is that these efforts to glamorize foreign policy are actually affecting what governments do and say. The power of soft news has given star entertainers additional leverage to advance their causes. Their ability to raise issues to the top of the global agenda is growing. This does not mean that celebrities can solve the problems that bedevil the world. And not all celebrity activists are equal in their effectiveness. Nevertheless, politically-engaged stars cannot be dismissed as merely an amusing curiosity in foreign policy.

Consider the most notable example of a celebrity attempting to move the global agenda: Angelina Jolie. Her image has come a long way since her marriage to Billy Bob Thornton. In February of this year she published an op-ed in *The Washington Post* about the crisis in Darfur, referencing her work as a goodwill ambassador for the United Nations High Commissioner for Refugees. During the summer, her press junket to promote *A Mighty Heart* included interviews with *Foreign Policy*'s website and a glowing profile in *Newsweek*, modestly titled "Angelina Jolie Wants to Save the World." In that story, former Secretary of State Colin Powell describes Jolie as "absolutely serious, absolutely informed. . . . She studies the issues." *Esquire*'s July 2007 cover featured a sultry picture of Jolie—but the attached story suggested something even more provocative: "In post-9/11 America, Angelina Jolie is the best woman in the world because she is the most famous woman in the world—because she is not like you or me."

What in the name of Walter Scott's Personality Parade is going on? Why has international relations gone glam? Have stars like Jolie, Madonna, Bono, Sean Penn, Steven Spielberg, George Clooney and Sheryl Crow carved out a new way to become foreign-policy heavyweights? Policy cognoscenti might laugh off this question as absurd, but the career arc of Al Gore should give them pause. As a conventional politician, Gore made little headway in addressing the problem of global warming beyond negotiating a treaty that the United States never ratified. As a post–White House celebrity, Gore starred in *An Inconvenient Truth*, won an Oscar and a Nobel Peace Prize, promoted this past summer's Live Earth concert and reframed the American debate about global warming. Gore has been far more successful as a celebrity activist than he ever was as vice president. This is the kind of parable that could lead aspiring policy wonks to wonder if the best way to command policy influence is to attend Julliard instead of the Fletcher School.

Joking aside, celebrity involvement in politics and policy is hardly new: Shirley Temple and Jane Fonda became known as much for their politics as their films. The template for Live Earth was the 1985 Live Aid concert, which in turn echoed the 1974 all-star concert for Bangladesh. Actors ranging from Ronald Reagan to Fred Thompson have taken the more traditional star route to power: running for political office.

Not everything old is new again, however. There is something different about the recent batch of celebrity activists. Current entertainers have greater incentives to adopt global causes than their precursors. Furthermore, they are more likely to be successful in pushing their policy agenda to the front of the queue. These facts have less to do with the celebrities themselves than with how citizens in the developed world consume information. Whether the rise of the celebrity activist will lead to policy improvements, however, is a more debatable proposition. Promoting a policy agenda is one thing; implementing it is another thing entirely. Regardless of what *Vanity Fair* or *Vogue* might want you to believe, celebrities really are just like everyone else. Some are competent in their activism, and some are . . . something else.

The Supply of Celebrity Activism

One reason for the newfound global agendas of celebrities is simply that today's stars have more autonomy than previous generations, and many of them recognize the benefits of being a popular saint. Stars may have always cared about politics, but they have not always been able to act on these impulses. Entertainers likely feared speaking out in the past, but the entertainment industry is not as authoritarian as it once was. The studio systems of yesteryear exerted much greater control over their movie stars. Mostly, the studios used this leverage to hush up scandals before the press found out about them.

In the decades since, celebrities have acquired more leverage in Hollywood. In some cases—see Winfrey, Oprah—they have become moguls themselves. This gives them the autonomy to adopt pet causes, policy initiatives and make their own publicity missteps. It also affords them the opportunity to manage their own "brand," as it were. Just as Nike or Pepsi recognize the benefits of developing a positive brand image, so do George Clooney and Sheryl Crow.

This leads to another, somewhat more selfish reason for celebrities to embrace policy activism: It distinguishes them from their tawdrier brethren. We now live in a world where the path to fame can be as fast as a 15-second YouTube clip. Paris Hilton became one of the world's most well-known faces on the strength of a famous name and a poorly lit home video. In such a world, marquee celebrities need to take steps to differentiate themselves from the lesser stars of stage and screen—or distance themselves from past scandals.[1] So when Angelina Jolie attends the Davos Economic Forum or sponsors a Millennium Village in Cambodia, she's not only trying to do good, she's trying to create a brand image that lets Americans forget about her role in breaking up Brad Pitt and Jennifer Aniston.

The final reason more celebrities are interested in making the world a better place is that it is simply easier for anyone to become a policy activist today. An effective policy entrepreneur requires a few simple commodities: expertise, money and the ability to command the media's attention. Celebrities already have the latter two; the Internet has enabled them to catch up on information-gathering. Several celebrities even have "philanthropic advisors" to facilitate their activism. This does not mean that celebrities will become authentic experts on a country or issue. They can, however, acquire enough knowledge to pen an op-ed or sound competent on a talk show. And when they look sexy doing it, all bets are off.

The Power of Soft News

Even as star activists aspire to appear on hard-news outlets, they dominate soft-news programs—a different but no less influential media format. Celebrity activism matters more now because Americans get their information about the world in different ways from a generation ago. Way back in the twentieth century, the available news outlets were well-defined: the major television networks, the weekly news magazines, *The New York Times* and the local newspaper. By relying on the same "general interest intermediaries," the best and the brightest editorial gatekeepers forced most Americans to consume the same information. Clearly, the gates have been crashed. Cable television, talk radio and weblogs have radically diversified the sources of news available to ordinary Americans. The market for news and entertainment has shifted from an oligopoly to a more competitive environment.

This shift in the information ecosystem profoundly affects how public opinion on foreign policy is formed. Matthew Baum has argued in *Soft News Goes to War* that a large share of Americans get their information about world politics from "soft-news" outlets like *Entertainment Tonight, Access Hollywood, SportsCenter, The View, People, US Weekly, Vanity Fair, Vogue, The Daily Show, The Tonight Show,* or Gawker, TMZ and PerezHilton. Although viewers might not watch these shows or read these magazines to learn about the world, any reporting of current events aired on these programs reaches an audience unattainable to *The New York Times* or *Nightline.*

In the current media environment, a symbiotic relationship between celebrities and cause célèbres has developed. Celebrities have a comparative advantage over policy wonks because they have access to a wider array of media outlets, which translates into a wider audience of citizens. Superstars can go on The Today Show or The Late Show to plug their latest movie and their latest global cause. Because of their celebrity cachet, even hard-news programs will cover them—stories about celebrities can goose Nielsen ratings. With a few exceptions, like Barack Obama or John McCain, most politicians cannot make the reverse leap to soft-news outlets. Non-celebrity policy activists are virtually guaranteed to be shut out of these programs.

The growth of soft news gives celebrity activists enormous leverage. The famous and the fabulous are the bread and butter of entertainment programs. Covering celebrity do-gooders provides content that balances out, say, tabloid coverage of Nicole Richie's personal and legal troubles. ESPN can cover both Michael Vick's travails and Dikembe Mutombo's efforts to improve health care in sub-Saharan Africa. MTV will cover Amy Winehouse's on-stage meltdowns, but they will also follow Angelina Jolie in her trips to Africa. They covered Live Earth for both the music and the message.

The power of soft news is not limited to television. *Vanity Fair* let Bono guest-edit a special issue about Africa, knowing that cover photos of Madonna and George Clooney would attract readers and buzz. Without intending to, those perusing the pages might form opinions about sending aid to sub-Saharan Africa in the process. Similarly, celebrity blogs can garner higher amounts of traffic. We may only speculate why Internet users flock to Pamela Anderson's website—but we know that while they are there, they can learn about Anderson's stance against animal testing.

Indeed, celebrities actually have an advantage over other policy activists and experts because hard-news outlets have an incentive to cover them too. Celebrities mean greater attention, and hard-news outlets are not above stunts designed to attract readers or ratings. Consider this question: If *The Washington Post* is deciding between running an op-ed by Angelina Jolie and an op-ed by a lesser-known expert on Sudan, which author do you think they are most likely to choose?

Do Celebrity Do-Gooders Do Any Good?

There is no doubt that celebrities have the ability to raise the profile of issues near and dear to their hearts. Highlighting a problem is not the same thing as solving it, however—and the celebrity track record at affecting policy outcomes could best be characterized as mixed. Star activism has been reasonably successful at forcing powerful states to pledge action to assist the least-developed countries. It has been less successful at getting states to honor these pledges and not successful at all in affecting other global policy problems.

There have been some significant achievements, though. In the 1990s, Princess Diana embraced a ban on the use of land mines. Her death became a rallying point that led to Great Britain's ratification of the 1997 Ottawa Convention to ban the devices.[2] The Jubilee 2000 campaign, which Bono championed, should also count as a success.[3] According to the Center for Global Development, the movement to assist highly indebted poor countries resulted in "the most successful industrial-country movement aimed at combating world poverty for many years, perhaps in all recorded history." Celebrity activism also helped fuel the pledge at the 2005 Gleneagles G-8 summit to double aid to developing countries. Bob Geldof, who organized Live Aid a generation ago, arranged the Live 8 concerts to coincide with the summit. Bono, George Clooney, Claudia Schiffer and Nelson Mandela all appeared on stage.

To be clear, celebrities were not the only reason that the Ottawa Convention was signed or the G-7 launched the Highly Indebted Poor Countries initiative. In each of these cases, celebrities were buttressing organized, grassroots campaigns to change the status quo. At a minimum, however, star activists raised the media profile, spurring politicians to act sooner than they otherwise might have.

But there have been failures, too. While Bono provided an invaluable assist in promoting debt relief, he has not been as successful in his (Product) Red campaign. The idea was for consumers to do good through consumption—by buying iconic products colored red, a portion of the price would go to the UN Global Fund to Fight AIDS, Tuberculosis and Malaria. The campaign was launched in January 2006 to great fanfare at Davos. According to Advertising Age, however, it has been a bust: After an estimated $100 million in marketing expenditures, the campaign netted only $18 million. (Product) Red has challenged the validity of these numbers, but the story invited media critiques of the campaign's strategy, denting its momentum and cachet.

Celebrity campaigns are also not always considered a greater good. Development expert William Easterly has argued that the celebrity focus on Africa's problems has been misguided. By focusing exclusively on the diseases of sub-Saharan Africa, celebrities have unwittingly tarnished an entire continent: "[Africans are] not helpless wards waiting for actors and rock stars to rescue them." Many African officials and activists share this sentiment, even heckling Bono at a development conference.

Though celebrities have a mixed record in promoting development aid to Africa, the record on other issues is even worse. The Live Earth concerts generated mixed reviews because of their disorganization. Promoters had to cancel the Istanbul venue because of a lack of local sponsorship, and the other concerts were less than sellouts. More significantly, some celebrity activists questioned whether the extravaganza even had a clear purpose. Bob Geldof told an interviewer, "Live Earth doesn't have a final goal. . . .So it's just an enormous pop concert or the umpteenth time that, say, Madonna or Coldplay get up on stage." Roger Daltrey of The Who concurred: "The last thing the planet needs is a rock concert."

Steven Spielberg came up for criticism in a *Wall Street Journal* article co-authored by actress Mia Farrow. The article warned that Spielberg, as an "artistic advisor" to the 2008 Summer Olympics in China, would become "the Leni Riefenstahl of the Beijing Games" if he did not speak out. The chastised producer later sent a letter to Chinese Premier Hu Jintao because he felt compelled to "add my voice to those who ask that China change its policy towards Sudan." Regardless of the reasons, Beijing has begun to pressure Sudan's government into cooperating with the United Nations on Darfur.

Richard Gere has devoted decades to the cause of Tibetan independence to little avail. Yet with one onstage kiss of Bollywood star Shilpa Shetty, he did manage to get himself burned in effigy across India—the reverse celebrity problem. On the whole, celebrities have made little headway in bringing peace to the world's trouble spots.

Even if celebrities are judicious and focused in promoting their causes, there are diminishing marginal returns to activism. A celebrity who repeatedly harps on a particular cause risks generating compassion fatigue with the general public. As Bono recently told CNN, "Look, I'm Bono and I'm sick of Bono. And I fully understand. . . . I look forward to a time when I'm not such a pest and a self-righteous rock-star. Who needs one?" Clearly, there is a fine line to walk between sustained focus and righteous indignation.

Hindered Hollywood

It is true that star activism can influence the global policy agenda. But as we've seen, when it comes to concrete achievements, celebrities have a spotty track record. They face a number of constraints on their ability to affect policy. Most obviously, celebrities might not be the most grounded community of individuals. While some celebrities have mastered the activist game, others seem out of their depth. Hip-hop singer and Live Earth performer Akon admitted to reporters that he didn't know what it meant to be "green" until the day of the concert. Sean Penn's recent fact-finding trip to visit Venezuelan president Hugo Chávez served little purpose beyond a story in *The New York Times* that gently mocked both men. Then there's Peter

Gabriel's idea for "The Elders," a group which includes Nobel Laureates Jimmy Carter, Nelson Mandela and Desmond Tutu that tries to "use their unique collective skills to catalyze peaceful resolutions to long-standing conflicts"—something that seems more at home in a Matrix sequel than in the here and now. For every Bono or Angelina Jolie, there are other celebrities who are less well-versed in their cause du jour. The problem for the savvy stars is that when other entertainers act foolishly, it becomes easier to summarily dismiss all celebrity activism.

Another problem is that some celebrity causes are more controversial than others—and controversy can still threaten a star's bankability. Tom Cruise's sofa pitch for Scientology (and against psychiatry) likely played a role in Paramount's 2006 decision to sever its business relationship with him. When the Dixie Chicks blasted George W. Bush on stage at a 2004 London concert, radio stations pulled their chart-topping single from playlists, affecting the record's sales.

None of these episodes ended a career, but they did sting. These cautionary tales reveal a clear constraint on celebrity activism: Most stars will be reluctant to risk their professional careers to take a controversial political stance. When Michael Jordan was asked to endorse a Democratic senatorial candidate during his playing career, he demurred with a famous reply: "Republicans buy sneakers too." There are certainly those who present exceptions to this rule, such as Robert Redford, Michael Moore and Susan Sarandon—but they are not the rule.

A deeper problem celebrities face is that the implicit theory of politics that guides their activism does not necessarily apply to all facets of international relations. The goal of most social activism is to bring greater attention to a problem. The assumption is that once people become aware of the problem, there will be a groundswell of support for direct action. This is not how politics necessarily works, particularly in the global realm. Any solution to a problem like global warming, for example, involves significant costs. As people become more aware of the policy problem, it is far from guaranteed that a consensus will emerge about the best way to solve it. It is therefore not surprising that celebs have had their greatest successes in touting humanitarian causes and almost no effect on ending militarized conflicts.

This increase in influence comes with a warning, however: With great power comes the great potential for blowback. A September CBS/*New York Times* poll revealed that 49 percent of Americans think celebrities should stay out of politics. Since 2003, the polling data suggests increasing public hostility towards celebrity activism.

Both elites and ordinary citizens have their reasons to resent star power. Celebrity activism rubs many policymakers and pundits the wrong way. To some, star power upsets their sense of fair play. Christopher Caldwell complained recently, "Philanthropy is a route through which celebrity can be laundered into political power." He makes an interesting point. Why should the leads of *Mr. & Mrs. Smith* be listened to on weightier affairs of state? Who appointed Bono the global secretary of development? Does Pamela Anderson merit attention for her causes ahead of learned policy experts? To other aspirants of the foreign-policy community, the offense is more personal. Power is a zero-sum commodity, and if celebrities are rising in influence, that means others are falling. This will not sit well with those who feel pushed aside, especially if they have toiled for years in graduate school and low-paying policy jobs.

Among "ordinary" citizens, celebrities are all too aware that the ingredients for a fall from grace are interwoven with the sources of star power. At its core, star activism hints that the famous are somehow better than you or me. Some Americans view celebrities who pontificate on politics and policy as taking advantage of a bully pulpit that they did not earn. There's a fine line between principled activism and righteous indignation, and the celebrity who crosses that line risks incurring the wrath of the common man or woman. Americans are addicted to celebrities because we like to see them on top but we also enjoy their fall.

Notes

1. For a very amusing skit that satirizes this point, see www.youtube.com/watch?v=e-ia__id_rm.
2. See Richard Price, "Reversing the Gun Sights: Transnational Civil Society Targets Land Mines," *International Organization* Vol. 52, No. 3 (Summer 1998).
3. See Joshua Busby, "Bono Made Jesse Helms Cry: Jubilee 2000, Debt Relief, and Moral Action in International Politics," *International Studies Quarterly*, No. 51 (June 2007).

III. THE PRICE OF FAME

Editor's Introduction

On August 31, 1997, Great Britain's Princess Diana died in a high-speed car crash in Paris. The driver of the car, Henri Paul, a hotel security manager, was instructed to avoid the paparazzi, who had pursued the vehicle. Though an official inquiry by French police determined Paul, who was intoxicated while driving, to be the cause of the accident, that fact has been largely lost to a more popular version of the event that blames the paparazzi. Ironically, the popular history of Diana's death was propagated by the very media outlets that pay paparazzi thousands of dollars for their revealing photos of celebrities.

Though the paparazzi may not have killed Princess Diana, they are a very real, very annoying, and very intrusive aspect of fame. And their powers and numbers have grown with the advance of technology. The advent of digital technology, mobile phones, and the Web means that anyone anywhere can be part of the paparazzi—and that anyone anywhere can be caught in a compromising position and have it broadcast to millions of people within seconds. You need only refer back to this volume's Preface for evidence of just how much we know about the sordid personal life of a celebrity like Britney Spears.

But privacy is not the only victim of fame. Critical taste is, as well. How can we as cultural consumers of music, film, and literature correctly judge the artistic merits of a piece when we know so much about its creator's personal life? If we know an actor engages in distasteful behavior almost daily, are we capable of watching his next potentially brilliant performance with critical equanimity? Perhaps, but most likely not. Therefore, the public suffers for its own hunger for information about celebrities.

Speaking of distasteful behavior, Simon Dumenco suggests in his article "Falling Stars" that the public secretly revels in the fall of celebrities—but it's not entirely our fault. "Of course," Dumenco writes, "part of the reason the Church of Celebrity stopped beatifying saints—there will never be another Audrey Hepburn or Jimmy Stewart—is because it gave away every last one of its mythmaking secrets. There are no more certified miracles in Hollywood." Using Anna Nicole Smith's tragic death in 2007 and the horrid media spectacle that accompanied it, Caryn James explores our macabre fascination with the darker side of celebrity in "Why Did We Watch? The Answer Isn't Pretty."

In the third piece of this section, "The Other Side of Fame," Mary Loftus details the psychological stresses particular to celebrity life. Specifically, Loftus discusses how the constant attention celebrities receive corrodes their sense of self. As if to prove Loftus's point, Katherine Monk tells the story of an incident involving actress Lindsay Lohan in her article "Falling Stars: Will Lohan Be the Next Celebrity Flame-Out?" In July 2007, Lohan was arrested for drunkenly chasing her personal assistant's mother. According to her companions that night, Monk reports, Lohan said, "I can't get into trouble. I'm a celebrity."

A distinctive lack of privacy is another aspect of our celebrity culture. Celebrity divorces in particular often take place in full view of the public. In "Right Time, Wrong Publicity," Caryn James chronicles David Hasselhoff's recent travails. In the midst of an acrimonious divorce, Hasselhoff, the star of *Knight Rider* and *Bay Watch*, was videotaped by his two adolescent daughters as he drunkenly ate a cheeseburger. The clip was soon widely disseminated. In the next piece, "Being Bad: The Career Move," Guy Trebay explores how bad behavior—drug use, for example—by celebrities or aspiring celebrities can actually boost a career.

For artists in general and musicians in particular, "selling out" is the gravest of sins. Greg Sevik analyzes this phenomenon in "What Price, Fame?"

In the final article in this section, "Screen Idols: The Tragedy of Falling Stars," Reni Celeste offers a philosophical analysis of the place of movie stars in the wider culture. "The 'star' in star studies," she writes, "is not an individual at all but a system of signs, a social construction, flattened into a text that has multiple meanings and that can be read as cultural product."

Falling Stars

By Simon Dumenco
New York, December 1, 2003

I'm looking at Michael Jackson's Santa Barbara County Sheriff's Department mug shot, and I'm thinking it's no longer technically a human face (it's Lily Tomlin melting, or Lily Tomlin as reconstructed by a mortuary makeup artist). It's now, chiefly, a metaphor. It represents, of course, self-transformation gone horribly awry, and self-hatred, and self-destruction.

But it also represents a collective fear: that it's not bad parenting, stolen childhood, or music-industry insanity that's to blame for Michael's ongoing meltdown. *Celebrity culture* has done this to him. And, so, by extension, have we.

He's *our* Michael, *our* icon—a (formerly) gifted artist—and we let him do this to himself. He's our American tragedy.

Michael Jackson's nose is just the crumbling tip of the iceberg.

The corroded 45-year-old man we see today is arguably just a logical outcome, an extreme outcome, of an off-the-charts case of celebrity-entitlement psychosis. The former King of Pop now seems to be, somehow, the perverse product of the limitless love he enjoyed from fans in his prime. He doesn't know he's been deposed; he lives in (clueless) exile in a hermetically sealed world tailored to his own tortured specifications. He's reimagined Neverland, his gated little patch of Santa Barbarian paradise, as not just his personal Disneyland but his private ancient Greece. Carnival rides plus man-boy sleepovers.

But as astonishingly reckless and delusional as Michael is (my God, love letters to a 12-year-old boy!), he's somehow still part of a celebrity continuum. He's an *Über*-freak, but of a type. Consider, for starters, his friends/former friends: Elizabeth Taylor and Liza Minnelli (and David Gest!).

And then consider the other conspicuously narcissistic celebrities (besides Liza and David) who have also suffered showstopping meltdowns lately: Paris Hilton and Martha Stewart and Rosie O'Donnell and Kobe Bryant and Rush Limbaugh. All of them caught in acts that betray their entitlement, their grandiosity, their neediness, their emotional greed, their expectations of blanket (or at least red-carpet-like) immunity. The world—with its petty little rules and restrictions and proprieties—is doing *them* a grave injustice.

Michael Jackson's face is celebrity culture's death mask.

Okay, yeah, we're more celebrity-obsessed than we've ever been. But the ground, in that regard, has shifted rather radically beneath our (and their) feet: Our relationship to celebrity—and celebrity's relationship to itself—has been so transformed over the past few years that these days it doesn't take much to crack the veneer of celebrity news (even seemingly positive celebrity news) to decode what celebrity now means to us as a culture.

Almost entirely gone is the presumption that we're interested in celebrities because of their talent or their work or because they're leading exemplary lives or because they're the first among equals in our supposedly egalitarian society, with America's celebrity-watching being some sort of less inbred version of Britain's royal-watching.

Rather, in the same way that, on the 40th anniversary of JFK's death, it's easy to observe that glamour has largely been drained from post-Camelot politics, we all regard celebrity glamour as a deeply suspect, ephemeral commodity. (Of course, the most salient feature of the JFK-anniversary TV orgy has been all the attention paid to the revelations about his medical ailments and sexual adventures. JFK's image, in this revisionist moment, is now perceived to have been as engineered as, say, FDR's.)

As celebrity has exploded, it's also simultaneously been reduced (the *Us Weekly* effect) and pathologized (the "Page Six" effect) and deconstructed (the *Behind the Music* effect) and cheapened (the reality-TV effect). It carries with it a whole new set of signifiers and layers of meaning.

Not that all consumers of celebrity culture, and players in the celebrity-industrial complex, seem to grasp this.

When, earlier this year, *Rolling Stone* owner-editor Jann Wenner sat in Charlie Rose's blacked-out studio and Charlie asked him why magazines are so celebrity-mad right now, Jann had a simple answer: "It's uplifting to read about."

Honestly, when I heard that, I practically did a spit take. In fact, I hit the instant-replay button on my TiVo to make sure he really said that (he did!). Then I thought, *What planet is Jann living on?*

Okay, on Planet Pop, where Jann owns several homes, I guess you could argue that stars are still gods. Bad behavior among rock and pop stars, of course, has traditionally burnished, not damaged, reputations. (Witness the unsettling sight of still-starstruck, supportive fans swarming Michael Jackson's SUV after his arrest.) In fact, Jann is not only one of the original celebrity-editors (along with Hugh Hefner), he's the *Ur*-fanboy-journalist, having created his magazine back in 1967 in large part to get close to the objects of his adoration. Jann and his team of golden-moment photographers (Annie Leibovitz and others) created one of the classic formulas for the deification of rock stars—a formula Tina Brown and Graydon Carter later adapted and turbocharged for Hollywood at *Vanity Fair* (where Leibovitz now works).

But the celebrity-industrial complex isn't, duh, about uplift any-more. Just ask Paris Hilton, whose sex-tape scandal—suspiciously timed to coincide with the premiere of her new Fox reality series—is hardly scandalous. In fact, the only achievement her celebrity has ever reflected is that she's a constantly-falling-out-of-her-clothes exhibitionist. A celebration of vapidness as a form of postmodern brand purity, Paris is a beautiful rich girl unencumbered by any agenda beyond ubiquity. Her sex tape merely reinforces her image: She falls all the way out of her clothes! And a video camera happens to be there! It was only a matter of time.

Meanwhile, elsewhere in Celebrityville, Queen of Nice Rosie O'Donnell, friend of chubby housewives everywhere, reveals herself to be a complete fraud [. . .] and proceeds to drive her eponymous magazine into the ground while berating a cancer-victim employee.

Homemaking goddess Martha Stewart takes an ungodly interest in the disposition of one foundering lit-tle chunk of stock among her vast holdings—as if selling on insider information, and lying about it, as the Feds maintain she did, is just as proper and artful as applying toile and acorns to a picture frame with a hot-glue gun.

Goody-goody Lakers guard Kobe Bryant allegedly turns into an arrogant [. . .] sexual predator [. . .]

Sadistic right-wing radio blabbermouth Rush Lim-baugh is struck suddenly silent when the news gets out that he's addicted to white-trash heroin OxyContin, which, it turns out, he used the help—his maid/dealer!—to secure for him.

Robert Blake molders in Hollywood, muttering slurs about his murdered wife, hoping Baretta will save the day.

> There's a compulsive-ness that these stars exhibit, making mistakes, sometimes over and over again, that are entirely in character.

And good old M. J.: It's déjà vu all over again, because, remember, he bought his way out of boy-trouble almost exactly ten years ago. (At least, so far, there doesn't appear to be video documenting his love life. His colleague R. Kelly—Michael was filming his new music video with R. in Sin City when the sheriff put out the warrant for his arrest—isn't so lucky. His alleged trysts with a 14-year-old girl, documented by a camcorder, are sure to air in court.)

There's a compulsiveness that these stars exhibit, making mis-takes, sometimes over and over again, that are entirely in charac-ter—effectively branding their misbehavior.

We're supposed to pretend to be shocked?

Of course, part of the reason the Church of Celebrity stopped beat-ifying saints—there will never be another Audrey Hepburn or Jimmy Stewart—is because it gave away every last one of its myth-making secrets. There are no more certified miracles in Hollywood.

Anti-glamour, or deconstructed glamour—or pure roguishness—sells now partly because mere glamour (already in oversupply) doesn't really sell on its own anymore. It almost always comes with myth-busting backstory.

As recently as the early nineties, the mechanics of glamour were largely opaque to the culture at large. Celebrity stylists and colorists and personal trainers and plastic surgeons were not celebrities themselves. *InStyle*—and before *InStyle*, the Condé Nast beauty magazine *Allure*—were just beginning to advance the *do*-it-yourself, do-try-this-at-home approach to celebrity glamour.

But since then, so many celebrities have let themselves unwittingly become walking infomercials—allowing the narrative that surrounds them to be about not only their "beauty secrets" but their conspicuous consumption and luxury-product choices—that *celebrity*, the word itself, has taken on its own stand-alone brand value. Drugstores stock the Hollywood Celebrity Diet and Celebrity White tooth bleach, and we understand implicitly what's being sold. Celebrity isn't about talent, it's about getting what you want—*now*.

The *InStyle* mentality, spread through-out celebrity culture, leaves the net impression that even the seemingly natural Hollywood beauty is actually a confection, a collage. To be in *InStyle* (or its many imitators), you must confess (without, it seems, even really apprehending that you're confessing) that you're the sum total of your hair and makeup and wardrobe. You are your image—what the image-makers on your payroll dreamed up. You are, in a word, a construct.

A construct that can come apart at the seams at any moment the media decide to part the curtain, it turns out. All the celebrity weeklies have done scalpel-happy cover stories this year—the most recent being *Us Weekly* clone *In Touch Weekly*'s plastic surgery secrets package (MEG RYAN: BATTLING RUMORS ABOUT HER LIPS; PAMELA ANDERSON: REGRETS BREAST IMPLANTS?).

And just in time for Thanksgiving (though, really, it felt like an early Christmas gift), *Star* magazine's STARS WITHOUT MAKEUP! COVER. A smaller headline reads LOTS MORE SHOCKING PHOTOS INSIDE!, but the photos, at this point, aren't all that shocking (Britney Spears is a little ragged, Cameron Diaz is plain, Renée Zellweger is blotchy, and Barbra Streisand is a hag).

Which doesn't make them any less irresistible, or at least salable. The makeup-less cover is already one of *Star*'s best-selling covers of the year—the tabloid's editor, Bonnie Fuller, is reportedly set to get a $10,000 bonus for hitting a new circulation high with it.

Bonnie, of course, is the celebrity editor who is most widely credited with masterminding the new celebrity "journalism" paradigm. Her current reign was enabled by Jann Wenner, who, in an inspired moment in early 2002, hired her to run *Us Weekly*. Never a corporate loyalist, she quit *Us* this past summer to run the *Star* and American Media's other tabloids for $3 mil a year.

The net effect of her tenure so far has been to reinforce the idea that not only is your average celebrity "just like us" (to use Bonnie's signature *Us Weekly*–era phrase), but that he or she is badly in need of an intervention. Of Britney Spears, a "source" (probably the mailroom guy at the *Star*) observes, "She looks very tired." The solution suggested: L'Oréal Touch-On Colour, Shimmering Bronze (just $8.99 at Walgreens). "Apply it," a makeup artist helpfully explains in the magazine, "on the forehead, nose, cheeks, and chin."

For the moment, the most perfectly realized form of celebrity—an old-school, untainted, high-glamour type of celebrity that allows the media, once again, to engage in undiluted hagiography—is the reality-TV celebrity. *Us Weekly* gives "Bachelor Bob," of ABC's *The Bachelor*, a cover and asks WHOSE HEART WILL HE BREAK? He's holding a red rose.

Johnny Depp, this year's "Sexiest Man Alive," is half-crowded off the cover of *People* by Bachelor Bob and his chosen mate, Estella. "We want to make it last," Estella coos in a big headline.

In Touch declares Trista and Ryan, of *The Bachelorette*, 2003's "Most Romantic Couple." (Jennifer Aniston, of Brad & Jen fame, is merely "Most Talked About.") ABC is giving the reality-TV couple's marriage—the culmination of their "televised true love story" from last season—royal-wedding treatment in a prime-time ceremony.

And just before Thanksgiving, Fox aired the *American Idol* Christmas special—starring Clay Aiken, Ruben Studdard, Kelly Clarkson, and Tamyra Gray—which, in its treacle and glee, recalled nothing so much as *The Lawrence Welk Show*.

Meanwhile, non-reality-TV stars—mere celebrity actors and singers who worked really, really hard to get where they are today—must continue their yeoman's duty of serving as avatars of dysfunction (even if it means moonwalking to jail).

We keep them on as temp workers—watching their TV shows and movies or not, buying their albums or not, depending on our whims. We not-so-secretly hope they'll crash big-time. (Ben and J.Lo. *Gigli*.) Until Clay succumbs to an autoerotic misadventure, or Bachelor Bob cheats on Estella (preferably with the paperboy), or Estella's sex video (preferably with Tamyra) ends up on the Internet, they're all we have.

Why Did We Watch?

The Answer Isn't Pretty

By Caryn James
The New York Times, February 10, 2007

Becoming famous is relatively easy: Anna Nicole Smith was born with a beautiful face, a big smile and a voluptuous body she was happy to bare for Playboy. Staying famous for nothing much is hard work, and that is the real story of Ms. Smith's life and death. Her desperation for fame was so raw that she didn't mind being the butt of the joke if it helped maintain her place in the spotlight. Her career started out tacky, went downhill from there and ultimately says more about the culture's fascination with celebrity than it does about Anna Nicole Smith.

While most stars play a clever cat-and-mouse game with the media, Ms. Smith's sport was Extreme Fame. Her sense of how to court attention was simply to show up, pose and practically say, "Come get me, use me." In that blatant desire for publicity she embodied the ultimate symbiosis of celebrity: between an individual who acted as if life out of the spotlight were worthless, and a press and public eager to indulge her craving for attention.

But without any actual career to back up her claim on the public, the question becomes: why did we watch? The unsettlingly vapid reason: because we could. She was a glittery spectacle who offered guilt-free voyeurism, as we watched her dramas with drugs and weight and inheritance laws. And the lesson of her fame is that there is no lesson.

All the attempts to justify her fame that have flowed in since her death on Thursday are hollow. She was not Marilyn Monroe; the closest Ms. Smith came to a real movie career was a small role in the spoof "Naked Gun 33⅓: The Final Insult." She was not a rags-to-riches inspiration; most little girls don't dream of growing up to be Playmate of the Year, marrying an 89-year-old billionaire and fighting for his money all the way to the Supreme Court. And she was not a cautionary tale; she courted attention too relentlessly to seem innocent or deluded.

There was the ring of truth in what her mother told "Good Morning America" yesterday: that her daughter said, "If my name is out there in the news, good or bad doesn't matter, good or bad I make money, so I'm going to do whatever it takes." It says a lot about the bubble Ms. Smith lived in that even her mother, Virgie Arthur, communicated with her daughter through the media. On "Good Morning America," Ms. Arthur said she had tried to warn her estranged daughter about her drug use, and had done so by appearing on the Nancy Grace show.

Ms. Smith's lust for fame coincided with a media explosion she could exploit. After her weight ballooned, and her modeling career declined, she latched onto the reality television craze. But her two seasons of "The Anna Nicole Show" on E! revealed how inept she was at shaping an image. Her speech was slurred, her voice was whiny, her manner was demanding, and the curiosity that fed the ratings quickly dissipated. She seemed beyond pathetic by 2004, after she became a diet-product spokeswoman and showed off her newly slim body in another slurry appearance at the American Music Awards.

Her story took an indisputably tragic turn in September, when her 20-year-old son, Daniel, died days after Ms. Smith gave birth to a daughter. Yet even then she couldn't rise above the lurid nature of her fame. She sold photographs of her son and newborn in the hospital room where he died to In Touch magazine; even now, video of her Caesarean section is available on YouTube.

> [Anna Nicole] Smith's lust for fame coincided with a media explosion she could exploit.

And soon an ugly paternity battle over the infant broke out in a flurry of media interviews, with two men claiming to be the father: Larry Birkhead, a former boyfriend, and Howard K. Stern, Ms. Smith's longtime lawyer and confidant. (He seemed glued to her on the reality show.) It's no surprise that Mr. Stern announced his fatherhood on "Larry King Live," with Ms. Smith by his side.

The messiness of her death—its unknown cause, the continuing legal battles about the inheritance and the little girl's paternity— have made its aftermath just as media-centric as her life, with cable news channels trotting out a parade of casual former boyfriends, sometime-friends and estranged relatives.

Donna Hogan, Ms. Smith's half-sister, talked to Larry King on the phone about her forthcoming book (announced long before Ms. Smith's death), predictably called "Train Wreck: Anna Nicole Unauthorized." Ms. Hogan said she hadn't seen her sister in about a decade.

And while commentators are struggling to find meaning in her life, the responses to her death in the hours just after it was announced may more accurately reflect the public attitude toward her as a joke who drew gawkers rather than fans.

Many reactions seemed to defy the usual courtesy of not speaking ill of the dead. A post by the Web site Wonkette.com said, "the dope-addicted floozy Anna Nicole Smith keeled over dead in a Florida hotel about an hour ago," a fast turnaround of irreverence even for the Internet. Geraldo Rivera on the Fox News Channel put the blame for Ms. Smith's sorry life on Mr. Stern, saying, "He's a pimp," who sold her to the media. (What does that make her?) And even

Larry King, the friendliest of anchors, told Wolf Blitzer that Ms. Smith was "not the smartest person in the world" before praising her good humor and good heart.

The news of her death brought the inevitable jolt that comes when anyone dies suddenly at 39. And there is the inescapable tragedy of a 5-month-old left without her mother. But Anna Nicole Smith's fame is as sad and shallow in death as it was in life, just as much of a tawdry compact between her and us.

The Other Side of Fame

BY MARY LOFTUS
PSYCHOLOGY TODAY, MAY/JUNE 1995

For some reason, perhaps because it's far removed from the L.A.–
N.Y. continuum, celebrities' siblings are drawn to Central Florida.
Not only that, but they feel compelled to become journalists here.

I've sat two desks over from Jennifer Beal's brother, Greg. Been at
newspaper parties with Susan Sarandon's brother, Terry Tomalin,
and shared journalistic turf with Gretchen Letterman, Dave's sis.

These relationships occasionally bring the mild-mannered reporters some fall-out fame. Terry, while on a backpacking trip with his
sister and her pal Julia Roberts, noticed that Roberts was listening
to Lyle Lovett cassettes on her Walkman, and set the two up for
their first date. Gretchen made the newspapers when her brother
dropped by for a visit in St. Petersburg and had a car accident.

But mostly, they're closemouthed about their celebrity sibs.

"It's not just that you get tired of people asking about them," says
Arthur McCune, a reporter whose stepbrother, Daniel Waters,
wrote *Heathers* and *Batman Returns*. "It's also that, in comparison,
you feel kind of like a failure. I mean, he comes home for Christmas
and has been at some exotic locale for his new movie, or just had
lunch with Winona Ryder, and then it's, 'So what's new with you?'"

Celebrity and success have become synonymous in a culture that
judges by how rich, seductive, and riveting the image; where the
name recognition of teenage waif models rivals that of Nobel Peace
Prize recipients.

"Celebrity [is] the reward of those who project a vivid or pleasing
exterior or have otherwise attracted attention to themselves," Christopher Lasch wrote in *The Culture of Narcissism*. "It is evanescent
. . . In our time, when success is so largely a function of youth,
glamour, and novelty, glory is more fleeting than ever, and those
who win the attention of the public worry incessantly about losing
it."

Stars, then, have their own problems, not the least of which is con-
templating their own half-lives. Some worries intrude from outside:
rabid fans, gold diggers, paparazzi, critics, competition. Others
gnaw from within: self-doubt, addiction, wanderlust.

Entertainers—whether actors, artists, evangelists, writers, musicians, politicians, or athletes—survive by peddling themselves and their talents to the masses. They're put on display, consumed, evaluated and achieve either dismissal or acclaim. Feedback is received through Gallop polls, Nielsen ratings, and box-office draw.

Like the tree-in-the-forest conundrum, this presents a philosophical puzzle: If a celebrity doesn't rivet the public's attention, does he exist?

Fame has always had a bad reputation among thinkers. Poets sung of its seductiveness, and its tendency to breed vanity and superficiality. But the worst you could say of the old kind of fame, the kind based on accomplishment, was that it clouded your vision. The new, less durable fame, the kind refracted through images, proves especially corrosive to the self.

"To be a celebrity means to have more than the usual assaults on one's ego," says Charles Figley, Ph.D., director of the Psychosocial Stress Research Program at Florida State University. "You're very vulnerable to the personal evaluations of other people. The public is ultimately in control of whether your career continues."

Figley, who is writing a book on the stresses peculiar to celebrities, conducted a survey in which 200 questionnaires were mailed out to names randomly selected from a list of the public's top-ranked celebrities. From 51 replies, he compiled a list of the primary sources of stress for celebrities and their families, as well as their reactions and solutions. Most of the questionnaires were completed by the celebrities, the rest by a spouse, friend, or adult child of the celebrity. The top 10 stressors, in order, were:

- the celebrity press

- critics

- threatening letters/calls

- the lack of privacy

- the constant monitoring of their lives

- worry about career plunges

- stalkers

- lack of security

- curious fans

- worries about their children's lives being disrupted

The celebrities's reactions to this stress were: depression, loss of sleep, crying over nothing, bad moods, acting out and misbehavior on the part of their children, lack of concentration, stomach problems, paranoia, over-spending, lack of trust, and self-hatred.

"There's a certain amount of insecurity," Figley says. "One of the respondents said that, at any time, he expected someone to come up and tap him on the shoulder and say, 'Go back to being a waiter. What do you think you're doing here, anyway?' There's a constant need for reassurance that they deserve what they've received."

Stress-busting solutions celebrities mentioned included: talking to friends or therapists, beefing up security, having friends outside the business, protecting their kids, laughing as much as possible, finding faith and religion, getting out of L.A.

"A sense of humor was one thing that kept coming up when they were asked about coping," Figley says. "One family had fun with it, and made a game out of trying various disguises to not be recognized." But another respondent, a well-known celeb, said he vividly remembers a painful moment when his family was going out for pizza, and his youngest child asked his mother, "Does dad have to come?"

"There tends to be a wide variation among the children," Figley says. "Some don't mind the attention, or even look forward to it. Others hate it." Gilda Radner spoke about dealing with fame in her autobiography, *It's Always Something*, written just before her death from ovarian cancer. "With fame, and the constant display of my image on television, came anorexia. I became almost afraid to eat," she said. But New York streets are filled with tempting kiosks. "During the second year of *Saturday Night Live*, I taught myself to throw up. I became bulimic before medical science had given it that name."

After her hair fell out from chemotherapy, Radner could go out in public and not be recognized. But with that freedom came the loss of her sense of self. "I started introducing myself by saying, 'I used to be Gilda Radner.' That was how I felt. I used to be her, but now I was someone else." Radner finally broke through the desolation and joined a cancer support group, where she established friendships and made people laugh. "Finding that part of myself again," she said, "was wonderful."

Drugs and Destruction

English actor Gary Oldman seems to take pride in finding the oddest roles imaginable; he's played Count Dracula, Beethoven, Sid Vicious, and Lee Harvey Oswald. "Acting comes too easy for Gary. He's a genius at the craft. It bores him" says Douglas Urbanski, Oldman's agent.

The nemesis Oldman is struggling to conquer is more challenging than a difficult screen persona. "He's 61 days sober as of today," Urbanski says. "Isabella (Rossellini), Gary, and I have been on the most incredible journey together. The work he has done on himself is awesome."

Oldman is the son of an alcoholic welder who abandoned his family when Gary was seven. While Oldman was gliding to the top of the film industry, his personal life was in shambles, with two broken marriages. "Sometimes acting gets in the way of living life," Oldman has said. "It's very consuming."

After five weeks of rehab, Oldman now plays his Steinway to relieve stress, attends AA meetings, and stays grounded by establishing a routine in his life. "He's got children, dogs, nannies, housekeepers, a whole menagerie up there [at his home]," Urbanski said. "But this is the first time he's experienced it all from a point of sobriety."

"People are naive about chemical dependence," Oldman now tells reporters, "about how destructive, powerful, and overwhelming it is."

David Wellisch, Ph.D., a professor of psychiatry at UCLA's medical school, says Oldman may well have two of the factors associated with alcohol abuse—a genetic predisposition and an environmental influence from childhood, with at least one parent modeling addictive behaviors.

But because of his talent, Oldman, like many celebs, had a third risk factor—one that Wellisch calls a "crisis of mobility," in which his fame transported him from one world to another. "He knew how to act when he was the son of a welder, but then he became a stranger in a strange land. His life had, at some level, lost its bearings. Drugs can be a stabilizer, at least temporarily, providing anxiety reduction, feelings of omnipotence and power, or a soothing, deep peace otherwise unattainable," Wellisch says.

For celebrities, especially in the entertainment field, the pressure is always on to turn in a perfect performance, to be better than before, to constantly hit the mark. At the same time, artists tend to be sensitive souls, in touch with naked emotions they mine for our perusal.

"Artists are the lenses through which life is transmitted. They show us what we think and feel in a way that is profound, intense, and highly emotional," Wellisch says. "They experience life more dearly than the rest of us." Drugs are a way to mute these feelings, which threaten to overwhelm.

And with the riches that accompany their fame, drugs are an escape route celebrities can afford at least for a while. The list of celebrity deaths from drugs is long, and continually updated—Elvis Presley, Judy Garland, Marilyn Monroe, Jim Morrison, Janis Joplin, Scott Newman, David Kennedy, John Belushi, River Phoenix.

"I think it has to be remembered that he was 23 and he made the choice," said Judy Davis, who was set to star opposite Phoenix in his next movie. "There's something about stardom and the way it empowers people—he thought he was immune." Fame, therapists agree, can draw stars into a kind of magical thinking, wherein the laws of humankind are suspended.

Or, perhaps, River Phoenix felt he was unworthy. "There's embarrassment and guilt among those who become superstars quickly," Figley says. "They may have a self-destructive streak."

Jib Fowles, professor of media studies at the University of Houston–Clear Lake and author of *Star Stuck: Celebrity Performers and the American Public* (Smithsonian Institute Press), found in a study of 100 stars from all fields—Hollywood entertainers, sports stars, musicians—that celebrities are almost four times more likely to kill themselves than the average American.

"It's an enormously stressful profession," Fowles says. "There is unrelenting pressure coupled with diminishing private lives. They have to be on every time they step out their front door."

In fact, Fowles found that the average age of death for celebrities, overall, was 58, compared to an average of 72 years old for other Americans.

Celebrities, he believes, are the sacrificial victims of our adoration.

> [Jib] Fowles found that the average age of death for celebrities, overall, was 58, compared to an average of 72 years old for other Americans.

"Never in a society has the individual been anywhere near as important as in contemporary America,' Fowles says. And, as old heroic figures—military, political, and religious leaders—have fallen by the wayside, entertainers have taken their place. "They are delivered to us as perfect human beings. We look to them as ideals, and that gives us orientation. But the burden falls heavily on them. There's an argument to be made that stars aren't paid nearly enough for the cultural service they provide."

"You have to wonder if anyone set limits for these people, if anyone said, 'You're nuts, you're going to the hospital,'" Wellisch says. "Take if from me, I've seen celebrities who are household names, and it's tough to tell them things. Everyone else is telling them what magnificent, otherworldly creatures they are, and you have to tell them they have clay feet and all these problems they need to deal with . . ."

Show business, like police work and medicine, is a high-risk profession, says Wellisch. "You experience too much, you see too much."

Some of the celebrities who have kicked drugs and come through to the other side attribute the change to settling down and having children. Actor Dennis Quaid battled drugs and alcohol for years, finally checking into rehab to kick a cocaine addiction before marrying Meg Ryan and having their son, Jack.

Children can pull their parents, famous or not, outside themselves. There is no longer the luxury of complete self-indulgence, if one takes parenting seriously. And, perhaps for the first time, there is someone more important, someone more deserving. For celebrities, who are at the center of so many orbits, it's especially important to have a little Copernicus around.

"As soon as Sam was born," said proud papa Michael J. Fox, "I knew that I would throw myself in front of a truck for him."

Privacy Protected

Sharon Stone, who's had a reputation for being outspoken and forthright in interviews, recently switched tacks. "My new policy is this: I have a life of my own. Just a little, tiny one, but it's mine," she told the *Entertainment Tonight* crew when they asked about her latest love interest.

Celebrities understandably become more protective when they achieve the level of fame where fans begin to swarm, track, or target them obsessively, says therapist Coe, whose office is across from the entrance to Warner Bros. Studios. "They'll buy burglar alarms, cars with tinted windows, guard dogs, bodyguards. Some of them even border on paranoia, like the stars who have four bodyguards with them at all times, even on a movie set, and change clothes five times a day. It's a fine line.

"You've got the up side, where celebrities have the freedom and opportunities to go places and do things that bring them wonderment and joy. But their boundaries are constantly being pushed back, physically and mentally. Also, their trust level is down. They don't trust a lot of people."

Through their prominence and visibility, celebrities become living Rorschach tests, valued by their adoring public not for who they are, but for who their fans want them to be. With the casual fan, this could mean confusing actors with the roles they play, or feeling a sense of false intimacy with someone they've never actually met. For the lunatic, it could mean that the celebrity becomes the fantasy half of a dangerous delusion. Take the woman who, after breaking into David Letterman's home, took to driving his cars and referring to herself as "Mrs. Letterman."

Michelle Pfeiffer has said that she acts for free—but charges for the inconvenience of being a celebrity. She tells about one day on the set of *The Age of Innocence*, when people were gathered around her trailer. "I kept trying to find a place where they couldn't see in. So I find myself in the back of the trailer and they can't see me, but I can hear them. Now, these are people who are usually like, 'Michelle, Michelle, we love you.' And I hear somebody say, 'Hey, man, I saw her and she looks old,'" Pfeiffer recounted, laughing. "I'm not worried about age. But I'm very aware that this is my window of time."

Moving away from fans to "get away from it all" might work too effectively, however. Garrison Keillor, radio host from the banks of Lake Wobegon, left St. Paul for Denmark, homeland of his Scandinavian wife. He claimed he wanted anonymity, the freedom to "live the life of a shy person." Eventually, he moved back to Minneapolis and resumed broadcasting live. Nothing's worse than adulation, till it's gone.

Family Ties

Celebrity parents may produce celebrity progeny: Janet Leigh begat Jamie Lee Curtis, Debbie Reynolds begat Carrie Fisher, Kirk Douglas begat Michael, Lloyd Bridges begat Beau and Jeff, Martin Sheen begat Charlie and Emilio, Henry Fonda begat Jane and Peter, who begat Bridget.

But for the most part, celebrities have ordinary moms, dads, dogs, and siblings back in the great American heartland who serve as touchstones in their lives. Families and old friends, say the stars, counteract the dizzying seduction of a world in which you can endlessly reinvent yourself, losing track of who you are and where you came from.

Sarah Jessica Parker, says she takes "self-appointed sabbaticals" from the demands of filming to "see my family, go to the market, and cook every day." Heather Locklear told Barbara Walters that her parents live nearby, visit often, and keep her sane.

When your parents are the ones who are famous, though, it can be a tough act to follow. It is the children who often pay the price of parental celebrity. The insecurity in the household, the tension, the career and mood ups and downs, the errant, hectic schedules, and the long absences all coalesce to shift a great deal of the emotional burden to the kids.

"I feel so for the kids," says Coe. "You're always dealing with having that name, or that face." No surprise, then, that the children of celebrities, like the prodigal minister's daughter, often act out in effective and embarrassing ways.

Alison Eastwood, now a model, grew up in Carmel as not only the daughter of actor Clint, but also as the rebellious child of the town's mayor. "I was feeling my oats," she said in a recent interview. "I dyed my hair orange and drove around fast with my stereo blaring. I was one of the big noise-makers in town. I bet people were happy to see me go to college."

The trappings of fame—frequent travel, drug use, affairs—can estrange celebrity parents from their children, preventing a normal relationship during their formative years. Actress Liv Tyler is the daughter of model Bebe Buell and Aerosmith's Steven Tyler. Raised in Maine, Liv was nine before she learned that Tyler was her father. Her mother blocked Tyler from his daughter's life due to his drug and alcohol abuse. "He was a screwed-up mess, and I chose not to have him in her life until he chose sobriety," Buell says.

Tyler's daughters now accept and acknowledge their rock-legend dad, although his daughter Mia says he does embarrass her sometimes while on stage. "I mean, he stands there and he's groping himself and he should not be doing that," she told *A Current Affair* in an interview. "It disgusts me."

Celebrities' children, like the children of the very wealthy, also run the risk of wasted lives due to dysgradia, a syndrome where there is a complete lack of connection between doing and getting. "This is extremely amotivational," says Wellisch. "You know that no matter what you do, everything's still going to be there."

> Hardest of all, perhaps, is the stress that fame can place on a celebrity's marriage.

In addition to blood relations, celebs often have extended "families" nearby, made up of friends, employees, and other stars. Celebrities often work out of their homes, scheduling appointments, reading scripts, conducting meetings, and having networking parties. "The household is filled with people always coming and going. There's quite a bit of entertainment. It's rather chaotic. Managers and agents who have been with them for a long time become close friends, and like aunts and uncles to their children," Figley says.

With a support staff comes a payroll, employees and associates who depend on the celebrity for their own livelihood. "That puts a celebrity under constant pressure to be famous,' Figley says. "So if an actor is in a movie that gets bad reviews or does poorly, he is inclined to self-blame, which leads to depression."

And, as always when there's a lot of money involved, there's the potential for corruption, for a trust violated. Indeed, celebrities are usually inundated by people who want to work for them. It can be difficult to scrutinize who to hire, never knowing what anyone really wants of you.

The Home Front

Hardest of all, perhaps, is the stress that fame can place on a celebrity's marriage.

Temptations are abundant. *Legends of the Fall* star Aidan Quinn, who has a wife, Elizabeth Bracco, and a young daughter, has women slipping notes to him even while he's getting his teeth cleaned at the dentist. "One time," he recounts, "I was out with my wife at dinner, and this woman walks up to the table and puts down a card with her name and number. She just laid it down and she walked away. I had to almost physically restrain my wife. [. . .]"

Without a separate, strong commitment to a career or other interests, it is particularly difficult for a celebrity's partner to maintain a clear sense of identity in a relationship. The attainment of celebrity almost automatically shifts the power balance. The spouse of a celebrity may live in constant fear of abandonment. What's more, the frequent absences of the celebrity mean the partner winds up with the extra burden of domestic responsibility. And the unpredictability of employment puts constant tension on the relationship.

But the biggest stress on relationships may come from the celebrity's own psyche. Does a star give up the role at home? The shift is almost always difficult for celebrities, therapists say. After a day in front of the camera, being catered to by teams of workers, not to mention sought out by hordes of fans, a request to take out the garbage can feel extremely claustrophobic.

Jennifer Sils, a Santa Monica therapist wed to comedy magician Mac King, says being in a relationship with an entertainer provides as many benefits as drawbacks to the spouse. Sils interviewed in depth eight women married to or living with men in the performing arts. Erratic schedules, long hours, unpredictable income, and periods of unemployment can make living with performers difficult, they admitted.

The financial ups and downs add a profound level of unpredictability in scheduling important life events, such as when to have children. There are difficulties in establishing a personal identity when married to a performer, who is often a strong personality. Parties and other social events supply more stress, because they tend to make the spouse feel unimportant. The frequent long absences of their mates require adjustments on leaving and reentry.

But, Sils found, most of the women said their relationships gave them opportunities they might not have otherwise experienced, like travel and rubbing shoulders with other stars. For the most part, said the women, their lives were exciting, filled with creativity, and seldom boring.

For celebrity spouses anchored by children, homes, and careers, however, home can be a long way from the latest movie set.

And then there are those celebrities who feel destined to stay single due to their star status. Joan Lunden, co-host of *Good Morning America*, bemoaned her lack of romantic companionship, three years after her divorce. "Since then, I've only had a few dates—and believe me, that hasn't been my choice. I can't understand why men are so intimidated. There must be someone wonderful out there. But I'm certainly finding him hard to find."

Media

Ah, the press. The Fourth Estate, defender of the First Amendment, the No. 1 source of celebrity stress.

The tabloids, both print and TV, lead the pack, certainly. But even the mainstream press has incredible leeway when it comes to reporting on public figures. Where a private person must prove only negligence to claim libel, public figures (such as celebrities, politicians, and others who have sought the spotlight) must claim actual malice or knowledge that the statement is false.

The creative-expression defense goes a long way with courts intent on upholding the freedom of the press. When *Hustler* magazine discussed Jerry Falwell having sex with his mother in an outhouse, the Supreme Court ruled it satire.

But those on the receiving end say the press can be relentless in trying to capture, then condemn, their celebrity prey.

"I was walking down the street to go and get a newspaper and I was followed by this van, and this man with a video camera was filming me," Julia Roberts said in an interview. "This popped up on TV a few days later. I mean, I'm going to get the paper, and it's early in the morning and I have my hair pulled back and I have on some little dress or whatever. This woman on the television had the nerve to be completely obsessed by how I looked.

> Just as we have created celebrities, we have created the hall of mirrors in which they so precariously exist.

"Now, I don't have a clue what she looks like when she's going to get the paper." Roberts continued, "but I doubt it is the same as she does on television. She was saying, 'Julia, I have the name of a great hairdresser.' I thought, well, why should I do my hair to go and get a paper on the off-chance that somebody is going to videotape it and put it on TV?"

Being constantly judged and evaluated by their appearance, whether attending the Academy Awards or stepping out to get a newspaper, denies celebrities any part of their life that is truly and exclusively their own. Therein lies madness . . . or, at least, resentment. Does buying a movie ticket, owning a television, or subscribing to a magazine give us automatic rights to 24-hour surveillance?

We build 'em up, just to knock 'em down.

Accomplishments

The late Tony Perkins, said his wife, Berry, never gloried in his cinematic successes. "He was very strong, and very intelligent, but I don't think he thought he really contributed a hell of a lot to this world, which is really sad."

"I've always felt . . . that it was a very exposable myth that I was somebody," Perkins told the *Saturday Evening Post* in 1960. "I've felt this was an absurd dishonesty and that if I were close to people, it would be instantly evident and that they would say, 'Well, gee, he's nothing at all. What do we want to see him for?'"

Many celebrities suffer from this "impostor phenomenon," says Harway, and attribute their successes to good luck rather than hard work.

Just as we have created celebrities, we have created the hall of mirrors in which they so precariously exist. For the famous today, said Lasch, self-approval depends on public recognition and acclaim.

"The good opinion of friends and neighbors, which formerly informed a man that he had lived a useful life, rested on appreciation of his accomplishments.

"Today, men seek the kind of approval that applauds not their actions, but their personal attributes," Lasch continued. "They wish to be not so much esteemed as admired. They crave not fame, but the glamour and excitement of celebrity. They want to be envied rather than respected. Pride and acquisitiveness . . . have given way to vanity."

Falling Stars

Will Lohan Be the Next Celebrity Flame-Out?

By Katherine Monk
The Ottawa Citizen, July 28, 2007

There's no shortage of fallen celebrity stars these days. The doors at pricey rehab centres in Southern California keep revolving—and the likes of Lindsay Lohan keep relapsing—prompting the inevitable question: What next?

Will Lohan be the next pretty face to fill a coffin, or will she manage to rise above the tragic archetype crafted by the likes of Marilyn Monroe to claim a place of credible fame instead of a fleeting slice of infamy?

The image of the doomed celebrity is as old as celebrity itself. The combination of a pretty face, a beloved screen star and a tragic end have proven to be a highly successful potion for mass publicity.

In this light, Lohan's recent post-rehab episode featuring an elevated blood-alcohol reading could be read—by the cynics, at any rate—as a slimy tool to promote her new movie, *I Know Who Killed Me*, which hits theatres without any positive word-of-mouth yesterday.

It certainly wouldn't be the first time a studio has taken to tapping into celebrity scandal to publicize a film. When Liz Taylor's marriage to Eddie Fisher famously exploded on the set of *Cleopatra*—which was overbudget and considered a flop before it even wrapped—steamy on-set pictures of Taylor and lover Richard Burton found their way onto the cover of *Life Magazine*.

The more awkward and embarrassing the descent becomes, the more power it has to fascinate the masses, and in turn, pull people into the theatre. Yet, as clever as the early studio bosses were, they didn't create the archetype of celebrity flame-outs. They merely exploited its primal power.

Marilyn Monroe may have been seen as a sexpot, a movie star and a bit of a bubblehead while she was alive, but in the decades since her death, she's been elevated to the level of secular goddess.

And when it comes to archetypal symbols of the epic battle between heroic selflessness and self-absorbed self-destruction that defines the modern celebrity experience, Marilyn is the template of tragedy. She reigns supreme over other platinum blond martyrs to fame such as Jayne Mansfield and Jean Harlow, who suffered from bad luck more than bad habits.

Material reprinted with the express permission of: "Ottawa Citizen Group Inc.", a CanWest Partnership.

The truly tragic demands self-destruction and so far, Lohan has done a pretty good job emulating the celebrity model. In news yesterday, a new audio tape and other details from Lohan's car chase and arrest this week reveal a woman pleading for help and witnesses saying the actress believed she was immune from punishment.

> In the long tradition of celebrity boozers and substance abusers, things generally end with a bang.

On the tape of a call to an emergency 911 line, which became public late Thursday, the woman being chased by Lohan—who police said was the mother of her personal assistant—describes what happened.

"We were just about to park our car. We were coming home and out of nowhere this huge white GMC came up. The gentleman jumped out of the car, and oh my God, they are following us," the woman told a 911 operator.

At one point, she can be heard yelling: "Oh my God, what is he doing?"

The men who claimed to be inside with Lohan told celebrity Internet site TMZ.com that, during the chase, Lohan boasted she would not be arrested. "I can't get into trouble. I'm a celebrity," one of the passengers claimed Lohan said.

Even Dr. Phil thinks it may just be a matter of time before the doomed starlet archetype swallows her whole.

And he may be right.

For instance, like fellow flame-out Judy Garland, Lohan rose to fame as a child actor—removing her from any semblance of normalcy at a young age. Combined with what appears to be a fame-obsessed parent-manager, Lohan and the deceased Gumm sister share a lot of unhealthy similarities.

Throw in some yo-yo-ing body weight issues, an ongoing battle with substance abuse and an apparent need to party with fame-sucking hangers-on, and Lohan could end up worse than Corey Haim, Tatum O'Neal and Winona Ryder combined: Alive but unemployable.

Worse still would be complete surrender to her apparent addiction. In the long tradition of celebrity boozers and substance abusers, things generally end with a bang.

If Lohan were to take the low road, and follow the careening career of River Phoenix or, more plausibly, Monty Clift—her string of DUIs would finally lead to a severe accident, possible disfigurement, and a short life addicted to pain killers and booze before the combination proved lethal.

She could also continue traipsing along in the path of Marilyn's pumps and create one scandal after another while pursuing an uneven film career—until she hits middle-age, that is, when she'll either die of a suspected suicide, become a plump has-been or turn into a Farrah Fawcett freak show.

Then again, she could pull off a Robert Downey Jr. or Robin Williams–style reclamation of her own destiny. Both men faced severe substance abuse problems after hitting the pinnacle of fame in their salad days, and managed—after more than one attempt—to stay clean and sober.

Right Time, Wrong Publicity

BY CARYN JAMES
THE NEW YORK TIMES, MAY 19, 2007

Burgers and alcohol have been an unlucky combination for David Hasselhoff, even more than we knew. First came the leaked video of him that flooded television and the Internet a couple of weeks ago: he sits on the floor, slurring words as he talks to his teenage daughter, so drunk he can't get a burger into his mouth. Now comes this revelation from his just-published autobiography, "Don't Hassel the Hoff." After a couple of stints in rehab, one that included a night-time escape from Betty Ford, he started drinking again and craved a midnight snack.

"The L.A.P.D. gave me a field sobriety test in the McDonald's parking lot on Ventura Boulevard," he writes of his 2004 arrest. Who would have dreamed that a drunken burger episode would become the best-known scene of his career?

The book is ludicrous; nothing in "Don't Hassel the Hoff" is as lively as its title or as revealing as its brief adventures in rehab. The video is just sad. Yet the media spectacle surrounding the Hasselhoff video and Alec Baldwin's leaked phone rant to his 11-year-old daughter have obscured some profound social issues. With their intensely personal moments made public, the celebrities represent oversize versions of the threats to privacy we all face at a time when the use of e-mail, camera-phones and other technologies has grown faster than common sense about them. If such betrayals can happen to stars, they can happen to us (with humiliation on a smaller scale). And the leaks themselves are the product of a celebrity culture as out of control as the stars in these uncontrolled moments.

The Hasselhoff and Baldwin recordings are not typical celebrity fodder, because both have become weapons in venomous custody battles. The identities of the people who leaked the material have not become public, but Mr. Hasselhoff and Mr. Baldwin have pointed in the direction of their ex-wives. However it happened, all the players are now involved in a high-stakes publicity war.

In her custody dispute over their two teenage daughters, Mr. Hasselhoff's ex-wife, Pamela Bach, recently hired Debra Opri, the lawyer who seemed to be on television every day when she represented Larry Birkhead, the Anna Nicole baby daddy. Mr. Baldwin's custody battle with his ex-wife, Kim Basinger, over their daughter, Ireland, became a tabloid staple years ago.

The legal wrangling here is all about custody. There is no law against the public's seeing and hearing these intimate scenes, and there shouldn't be. But just because we can know doesn't mean we deserve to. These tapes are not like Linda Tripp's recordings of Monica Lewinsky, an enormous personal betrayal with bigger implications. They're not even like the embarrassing leak of Prince Charles's phone call to his then-girlfriend Camilla saying that he wished to be her tampon; he's the man who will be king. These new leaks simply draw all of us into family battles where we don't belong.

Beyond the humane idea that some things really should remain private, even for fame-mongers, these leaks have an insidious snowball effect on the culture. As the celebrity press goes into overdrive, the stars on the defense are forced into weirder and weirder contortions of spin. Mr. Hasselhoff began by issuing a long, straightforward statement about his recovery and relapse as an alcoholic, making some accusations about his ex-wife along the way.

"She will resort to any means to obtain the attention of the media," his statement said. Even with a book coming out, he couldn't have wanted this kind of attention: his visitation rights were temporarily suspended in light of the video, with a hearing about visitation scheduled for Monday.

But he also has a career to protect, and he's already yukking it up about the burger. "Party at my house tonight, Red Bulls and burgers," he joked the other day during a taping of the NBC show "America's Got Talent," the "American Idol" clone on which he's a judge. That clip appeared Tuesday on the NBC-owned "Access Hollywood" and its Web site, accesshollywood.com, a blunt network effort at cross-promotion and damage control.

It's hard to imagine that Mr. Baldwin actually wanted to be scrutinized again while explaining himself on "The View," or to have a private chat with Dr. Phil, who had offered his help via "Larry King Live." Mr. Baldwin took him up on the offer and authorized the doc to talk publicly about the conversation later. Did he have much choice? And who asked Dr. Phil to get into the act?

On Mr. Hasselhoff's Web site, hasselhoff.com, there is now only a giant photograph of him ending his recent Las Vegas run of "The Producers," with a message that the site will be back soon. Mr. Baldwin's site, alecbaldwin.com, is still up, with a message that he plans to shut it down on June 30 and return in the fall with a site devoted to his new book projects and their subjects, custody and parental alienation.

Mr. Hasselhoff's much fluffier book, written "with" (or should it be by?) Peter Thompson, reads like a cut-and-paste job padded with plot summaries of "Baywatch" and "Knight Rider." If you didn't care about KITT the talking car back then, you really won't care now.

But his book becomes accidentally illuminating about the lure and pitfalls of fame when he describes meeting Princess Diana. It seem that even stars can be star-struck. The princess, he says wondrously, flirted with him. (He probably shouldn't have taken that so personally.) He quotes a full paragraph from her brother's eulogy, the part about how she was "hunted" by the press. The book's final upbeat word on publicity, though, is that "tabloid smears can't damage me," a line that is one of his less convincing efforts at spin.

And that spinning has just begun. The new season of "America's Got Talent" begins on June 5, the same day a court hearing is scheduled about who leaked the Baldwin message, and the very day Paris Hilton is supposed to start serving her prison term. That day may turn out be the oddest celebrity trifecta ever.

Being Bad

The Career Move

By Guy Trebay
The New York Times, April 20, 2006

It would probably require a stopwatch to clock the lag time between sin and redemption lately, as media disgrace is transformed into a bargaining chip in a celebrity's career often before a bad boy or girl has stumbled home from the crime scene and showered off the taint of shame.

What seems evident is that public humiliation has lost its barb. There might have been a time when being caught on camera in flagrante delicto or hoovering up lines of coke would have ended a career. But as Paris Hilton proved, being videotaped by one's boyfriend in a zonked-out state and naked on all fours does not put a hitch in one's five-year plan. If anything, the bubble-gum divinity apotheosized on the basis of a homemade pornography loop, a moronic catchphrase and a mental vacancy cavernous enough for storing yellowcake appears set to enjoy a media half-life about as long as that of a spent plutonium rod.

And this odd realization goes a long way toward explaining recent events in the life of another creature of the age: the model Kate Moss.

The recent career arc of this British model, style emblem, rocker's moll and anointed reprobate of the fashion world could be found unexpected only by those whose attention has strayed from the celebrity mosh pit that now crams the main stage of pop culture. Readers whose Star subscriptions have lapsed may not recall that it was just seven months ago, on Sept. 15, that The Daily Mirror of London ran front page photographs that, it claimed, showed Ms. Moss cutting and snorting cocaine in a London photo studio where Babyshambles, the band of her boyfriend, Pete Doherty, was in the middle of a recording session.

The pictures looked gritty, candid and sufficiently libel-proof that both images and coke-snorting allegations were soon plastered like sleazy wallpaper across the blogosphere. The immediate effect on Ms. Moss's career was less than promising. She was booted by a group of the clients who had made her one of the richest women in her industry, with estimated annual earnings of $9 million. The Swedish retailer H&M, Europe's largest clothing chain, led the charge, dropping her from an advertising campaign showcasing clothes designed by Stella McCartney after first coming to Ms. Moss's defense.

"If someone is going to be the face of H&M," a spokeswoman said at the time, "it is important that they be healthy, wholesome and sound."

Ms. Moss simultaneously discovered that lucrative contracts with longstanding clients like Burberry and Chanel were not renewed or else dropped. And while she stopped short of admitting to drug use, Ms. Moss did what spin doctors always advise troubled clients to do in a pinch: issue an apology and head for the hills. In Ms. Moss's case, the hills surrounded an Arizona clinic where she went to treat "the various personal issues I need to address," as she said in a prepared public statement, "and to take the difficult yet necessary steps to resolve them."

Yet a strange thing happened to Kate Moss on the way to rehab. Far from becoming a pariah or experiencing a serious fall from public grace, she developed an unexpected level of luster. The 32-year-old woman who has been the subject of controversial press since she was discovered at 14, the onetime waif, the person pilloried for allegedly promoting anorexia, the freewheeling seductress of the British tabloids, the tempestuous destroyer of hotel rooms, the confidante and bosom buddy of Anita Pallenberg and other rock chick survivors from the heyday of hard drugs, found herself bumped up a notch to the status of that most nebulous of beings, the cultural avatar.

Even as the London police were questioning [Kate] Moss in January, clients were clamoring for her services.

And even before the model had checked out of the drying-out clinic, she was inundated in attention and work. W magazine ran a cover story on Kate Moss in November 2005. Vanity Fair made her its cover subject the following month. An issue of the influential fashion magazine French Vogue was dedicated to Ms. Moss, who also served as guest editor.

If her notoriety was bad for the brand, it is hard to see how. Even as the London police were questioning Ms. Moss in January, clients were clamoring for her services. Already by early 2006 she had booked campaigns with Virgin Mobile, Dior, Roberto Cavalli and CK Jeans. She had renewed her contracts with the leather and accessories company Longchamp and, it was rumored in the industry, also with Burberry, whose runway show in Milan she attended in February as the front-row guest of Rose Marie Bravo, the company's chief executive. "It shows how relevant she is," Jenn Ramey, Ms. Moss's American agent, said this week, just days after Nikon introduced a new campaign for its Coolpix S6 digital camera built around a series of photographs of a mostly naked Ms. Moss.

"Kate is the height of style and sophistication," said Bill Oberlander, the executive creative director of McCann Worldwide, the agency that created the Nikon ads, for which Ms. Moss is reputedly being paid several million dollars. "She has this almost superhuman quality."

For Anna Marie Bakker, the director of communications at Nikon, Ms. Moss seemed an obvious choice to promote a brand aggressively trying to shed its fusty image and seduce the notoriously fickle imaginations of young consumers. "Part of the appeal is that she is truly an enduring style icon," Ms. Bakker said. "But most importantly, she appeals to Nikon as we try to move our product forward, because she has an edge."

Doctoral dissertations could be written on the layered meanings of "edge," the most overused marketing term of the last decade and one most often deployed to lend freshness to ideas and objects whose use-by date has clearly expired. Yet Kate Moss, whose cool not only fueled an 18-year career at the top of her profession, but also attracted the attention of artists from Lucien Freud to the British sculptor Marc Quinn, can now fairly be said to have added "edge" to her résumé, largely on the basis of her sporadic relationship with the unregenerate bad boy, Mr. Doherty, and the resulting brouhaha about a druggy night spent in a London studio.

"She's ubiquitous, she never speaks publicly and so she's someone who has this muteness, this silence that allows people to project onto her image," said Mr. Quinn, whose painted bronze sculpture of Ms. Moss, in an elaborate yoga posture and with her feet behind her ears, will be the centerpiece of a show opening in May at the Mary Boone Gallery in New York. "Her image has a life of its own. What was interesting when she had all those troubles with the tabloid press about her drug-taking was that the image and the drug-taking didn't fit and people couldn't take that."

Yet just as likely the reverse is true; Ms. Moss's tabloid adventures added to the nest of magpie details that, wittingly or not, we all now seem to accumulate about celebrities and then mold into specious narratives about people we've never met. "And that, after all, is what a brand is," said James Twitchell, an author and professor of English and advertising at the University of Florida. "Celebrities are these extraordinary characters who have no plot, but who are in many ways the easiest characters to follow. They don't violate expectations because there really are none."

And so Ms. Moss's cool—the historical cool of bad boys and girls doing things that most of us, being properly middle class, might wish to do but will never get around to, explained Dr. Michael Brody, chairman of the media committee of the American Academy of Child and Adolescent Psychiatry—becomes something different and better in a marketing sense when one adds a dollop of scandal or edge.

"Edge denotes shame," said Dr. Brody, the kind invoked when, for example, one is caught by a camera huddled over a mound of white powder, neatly chopping lines. "People use cameras to take all kinds of pictures now," he added, alluding to the proliferation of too-intimate images widely available on sites like Craigslist.com or MySpace.com. "If you're selling a camera in our celebrity-obsessed culture, why not use a celebrity and one who was captured at the scene of a crime?" he said.

The idea is not just sexy, in a dubious but distinctly transgressive fashion. It is also a shrewd exploitation of brand. "From the minute her name came up, we loved the idea of Kate endorsing a camera," said Mr. Oberlander, the McCann Worldwide executive. What could be better, Mr. Oberlander said, than giving a camera to the woman who has spent her life as the focus of its gaze and letting her "take the lens and turn it on the audience?"

What Price, Fame?

By Greg Sevik
Popular Music and Society, Fall/Winter 2001

Music is a wonderful art form. It has the lyrical properties of poetry and the unique expression that can only come from seven notes: seven pitches of sounds arranged in infinite variety. The full spectrum of feelings and emotions can come through in this medium, and through the ages, the music of a culture has been a great reflection of its people and society. This is quite true of today's music; it reflects a materialistic society in which the pursuit of wealth is also the goal of existence. In fact, many of today's musicians are artists to a decreasing degree and increasingly resemble entrepreneurs, hocking their profitable commodity. Some of today's musicians are losing a sense of artistic integrity because of the emphasis on the acquisition of fame and fortune. The media often promote such ideas about musicianship not as an art form, but as a business venture.

An ad for Sennheiser vocal microphones featured in the December 1997 issue of *Guitar One* illustrates a common advertising dynamic. The physical details of the ad itself are material to the overall effect. In the extreme foreground, bold red letters brandish Benjamin Franklin's famous quote: "What price, fame?" At the bottom, also in the extreme foreground, is Sennheiser's clever retort: "Not as much as you think." Benjamin Franklin's $100 bill portrait, slightly modified, occupies the middle foreground. The winking Franklin evidently knows something that we do not. A large-as-life picture of the microphone itself lies dead center, leaning toward the prospective musician, beckoning him to step up to the mic. The ad sits on a background which is immediately recognizable as a sell-out crowd for a huge concert, which, in this case, just happens to be Woodstock '94, a name synonymous with the heart of rock and roll. The crowd itself, nothing more than a mass of intoxicated youth, is reaching, hands raised and eyes aglow with adoration and admiration, seemingly grasping for the musician on stage who is represented only by the oversized microphone.

The ad makes the promise, then, that if you buy a Sennheiser vocal microphone, you will be one step closer to becoming famous. To Franklin's profound rhetorical question, this ad answers "not as much as you think." In other words, if you buy the microphone, you too can be famous. Only the microphone, not a human being, is standing tall before the crowd, suggesting that the consumer-musician cannot be responsible for his own destiny, but must rely on a microphone to make him famous. The crowd is a powerful motivator because the musician sees the crowd and begins to hope that, with the aid of a new microphone he, too, will be loved and admired by countless people.

The microphone is, of course, not destined to live up to its promise. The ad itself apologizes for so shrewdly persuading the consumer into buying Sennheiser's microphone by saying that "we cannot guarantee that you'll be performing in front of half a million people tomorrow," but "we *do* ensure that you'll sound better wherever you play." In fact, the ad turns its own promise into a sort of joke by admitting that it is unreasonable. Mark Crispin Miller, in his essay "Deride and Conquer," explains this phenomenon, noting that an ad "solicits each viewer's allegiance by reflecting back his/her own automatic skepticism toward [the ad]" and thus "protects itself from criticism or rejection by incorporating our very animus against the spectacle into the spectacle itself" (444). Everyone knows that the promises that advertisements make are unrealistic, so the advertisers mock themselves to show us that the ad is benign. At this point it would be easy enough to dismiss the ad as harmless, even funny. However, there is something deeper at work.

The Sennheiser ad is telling us something important about what it means to be a musician, providing us with a definition of the ultimate goal of musicianship as fame and fortune. Franklin's quote, "What price, fame?" was originally intended as a comment on the evils of fame: lack of privacy in the public eye, not knowing who one's true friends are, and tremendous responsibility, to name a few. The advertiser intentionally misuses the quote. Instead, the ad implies that Franklin meant to ask "what does a guy have to do to get famous?" A winking Ben Franklin in the ad confirms this, and the use of Franklin's $100 bill portrait emphasizes that money is also a big part of what it means to be a successful musician. The crowd, however, is probably the major promoter of fame in the ad. Presumably, the musician-consumer, seeing the crowd in the ad, and being touched by the love and admiration expressed by the drunken mass (who might just as easily lavish such affection on a candy bar or cigarette), will say to himself: "Maybe my music can make me famous." After all, this ad clearly portrays such fame very powerfully as the possibility of being great—an example to others instead of a follower—and of becoming extremely wealthy in the process.

The real danger of the ad, then, is not the fact that it makes empty promises—we knew that already. The danger is that the ad, like much of the media, defines musicianship as a commercial venture, and thus takes the emphasis away from artistry in music by harboring the desire to be famous. Of course, one ad does not have the power to change us, but as Jean Kilbourne says in her documentary *Killing Us Softly*, these effects are "cumulative and unconscious."

When we consider that by the age of 65 the average person has seen two million television commercials and countless hours of TV and movies ("Statistics on Television's Impact"), we must realize that the media will inevitably shape our attitudes, even without our awareness.

What makes this ad, and popular culture at large, most powerful and effective is that it does not offer us any alternate definitions. If the ad did not sell us a definition of a good musician as one who becomes famous, then the advertiser might have a hard time getting us to constantly purchase to relieve ourselves of the guilt and shame of private life. We might become bad consumers. The media would certainly have nothing to gain by portraying the aim of musicianship as, say, a medium through which to express oneself artistically, a sort of therapy by which to express and better understand one's own emotions, or a medium by which to enlighten and educate an audience. By these definitions, the need to become rich and famous and the need to purchase expensive new equipment become obsolete. After all, one's prominence and financial status have nothing at all to do with one's talents, abilities, creativity, or musicianship.

These definitions of musicianship, however, have failed to be the most popular ones. The definition of music as a commercial venture has been promoted, quite powerfully, by the musicians who themselves possess the media-sponsored image of happiness: wealth, power, and the adoration of the public. For many musicians their careers are so focused on their fortunes that even the music itself is about money. This is especially evident in rap music, where "artists" such as Puff Daddy have been so overcome by fame that "materialistic boasting now constitutes Puff's entire message" (Shift 59). The audience for rap has no way of relating to lines like I "got a Benz I ain't even drove yet" (qtd. in Shift 59), which virtually no one can relate to. This leads to a certain dubiousness about the value and importance of such music.

The confusion that musicians face in light of the relationship between money and music is perhaps exemplified by the Reel Big Fish song "Sell Out." The song is about an aspiring musician who has just gotten his "big break" and is apparently struggling with the decision of whether or not to sign a contract with a record company. The "artist" seems aware that this decision may corrupt his artistry as he sings "They say they're gonna give me lots of money if I play what they want you to hear." He even seems to acknowledge that the goal of becoming rich and famous is not entirely his own, "'cause *the man* said that's the way it is and *the man* said it don't get better than this" (emphasis added). In fact, the song leads the listener to believe that the "artist" understands that his integrity will be comprised at least, and at most that he will lose creative freedom altogether by signing the record contract. However, he gives in to the desire to be a rock star as he declares in closing that he can't flip burgers for the rest of his life. The song's ending attempts both to justify his decision and, at the same time, sung with a note of sadness not present in the rest of the upbeat tune, to emphasize that he has given up something precious. Ironically, for Puff Daddy, Reel Big Fish, and others who sing about money, the very thing that compromises their artistry has become the subject of it.

The phenomenon of "selling out" has become alarmingly common among today's musicians. Many musicians are now selling the rights to their songs to large corporations for use in commercials to sell products ranging from cars to computer software. Such deals are disturbing evidence of the growing acceptance of musicianship defined as a quest for material wealth. The most well-known of such deals occurred when the Rolling Stones sold the rights to their song "Start Me Up" to Microsoft for $3 million. Most "artists" do not seem to think this is a big problem, such as James "Diamond" Williams of the Ohio Players, who said of his band's licensing the song "Love Rollercoaster" to Microsoft: "This is a beautiful thing. The song is back in heavy rotation" (qtd. in Boehlert 24). With this statement Williams betrays his attitude toward artistry versus music as a commodity. To him, it is not the song, the piece of art, that is beautiful, but rather it is the fact that the song is in back in the public eye; he is famous again and making money.

This, like the promises made by the media, may seem harmless at first, but many musicians such as John Fogerty, Neil Young, and Pearl Jam see the potential threat. Trey Anastasio from the group Phish says that the corporate cash in wave of the '90s is wrong because it breaks a fundamental trust between audience and artist. If a song that touches a listener deeply one year is wrenched out of context to become an advertising jingle the next, what does that say about the intent, integrity and sincerity of the artist who made the song? (qtd. in Kot E-3)

The answer to that question is an obvious one: it shows a decided lack of integrity on the part of the artist. This lack of integrity, though, has more far-reaching implications than one might think. As music becomes a quest for financial gain, this goal will detract artists away from nobler aims. If the trend toward the commodification of music continues, so then will the trend toward declining artistic integrity. Furthermore, as musicians realize that they can make their fortunes by selling out to big business, their songs will bear an increasing resemblance to the jingles they have replaced. Musicians will cease to write for themselves and for their generation, but will write instead for their new audience of producers and advertising executives, an audience looking less for good art than for a catchy tune.

This is the direction in which music currently moves. A decline in artistic integrity can be traced back to the prevalent notion that the goal of musicianship is to become rich and famous, which, in turn, comes from ideas commonly promoted by the media. In "Seller's Market," Jeremiah Creedon remarks that though "today's tremendous wealth should be funding a time of great creativity and free expression . . . this may be one of the great conformist eras, perhaps even more so than the 1950s" (Creedon 53). We have simply become assimilated to the decline in artistic integrity, or, as is the case with many young people, we have had to turn back to the music of richer cultural eras. It may be that we have to wait around for another social and cultural revolution which will spawn great musical innovation and artistry, or it may be that much of our music will be lost in a tide of crass commercialism. The final answer to Franklin's question "What price, fame?" may just be the demise of our music.

Works Cited

Boehlert, Eric. "Bitter-Sweet Synergy." *Rolling Stone* 19 March 1998: 24, 26.

Creedon, Jeremiah. "Seller's Market." *UTNE Reader* Nov.-Dec. 1999: 52–54.

Kot, Greg. "'Selling Out' Is in as Rockers Cash in on Commercialism." *San Diego Union-Tribune* 24 Oct. 1999: E-3.

Miller, Mark Crispin. "Deride and Conquer." *Media Journal*. Ed. Joseph Harris and Jay Rosen. Needham Heights, MA: Allyn and Bacon, 1986. 435–44.

Sennheiser. Advertisement. *Guitar One* Dec. 1997: inside back cover.

Shift, Mireille Silcott. "Rhyme Pays." *UTNE Reader* Nov.–Dec. 1999: 58–59.

"Statistics on Television's Impact." 16 June 1998. *TV Free America* 30 June 1998 <http//:www.tvfa.org/stats.html>.

Discography

Reel Big Fish. "Sell Out." *Turn the Radio Off.* Mojo Records. UD-53108. 1996.

Filmography

Kilbourne, Jean. *Killing Us Softly*. Videocassette. Cambridge Documentary Films. HF 5827. K55. 1979.

Screen Idols

The Tragedy of Falling Stars

By Reni Celeste
Journal of Popular Film and Television, Spring 2005

In the cinema, love and death, victory and disaster play out across a unique body. Even though the earliest cinema has been called a starless cinema, a "cinema of attractions" (Gunning 56), the magnetic force of the fascinating individual rapidly took over and became the engine of the industry, leading to its expansion from nickelodeon sideshow to global phenomenon. The explanation for this development has been described in economic and sociological terms, but the magnitude of the question of stardom as it emerged in twentieth-century cinema has only begun to be thought about.[1] The allure of the star is inseparable from his or her heroism and ruin.

Although the star has become one of the most influential and highly paid figures in film production in the post-studio era,[2] the concept of the individual is considered a dubious one. It was not one of the priorities of the early avant-garde cinemas. Early Soviet cinema, for example, aligned stardom with the fall of Western cinema to entertainment and the ambitions of bourgeois capital. The force of the early Soviet cinema was understood as the political insight engendered from film form, specifically rapid montage. The individual was merely the product of world conflicts and could be replaced.[3]

Furthermore, foregrounding the question of the star would tend to encourage the same problems that limited auteur theory—the individual threatens to become the classic modern subject, understood as the origin of all action, possessing a coherent identity and certain innate expressive capacities. And, yet, discourse about the star only begins to emerge with any seriousness with edited collections inspired by the work of Richard Dyer in the 1980s. The discourse of "star studies" promised to take a very different route, offering, like genre theory, to provide a means of escaping the boundaries of the film screen by asking questions about reception, spectatorship, industry, and cultural politics. Rather than reducing the field to the individual, star studies offered to expand it to include film text, industry, and audience all in one view (Jancovich and Hollows). The "star" in star studies is not an individual at all but a system of signs, a social construction, flattened into a text that has multiple meanings and that can be read as cultural product. But can there be drama without 'individuals'? Are individualism and stardom necessary to the dramatic work, or are they supplemental, a mere appendage of modernity? Furthermore, it is not the stage but cinema that is the dramatic medium of the age of the machine and mass production, the rise of the institution, and the death of the modern subject.

Why, then, has the cinematic star emerged as such an undeniable force in the development of the film industry and the cultural landscape of the past century? Is there another way to understand the phenomenon of the star without flattening him or her into a semiotic text or exalting him as maker and origin of value? In this article, I consider that, rather than postmodernism being the death of the individual, this figure is essential to new structures of thought and culture. The cinematic star is not merely a discursive text but the tragic heroine of popular culture.

The One and the Many

Just as the printing press made possible the proliferation of ideas, news, and commerce, the moving camera made possible the proliferation of individuals. What was once loved privately in the quiet of the home could now be shared and worshipped throughout the world: the unique and irreplaceable individual close up. With the emergence of camera culture, a contradiction arises between mass reproduction and the coveting of unique individual appearance. It is a disparity found at the core of tragedy, where the one and the many, the sensuous and the abstract, the singular and the infinite, converge in the dramatic act. Understanding the modern celebrity begins with a study of this basic agonistic structure. The star occupies a position of strife.

Walter Benjamin argues that art in the mechanical age moved from being based on aura, or the unique appearance of a one-of-a-kind object, to being based on politics and mass production. He heralded the decline of the aura and the end of the auratic arts. I would argue that, in the star, the aura of unique things and the anonymity of mass production exist *simultaneously*. The existence of the star demands that we think absolute singularity and the popular together. The aura has not vanished but has become undecideable.[4] There is no stardom without both individualism and mass reproduction.

Charlie Chaplin was one of the first major stars to exemplify this strife. Without uttering a word, Chaplin became easily recognizable around the world by a series of simple gestures and objects of apparel. The little tramp represented one of the dominant themes of modernity, the convergence of man and his clothing, man and his machine, the transformation of unique man into a thing, an object, and an image. Chaplin could be represented and recognized by his props: moustache, bowler hat, cane, and clown shoes.

Henri Bergson wrote an essay on laughter in which he argued that the source of comedy is the conversion of a human being into a machine. In *A Short History of the Movies*, Gerald Mast wonders whether it may not be a coincidence that this essay was contemporaneous with the early films of director Max Sennett. As he points out, Sennett specialized in this conversion of people into objects, moving his characters around like mechanical toys, tossing pies and bricks, crashing into furniture and walls. He heightened this mechanization of the human by undercranking the camera, recording at a slow speed and projecting at normal speed, in this way exaggerating the jerkiness and frantic movements of these machine persons. In Charlie Chaplin, Sennett had found his ideal (Mast 83).

The analogy between man and machine in modernity was overdetermined, serving as a dream ideal as well as a social critique mourning the loss of humanity and individualism to the industrial machine age and mass production. It was modernity's tragic/comic self-interpretation. Sennett's comedies conveyed this loss through film, an industry that would model itself on the Ford assembly line and produce the ultimate modern machine—a machine whose fuel was humanity itself, the magnetism of the human image. The individual was not wholly objectified from the toil and sweat of the factory line or by walking the Kafkaesque corridors of modern institutional bureaucracy—he only truly became an object under the lights of the camera.

Sixty years later, it became possible to turn the Industrial Revolution that gave rise to cinematic culture into an art project. Modernism had lapsed into postmodernism. When Andy Warhol named his art studio The Factory, he began one of the earliest attempts to engage reflexively with the condition of media culture. In doing so, Warhol and other pop artists obscured an already fading boundary between fine art and the popular. It was not incidental that Warhol became one of the most popularized artists in the fine arts. Stardom and its mechanism were at the base of Warhol's oeuvre and, for him, the very essence of popular culture. Beyond the cultivation of his own personality, Warhol collected personalities, faux stars he coined "superstars." Warhol produced a number of films in which these figures were filmed as living headshots, the camera simply staring at the individual while he or she did nothing but awkwardly return the gaze. This uncomfortably long confrontation with an individual could make anyone seem perfectly exceptional. These stars were ready-mades and fabrications, individuals off the street, and yet performing their own individuality as a mask, a style, a pseudonym, and a personality. They stood before the camera nude and disguised, utterly false and painfully real, and infinitely far and uncomfortably near, thus representing the central paradox of modern stardom and camera culture.

Warhol's celebrity prints represented an assortment of idols from movie and rock stars to political figures, not only mass produced in the printing process but often in duplicate within the frame, as in

Double Marilyn and *Double Mona Lisa*, or in repeating series, such as *Sixteen Jackies*, where four images repeat four times each. In *Double Marilyn*, Monroe is visualized in photo negative, two identical headshots side-by-side, identifiable only by the light patterns that mark her signature eyes, lips, and brows. Like the Chaplin moustache and bowler hat, she is instantly identifiable. She is not a particular woman but a particular arrangement of features and patterns of light that make up the star Marilyn Monroe. She is the fetish of the particular.

Similarly, Elizabeth Taylor's portrait is a duplication of a familiar photograph. Taylor appears in simple block colors, bearing none of the nuance of tone and shade of realism. She is a heavily made-up head, bearing the mythic black hair and pure white skin of Disney's Snow White but with blue eye shadow and a smile painted on with lipstick. From a distance, it is the smiling face of Taylor. Up close, a grotesque incongruity between the lipstick and the lips becomes visible, and suddenly she bears the hidden sorrow of a clown, her smiling personae literally painted over her, her emotions a curly line of lipstick drawn over a pout. Here lays her fascination—she promises to conceal secrets.

Mass reproduction both destroys and invents individualism. The cinema opens up a screen on which fascinating individuals can exert force through several layers of disguise or fiction—the screen character, the public image generated by tabloids, and the movement of that body through time.[5] And yet in turning the individual into image, the truth of the singularity that is sought is lost to this repetition, invention, and disguise. This is one of the primary seductions of the star. The star is a portal, an invitation to an elusive truth that withholds disclosure. A place is desired that cannot be reached and may not even exist. These are the rules of seduction, which in cinema becomes known as *glamour*.

Glamour, or I Must Know You

Mass production has been described as the technological possibility of modern stardom, but technology alone does not introduce into existence something as significant as the star. The foremost condition of the star is the fan. Star power is the product of a relation, the most basic relation in dramatic art, that between spectator and stage. Star and fan are each other's origin and do not exist independently. Anyone can occupy either of these positions or both simultaneously. Warhol, in his famous credo that in the future everyone will have fifteen minutes of fame, points to this democracy of stardom, its shifting roles, and the way its pleasures have themselves become a commodity that could be marketed in a utopian future.[6] The roles of star and fan precede and exceed the individuals. Nevertheless, there is nothing abstract about this union. Star power is a love affair. Although this position is a role, the star is pure singularity, what cannot be replaced—just as the beloved object cannot be replaced. Even if the object of love is not an erotic object, the star is always a passion to be pursued. To love a star is to love an image of singularity. But seldom is the lover satisfied with an image.

The fan is compelled by fascination to learn more or to uncover and expose the nudity of the star. Love of the star is a movement from glamour to defilement. Andy Warhol confessed that he became incapable of love by the end of the 1960s. Instead, he became *fascinated* by certain people (Warhol 27). This new euphoria, or trance, is the perfect description of star power. The star's glamour is not so much that she possesses high stature, like a queen, and is as such an ideal without a body, but the discovery that she is flesh, that she is also low, soiled, even foul. Warhol was fascinated that stars ate at the same fast-food restaurants as everyone else and had body odors and personal problems. An encounter with stardom was a form of disclosure and revelation. In a traditional metaphysics, this process of pursuing nudity would be understood as a pursuit of truth over falsity, where the image is false and the original true. This rhetoric still exists in the language of reality programming, which promises "real life" and "real events." Baudrillard foresaw the market for reality programming when he argued that the more hyperreal or image intensive modern culture became, the hungrier the spectator would become for this elusive "real."

But if we try to think of the disclosure of the star in a more hermeneutic or deconstructive manner, in terms of unconcealment rather than truth, we can think of star seduction in layers,' as an act of disrobing. Nudity or full exposure is the goal, and yet this nudity's value is precisely in its hiddenness. Truth here is not identity or correspondence but the play between concealment and exposure.[7] This play can be understood as glamour, the uncanny confrontation of opposites. Glamour appears as a glistening or shining. This is the light of the stars. It is a nearness that can only be seen at a distance.

The camera's basic paradox is revealed as well in its literal manipulation of scale, from extreme close-up to long range. The magnitude of cinematic star power is unthinkable without the close-up. The close-up was the subject of much discussion in early film theory. Through the close-up, viewers and critics fell in love with cinema and its faces. Jean Epstein called the close-up the soul of cinema and spoke so passionately about the experience of magnification on a screen that it is impossible to read his words and not wonder if the power of love is a question of scale. Love is the desire for proximity in a world of landscapes.

> I will never find the way to say how much I love American close-ups. Point blank. A head suddenly appears on screen and drama, now face to face, seems to address me personally and swells with an extraordinary intensity. I am hypnotized. Now the tragedy is anatomical: The decor of the fifth act is this corner of a cheek torn by a smile. [. . .] The mouth gives way, like a

ripe fruit splitting open. As if slit by a scalpel, a keyboard-like smile cuts laterally into the corner of the lips.

[. . .] Even more beautiful than a laugh is the face preparing for it. I must interrupt. I love the mouth which is about to speak and holds back, the gesture which hesitates between right and left, the recoil before the leap, and the moment before landing, the becoming, the hesitation, the taut spring, the prelude, and even more than all these, the piano being tuned before the overture. The photogenic is conjugated in the future and in the imperative. It does not allow for stasis. (Epstein 9)

This passionate proximity combined with a tragic distance is the core of fandom. The relationship between fan and idol suffers from a tragic alienation or lack of consummation. The media exist to capitalize on this and other distances, promising to provide a link between the pair through gossip and exposé. The gossip columns pursue the hidden—personal lives, the overheard and overseen. The talk shows introduce actors and actresses as individuals with histories, secrets, childhood illnesses, and pains. Star confessions expose childhood neglect, abuse, alcoholism, and homosexuality. The emphasis is on the corrupted and wounded body—scandal, disease, divorce, addictions—anything that will bring closer the realism or vulnerability of the body of the star. Media, as mediator, must walk the fine line between exposure and concealment to generate and maintain fascination and fandom.[8] This was never more clear than in the 1920s, when the early star apparatus generated too much scandal and excess and brought the wrath of the American public on Hollywood, leading to the film censorship of the notorious Hays Office. Careers were lost overnight to tabloid scandal.[9]

The print and broadcast media exist to serve the interest of both star and fan. The advent of star power is unthinkable without this basic union of two gazes: cinema and the media. This union has been credited with the generation of tremendous ticket sales and the rapid expansion of the industry, but its influence is more profound. It is here that the breakdown between screen and world, the postmodern condition, is materialized. Gossip is not merely frivolous. The star body becomes the medium that links worlds that had previously been distinct: fiction and life. The star is not merely a character, a figure that shines on the stage in dramatic narrative. The star moves the light from screen to world. Star spotting is most fascinating when the star is seen simply eating at a café, entering an elevator, or using a lavoratory. What happens off the screen will be as important as what occurs on it, and even undistinguishable. The screen now extends metaphorically beyond the theater to the living room through the media, a virtual stage embracing both observer and observed. Tragedy is closer in the popular sphere than it ever approached in the classical. We could even say that popular media culture is the product of cinematic fandom's modern exports:

desire, alienation, and *fascination*. And that it is this triangle—fan, the media, and star—that makes up the structure of popular culture. The media serve the role of connecting, but mediation is also separation. It marks the tragedy or impossibility of the star/fan enterprise.

The Mortal Body

The ultimate level of nudity exposed by the devoted fan is mortality, the vulnerability of the organic and mortal body of the living star. Exposure can come through disease, violent physical death, or gradually through the aging process of the body. There is perhaps no greater desire than to kill the star or to bear witness to this event or process. J. G. Ballard imagined a world in his novel *Crash* in which the body's prime desire was to merge with its technology. Placed at the altar of this fetish was the body of the deceased star, mangled in the metal of her automobile crash. Like the star, the automobile was the incarnation of American fantasies of freedom, mobility, and power. Vaughn, one of the novel's leading figures, is obsessed with restaging the automobile disasters of James Dean, Jayne Mansfield, and others for a stadium of passionate fans. Similarly, Andy Warhol created his disaster series at the same time as his celebrity series, placing the disembodied head of Mao over the electric chair. For Warhol, celebrity and disaster were not unconnected events. It is the star's beautiful plastic face that opens up the site of the disaster. Glamour and disaster are the two major commodities of a media culture. Glamour, and its process of mystery and exposure, could even be called the face of disaster and death. By moving away from the organic toward the plastic or inorganic, one becomes something of a mask, a sign for death. The living star is already a ruin, a tombstone. And ruins have always inspired dreams.

Film has only in the past fifty years aged sufficiently for the medium to reflect on its own relation to death. Films such as *Sunset Boulevard* (1950) and *Whatever Happened to Baby Jane* (1962) were not possible before the 1950s. Even though disaster was a critical component of modern stardom from the beginning, and suicide, murder, and accidental death intrinsic parts of celebrity, it was not until the 1950s that the aging process of the first generation of stars exposed a glamour worn thin. The young narrator of *Sunset Boulevard* refers to the buddies of his benefactor Norma Desmond, the silent film star, as the "wax works." Buster Keaton plays a cameo role as a member of this sad entourage of icons who have outlived themselves. These films reveal through the aging of celebrity bodies the mortality of the spectators and cinema itself. In beholding the shot, a sense of responsibility and impotence overwhelms the viewer. Roland Barthes's description of the photo as *memento mori* comes to mind (96). To look into a photo is to see a scandal. The fate of those individuals depicted seems sealed. We know already what will become of them, and yet we cannot issue a warning, our voices cannot penetrate the frame. They appear to us trapped within the time they once occupied, a time whose very appearance is in the form of an alert—*this time will pass*, which is the same as *this time is gone forever*. "Whether or not the subject is already dead, every photo is this catastrophe," according to Barthes (96). By being photographed, they do not die for us, they die before us. We are silent because we know that their fate is merely a reflection of our own procession.

If the star's body represents the attempt to bridge the limit between finite and infinite forces, it also lends itself to religious symbolism. The most obvious correlation is the fascination in Christianity with the suffering body of Christ. It is important in making this comparison to first assert that the Christian narrative is the ultimate nontragic force.[10] Nevertheless, the modern star can be understood as the failure of Christian heroism. If we compare stardom to dominant Christian narratives, Christ's appearance in the world was understood as an act of transubstantiation between the spiritual and material. He was the father incarnate in the son. He gave the divine a temporal body situated within the world. The New Testament sought to bind itself to Judaism by understanding itself as the answer or prophecy of the Old Testament, and as such already an interpretation of Judaic order. But the break is radical, foremost because the divine is not the "Word," what cannot be visualized or formalized, but the collapse of the mortal body in the figure of Christ. The Christ figure suffers from an excessive corporeality, and it is this materiality that must be overcome for mankind to be redeemed. The Stations of the Cross evaluate at each moment in time the suffering of the body—hunger, thirst, fatigue, the stigmata, the moment of death. To accomplish his task as Christ, he must survive the body. Torture of the body, death, and resurrection are the path to the infinite. Likewise, the star must suffer, die, and survive the body, all its excesses, addictions, obesities, and diseases, to be reborn as pure image and immortal icon. Not only are stars the objects of myths about their continued existence (Jim Morrison, Elvis, Walt Disney), but their image literally survives them by becoming legal property. Sartre argued that beings desire to become objects as part of a larger quest to become God (171). To desire the stars is to have great ambitions, to seek nothing short of immortality, or the other side of time.

Filmmaker Kenneth Anger set his eyes on the stars, and reflected in this fire he saw eternal life's twin sister, death, through the figure of the fan. If Breton saw the face of God in a gas tank, Anger saw the infinite reflected in the metal of a Harley Davidson motorcycle and in the gaze of a beautiful gay boy. Besides publishing two books documenting and exemplifying the sordid underside of Hollywood glamour and tabloid excess (*Hollywood Babylon* and *Hollywood Babylon II*), his most significant contribution to popular culture came with his film *Scorpio Rising* (1963), a mystical snapshot of gay motorcycle subculture. The film is impossible without the rock 'n' roll youth culture that emerged in the 1950s, and it is one of the first works to reverse the hierarchy of image and music, bringing its nonstop soundtrack of top-40 hits into the foreground, where it will serve a structural and narrative function in the film. The distinction in film theory between background and diegetic music begins to be deeply challenged. In this equality of image and popular music, cool is being defined, not as a sociological construction but as the sensation or atmosphere of the mystical. The film transpires as a movement from the interior of the individual's room to communal party space and event. This movement is a rhythm and a pace that gradually mounts, moving from stasis (pose, interior) to ecstasis (community, event, speed, racing) and back again to stasis (death). Along the way, an analogy between the first and second stasis, fashion and death, is achieved.

The film begins with Anger's camera panning an assortment of objects in the bedroom of the individual as he prepares for an evening of drunken revelry and drag racing. The objects and images are fetishistic expressions of fandom and mass circulation—James Dean and Elvis Presley posters, comic books, newspapers, Dick Tracy, press photos, and a skull flag. The details are essential as individual items and as collections. The camera is documenting a preference, a collection, a series of choices—the new ingredients for culture and individualism. The community is nothing other than a gathering of fans and a collage, a shared valuation of selections from the river of commodities. The bodies in the room are treated with the same interest as the objects. A slow pan moves up and down the body of the boy dressing, an object to be desired, possessed, and consumed. This preparation for style, appearance, and event resembles the preparations of the body of the dead for display and internment. The pose is the language of this new rhythm. The pose is the body's simulation of a snapshot. It is a natural photograph, a lightning flash of perfection and power, a ruin, a step outside of time. The boy poses for the camera, fingers in pockets of tight white pants, no shirt, leather jacket, tilted cap, shades, cool. This is a perfect moment, a portal to timelessness. He is ready to be displayed and sacrificed.

The film is a visual display of musical, Dionysian drives, driven by pace, rhythm, and scale. The pace of the montage will grow gradually throughout the film, from slow pans and long takes to the cross-cutting of rapid-fire shots that hardly appear long enough to deliver their meaning. Similarly, the scale of the shots will shift from extreme close-ups of hands, objects, preparations, and individuals to long shots of cultural entourages and mass movements. From the bedroom, we move to the group. The party scene stages a masquerade, individuals dressing up as death, wearing masks and skeleton costumes. Death is a game of musical chairs. The playful torture of a drunken guest is set to a top-40 hit "Torture." Irony is in the air.

Cuts quicken, and pans begin to swish rapidly. The changing rhythm is essential to understanding the journey, a transition from the solitude of the bedroom, the festival of the group, to death.

The climax of the film emerges when Anger begins to crosscut between cycle racing and the journey of Christ and his followers, drawing a direct analogy between the cultic value of popular culture and the presence of Christ amidst his fans. Equivalences are drawn around the iconic figures of Hitler, Christ, and James Dean. Celebrity is seen not only as a pagan form of religious idolatry but also as the very possibility of culture, cult, and community. The backdrop of this analogy is death, which appears as one of the many commodities, objects, or symbols in the frame until the final scenes conclude the film with the actual motorcycle crash and sirens.

Anger's film is foremost a portrait of fandom, not stardom. The fan is the tragic figure in *Scorpio Rising*. What we witness in this work is the breakdown of mediation, the collapse of the fan into the starry night of his dreams. The celebrity exists as a photograph or mirror in which the fan experiences his own tragedy. Anger documented in this film a decisive moment occurring in visual culture and media from which there would be no return. He showed how pose, attitude, style, and rhythm were the new languages of the popular. And that perhaps the popular was the new portal to the mystical, a realm in which one was impelled irresistibly into the void.

Andy Warhol fashioned his entire persona around this collision of fashion and the void. He was a walking pose, a void, a medium through which others spoke. He refused the notion of depth and interpretation. When his fans sought to discover in him a hidden content, he insisted on the one-dimensionality of his persona, stating that "if you want to know anything about me or my work, look at the surface of my artwork, and there it is" (qtd. in MacCabe). He was fascinated by Hollywood. He believed that the glamour and seductive appeal of Hollywood was based on its fakery, and he modeled his own star persona on this vapidity. As he said, "this is what made Hollywood more exciting to me, the idea that it was so vacant. Vacant, vacuous Hollywood was everything I ever wanted to mold my life into. Plastic. White-on-white" (qtd. in Osterwold).

When Valerie Solanis fired three shots into Andy Warhol's body, she chased him into the void. She expressed the desire both to break out of the image and to complete the image of the star through the destruction of the body. To kill the star is to attempt the impossible goal of union—the closure of mediation, the collapse of the distinction between observed and observer. The star is brought down to the level of the fan, and the fan is simultaneously lifted up to the star through infamy. The death of the star completes the image, fulfilling the *telos* of stardom. In the survival of Andy Warhol, Solanis's act was an apparent failure, and yet it is well known that Warhol never fully recovered his faith in the image. A new dementia had set

in that corresponded in many ways to the confusion of the present—
the advanced stages of representation in a culture still based on a
logocentric conception of truth.

> I am trying to decide if I should pretend to be real or fake it. I
> had always thought everyone was kidding. But now I know
> they're not. I'm not sure if I should pretend that things are real
> or that they are fake. You see to pretend something is real, I'd
> have to fake it. Then people would think I'm doing it real. Well, I
> guess people thought we were so silly and we weren't. Now
> maybe we'll have to fake a little and be serious. But then, that
> would be faking seriousness which is sort of faking. But we were
> serious before so now we might have to fake a little just to make
> ourselves look serious? (qtd. in Osterwold)

The star, then, is an invitation to expose or arrest a particular
truth from the body on display. This exposure is photographic and,
ultimately, a contradictory goal—the attempt to stabilize or freeze a
process, to complete an image of existence. The star is mortality in a
box, being-toward-death in a frame. The temporal range exposed by
the star is fascinating and strange, like a flower viewed under stop-
motion photography, sprouting, growing, blooming, and dying. The
photographic medium and mass communication arrest this process
by seeming to stop time in the image and, by presenting a succes-
sion of changing or developing images, permit it to be captured in its
beauty and decay. The pleasure of revelation makes bearing witness
to the fatality and the glamour of mortal existence a coveted obsession.

The Beauty of Falling

Star power is a perfect example of the postmodern sublime
employing both the mathematical (measure) and dynamical (might).
The idea of measure can be seen in the importance of rising and falling in stardom—how far the star transverses a vertical axis. Classical tragedy is a form that derived pleasure from the display of the
disastrous fates of kings and gods, Tragedy in its origin is a product
of paganism and polytheism. It had been Christianized by the time
of its incarnation in eighteenth-century aesthetics, where it came to
serve as a catalyst or embodiment of the emerging concept of "fine
arts," a value based on Genius[11] or exception and an ideal deeply at
odds with the emergent liberalism and modern democracy. In both
Classical and Renaissance tragedy, the hero had to be high so that
he could make a great fall. He was a sacrifice, and, within a monar-
chy or a Christian culture, no other figure had the necessary authority. The peasant's fall was not a catastrophe and could not be
universalized.

Many critics of tragedy in modernity insist that democracy itself
rendered tragedy defunct. But the modern star is proof that a new
kind of tragedy emerges in the popular. Social mobility is the source

of authority in modern capitalistic democracy, where the ultimate value is the rise of the individual.[12] The modern star is the ultimate product of democracy, moving easily back and forth between the poles of high and low, depending on whether a comeback is in the works. It is this mobility itself that maximizes the satisfaction of popular tragedy. The greater the distance between the bottom (origin) and the top (rise), the greater the star and the pleasure taken in the descent. As a result, high birthright can even work against the modern star. The most coveted icons often come from the lower classes or have secret pasts involving uncertain parentage, abuse, and survival and success despite hardships. Marilyn Monroe was an orphan. Tragedy is a form that capitalizes on the beauty of falling things. The more gained in the rise, the more lost in the fall.

> Warhol sought with his superstars to demonstrate the artificial nature of modern celebrity.

Classical tragedy was invested in the ideal, the God figure or the hero. The hero is still very much alive in comic myths, but he is a *superhero*, a figure of the age of democracy, and as such he emerges from the norm. Clark Kent divided his life between being the most ordinary midwestern American citizen, bearing no sensational attributes on the surface, to superhero-ism in the figure of Superman. His return to his extraordinary birthright was a reversal of his life in the norm, existing in a separate and secret sphere in which he could freely reveal his power to exceed the bounds of natural and civic laws. Likewise, the cinematic star is the glamorization of the norm. Norma Jean became Marilyn Monroe. The shadow of the mask of Marilyn is Norma Jean. Both are essential to her myth. The one is buried beneath the other. But she does not represent a "norm" or "mass" in an allegorical manner, where she is just one example of a universal. She is absolute singularity. She can be copied, made into a stereotype, but she cannot be replaced.[13]

In a democracy, everyone can potentially occupy the role of the star, but a star cannot be everyone. A star is singular. So it is nearly impossible to provide a coherent law or recipe for stardom. Andy Warhol believed stars were constructions or patterns that could be duplicated to infinity and, as such, figures of pure falsehood or disguise. His biggest success, Edie Sedgwick, revealed the matter to be more complex. Edie Sedgwick did not come from lowly origins. As a young heiress, a child of wealth and privilege, her immersion in the New York underground art scene, with its drugs, fashion, and pop culture, was more of a fall than a rise. To complicate matters, her stardom was not legitimate—she was a fabrication of stardom, an art project about stardom. She both understood and accepted the artistic level of irony and felt humiliated and wanted to be a "real star" (Warhol and Hackett 127). Ironically, her actual fall from pseudo-stardom is captured on film by John Palmer and Robert Weisman in *Ciao! Manhattan* (1973). The film charts the years following her departure from New York, when she moves back into her mother's home, takes up residence in the dried-up, outdoor swimming pool, and tells her story with slides projected onto the pool walls and a series of black-and-white photos/flashbacks, between being serviced and shuttled to and from shock therapy treatments by the half-witted, young male narrator. Edie is topless, drunk, inarticulate, and high on psychiatric meds throughout the film. The swimming pool where she projects her old clips and films for the bored narrator becomes a metaphor for stardom. Despite narration, photography, and various editing techniques that juxtapose the two places and times, the distance between N.Y. and L.A., her present and her past, is unbridgeable.

Warhol sought with his superstars to demonstrate the artificial nature of modern celebrity. His "stars" were twice removed, images of images, constructions of constructedness. And yet, in this film, we can see the borders between the real and the fake becoming impossible to mark. Screen tragedy and the tragedy of existence are indistinguishable. Despite the irony of the production, and the doubling of Edie's falseness, the film is a terrifying document of exposure and truth. Edie died of a drug overdose three months after completion of the film. In the case of Edie, faux stardom was an even greater burden than stardom, a form of homelessness, an empty pool in which to drown.

The star is the combination of truth and disguise, beauty and decay, rise and loss. If the star possesses enough fascination, death becomes a portal through which he or she becomes non-corporeal, immortal, like a building or part of the boulevard. As such, the star can be understood within the aesthetic category of magnitude. During the filming of *Empire*, a film in which Warhol set up a moving camera in an adjacent building and filmed the Empire State Building for eight hours, he said at least three things of interest to his assistant:

> The empire state building is a star!
> [. . .]
> Henry, what is the meaning of action?

(qtd. in Malanga 85–88)

What does it mean to compare a building to a star? Or to compare a building to a body part? The building and the body are literally interchangeable for one another, standing in the same relation as the cinema to the individual. Cinema is the architecture of the human body. As the star becomes an inorganic image or object, those things in proximity to the star take on the aura of the star. Not only does the subject become object, but vice versa—the room begins to breathe.

Second, *Empire* expresses the relation between stardom and magnitude. The Empire State Building is sublime. Its magnitude invokes an awe bordering on terror. Similarly the star, by becoming gigantic, by generating massive exposure, becomes a force of magnitude akin to the phenomenon of architecture, something on one hand more stable, more immortal, more massive than the corporeal body. When Kant laid out the analytic of the sublime to explain raging beauty, the experience of magnitude, that torment and pleasure where the limits of the human faculties are reached and surpassed, he used nature as his model, conjuring storms at sea and vast mountain ranges (97).

By the end of the twentieth century, media culture had developed to such a level of immensity as to achieve sublimity—skyscrapers, nuclear bombs, modern warfare, and mass media. The star is such an achievement. The media technology of the star became so gigantic as to be the very source of aesthetic pleasure. Just as special effects in cinema evoke both the pleasure of believing in a fantastic event as well as the pleasure of witnessing the power of technology, the machinery of media stardom quickly became its own object of pleasure. Stardom in this scenario is self-perpetuating. The bigger the star becomes, the more the source of pleasure becomes the magnitude itself. The star and his or her unique individuality are just one of an array of values. The star does not even need to prove longevity but can himself be a moment in fashion, a product of the "now." The "cinema of attractions" that Gunning described of early cinema, where spectators came to see the magic technology of the camera, has returned, including circus rings for star, spectator, and apparatus.

Within this spectacle, the entrance of the star can be thought of as "the screaming point" (Chion) of aesthetic pleasure, both the sexual climax and the beginning, the arrival of the event. In *Gilda*, we must wait twenty minutes before we witness the magnificent image of Rita Hayworth throwing back her hair and asking, "Am I decent?" The magnitude of the moment is increased by the pact the males have taken to exclude women and by having her voice precede her appearance—as the men ascend the stairs toward the surprise, a female voice is heard singing in the distance, a voice recognized by both men.

If we look at a more contemporary example from popular music we see that this structure continues to be essential to the aesthetic and that it has become even more complex. At the MTV Music Video Awards of 2000, Eminem appeared through three levels of introduction to perform two central hits from *The Marshall Mathers LP*, "The Real Slim Shady" and "The Way I Am," both highly invested in the question of stardom. He was introduced by the major comic film star of the day, Jim Carrey, who was in turn introduced by the Wayans brothers. His approach, with a staged army of Slim Shadys, was filmed as a movement from the streets into the theater, breaking down all separations between stage, live audience, media, and television viewer. Slim Shady had become the fictionalized ground on which fan and artist collapsed into one another as a mobilized unit of force, rage, and magnitude.[14] The media filmed his approach, the mock fans, the streets of New York City, the live audience, and themselves documenting his entrance. Continuity and unity were created by a long mobile take from exterior city to interior architecture and by the rap, where an uncanny correspondence between lyrical content and event was achieved.[15] Eminem's entrance on this night resembled the Empire State Building—a feat of modern architecture.

The pleasure of media magnitude is reflexive—the pleasure of seeing oneself seeing, or of seeing everything at once. This is an advanced stage of spectators hip. This desire to see everything at once is also expressed in reality television and in the growing marketing value of bonus features packaged with DVDs, including commentaries, deleted scenes, special effects secrets, descriptions, and images of the production process. These details have become almost as important to spectatorship as the production itself. The sum total of components and dimensions contribute to the magnitude of the product or event. The search for totality and full disclosure moves from star body back to star apparatus to world. What this movement discloses is the goal of desire, and it bears an uncanny likeness to Socrates's description in the *Phaedrus* of the journey from a beautiful boy to Beauty (Plato). But what is being described is not Socraticism, logocentrism, or mysticism. Tragedy must be distinguished from mysticism, because tragedy is the failure to fully arrive at a destination or closure. In "Metaphysics of Tragedy," Lukàcs makes this important distinction:

> In this way the mystical and the tragic modes of experiencing life touch and supplement one another. Both mysteriously combine life and death, autonomous selfhood and the total dissolving of the self in a higher being. Surrender is the mystic's way, struggle the tragic man's; the one, at the end of his road, is absorbed into the All, the other shattered against the All. (160)

Although this shattering appears destructive, tragedy is ultimately being described as form producing and creative. Selfhood is form that cannot vanish or be dissolved or incorporated. No matter how it moves to the All, it is repeatedly reduced to fragments, forms, and individuals. The star is not the dissolution of individualism into death and oblivion but the freezing of particularity into an eternal image of itself.

> The wisdom of the tragic miracle is the wisdom of frontiers. A miracle is always unambiguous, but everything unambiguous divides and points in two directions. Every ending is always an arrival and a cessation, an affirmation and a denial all at once, every climax is a peak and frontier, the point of intersection between life and death. (Lukàcs 160)

The photograph is the imprint of light, the manifold in which singular objects and events appear in a frame. What is revealed in the light is not just a table but this table, this chair, this doorway, this corridor, my lover's face in the morning. Of all the forms the light illuminates, it is the human form that shines the brightest, that evokes love, and whose singularity is the most seductive and elusive. The cinematic event is tragic, a mortal moment living and dying simultaneously. The star is an invitation to this moment, the bridge between here and there.

Notes

1. Film historians trace the rapid growth of the industry to Carl Laemmle's decision to capitalize on fan interest. See, for example, Cook (40).

2. The history of the film star has been a movement from the capitalization of studio system formulation to free agency. Stars today often produce their own vehicles (Tom Cruise in Mission Impossible [2000]) or negotiate shares in the box-office profits.

3. Eisenstein and Vertov sought to create a revolutionary and classless cinema using unscripted citizens, no face or personality privileged over another.

4. Jacques Derrida's term for how the instability of the signifier/referent relation renders decisions to always be based on inconclusive terms.

5. I do not mean merely to discuss individualism as pure performativity, although many interesting things have been said about the drag queen and the performance of the feminine in stars such as Marilyn Monroe. Disguise, or illusion, is just one angle of the duplicity of the individual, who is more deconstructive, truth *and* untruth. It is this double bind that defines the tragic nature of the star.

6. That future Warhol described has come to pass in such programs as MTV's *Becoming*, where, for one day, a fan is converted into the star of their choice through the mock reproduction of their star's music video.

7. I refer here to Heidegger's conception of truth as *aletheia*, truth and untruth, concealment and unconcealment as described in "The Origin of the Work of Art."

8. Programs such as VH1's *Behind the Music* seem to indulge in overexposure, introducing the audience to the self-doubts and fragile egos of their heroes, tearing down the kind of illusions that sustain rock iconography.

9. The career of Fatty Arbuckle, one of the highest paid comedians of early cinema, was destroyed by scandal.

10. However, in Kierkegaard's description of faith, the Christian "believer" is surely a tragic figure. Nevertheless, Kierkegaard's text is a diatribe against traditional Christendom, which modernist thinkers saw as one of the destroyers of Greek tragic forces in western culture.

11. The concept of Genius is very important in the early aesthetics of romanticism because such a figure provided the mystical link between nature and culture.

12. *Citizen Kane* is a cinematic description of this new rise/fall inherent to Americanism.

13. Jayne Mansfield, for instance.

14. All three albums thus far develop this theme to infinity: Marshall Mathers, the "real" name of Eminem, exposes Eminem as another site of construction, placing him on the same level of Slim Shady, and so on.

15. The lyrics of "The Real Slim Shady" reference an award ceremony with Britney Spears, Christina Aguilera, and Fred Durst as spectators. He performs these

lyrics at the Music Video Awards 2000 ceremony as he passes them in the audience.

Works Cited

Anger, Kenneth. *Hollywood Babylon*. San Francisco: Straight Arrow Books, 1975.

———. *Hollywood Babylon II*. New York: Dutton, 1984.

Ballard, J. G. *Crash*. New York: Noonday, 1994.

Barthes, Roland. *Camera Lucida: Reflections on Photography*. Trans. Richard Howard. New York: Hill and Wang, 1981.

Baudrillard, Jean. *Seductions*. Trans. Brian Singer. New York: St. Martin's, 1990.

Benjamin, Walter. "The Work of Art in the Age of Mechanical Reproduction." Illuminations. Ed. Hannah Arendt. New York: Schocken, 1968. 217–51.

Bergson, Henri. Laughter: An Essay on the Meaning of the Comic. London: Macmillan, 1911.

Chion, Michel. "The Screaming Point" *The Voice in Cinema*. Trans. Claudia Gorbman. New York: Columbia UP, 1999.

Cook, David A. *A History of Narrative Film*. 3rd ed. New York: Norton and Norton, 1996.

Dyer, Richard. *Stars*. London: BFI, 1979.

Epstein, Jean. "Magnification." Trans. Stuart Liebman. *October 3* (Spring 1977): 9–15.

Gunning, Thomas. "The Cinema of Attractions: Early Film, Its Spectator and the Avant-garde." *Early Cinema: Space-Frame-Narrative*. Ed. Thomas Elsaesser with Adam Barker. London: BFI, 1990. 56–62.

Heidegger, Martin. "The Origin of the Work of Art'" *Basic Writings from Being and Time (1927) to The Task of Thinking (1964)*. Trans. David Farrell Krell. New York: Harper & Row, 1977. 143–87.

Jancovich, Mark, and Joanne Hollows, eds. *Approaches to Popular Culture*. New York. St. Martin's, 1995.

Kant, Immanuel. *Critique of Judgment*. Trans. Werner S. Pluhar. Indianapolis: Hackett, 1987.

Kierkegaard, Soren. *Concluding Unscientific Postscript*. Trans. David F. Swenson. Princeton, NJ: Princeton UP, 1974.

Lukàcs, Georg. "The Metaphysics of Tragedy." *Soul and Form*. Trans. Anna Bostock. Cambridge. MA: MIT P, 1974. 152–74.

Malanga, Gerard. *Archiving Warhol: Illustrated History*. London: Creation Books, 2002.

Mast, Gerald. *A Short History of the Movies*. 7th ed. Boston: Allyn and Bacon, 1999.

MacCabe, Colin, Mark Francis, and Peter Wollen, eds. *Who Is Andy Warhol?* Pittsburgh: BFI and the Andy Warhol Museum, 1997.

Osterwold, Tilman. *Pop Art*. New York: Taschen America LLC, 1999.

Plato. *Phaedrus*. Trans. Alexander Nehamas and Paul Woodruff. Indianapolis: Hackett, 1995.

Sartre, Jean Paul. *Being and Nothingness*. Trans. Hazel E. Barnes. New York: Philosophical Library, 1956.

Warhol, Andy. *The Philosophy of Andy Warhol: From A to B and Back Again*. New York: Harvest, 1975.

Warhol, Andy, and Pat Hackett. *POPism: The Warhol Sixties*. New York: Harvest, 1980.

IV. THE DEMOCRATIZATION OF CELEBRITY

Editor's Introduction

In January 2007, the Pew Research Center released "A Portrait of 'Generation Next.'" This report reveals that among those surveyed between ages 18 and 25, 81 percent chose "To get rich" and 51 percent chose "To be famous" as one of their top two goals in life. While those percentages are remarkable in themselves, what is more significant is that both responses were not qualified in any way. In other words, in their answers, the respondents did not include *how* they would get rich or *what* they would be famous for. That such a large portion of young adults considers wealth and fame worthy goals in and of themselves is quite telling.

Consider what the group that Pew Research surveyed, who were born between 1983 and 1989, grew up with. They probably have not known a world in which a typewriter was required to compose a school paper. In fact, for them the Internet has long been a viable research and entertainment option. Furthermore, many of them came of age just as the social Web, or Web 2.0, offered increasing control over their digital content and expanded their social horizons beyond the limits of geography, through such sites as MySpace, Facebook, and YouTube. Finally, such tools that enable us to be the masters of our own digital domains—that make us the center of our media universes—must not have seemed so foreign to this group. After all, they had already been tuning into reality TV programs that make stars of regular people.

Therefore, it is with an eye toward this emergent trend that we conclude this volume with a collection of pieces documenting the democratization of celebrity. We begin with "Open-Source Celebrity," in which Jonathon Keats examines how interactive media have made celebrity a participatory sport. That is anyone with the requisite technology can produce content for mass consumption.

Lakshmi Chaudhry next looks at the double edge to the digital democratization sword: excessive self-expression and narcissism. In her article, "Mirror, Mirror on the Web," she points out that although a number of online celebrities are justifiably renowned for doing something while others have leveraged their virtual success to forge lucrative careers, it is no longer necessary to do either in order to be famous. Fame is now reduced to its most basic element—public attention—and that attention does not have to be positive.

From Internet sensation to reality TV star, Tila Tequila provides an illustrative example of this new form of celebrity. Guy Trebay discusses Tequila's recent ascent up the celebrity ladder in "She's Famous (and So Can You)." While Trebay notes that Tequila does not display any distinctive talent, that is no reason to dismiss her, "to sniff from the sideline about the depths to which the culture has sunk." Ultimately, Trebay concludes, "in her own way, [Tequila] has divined truths about the marketplace that academics and industry are still laboring fully to comprehend."

Open-Source Celebrity

The Wisdom of the Audience

By Jonathon Keats
Wired Magazine, May 22, 2007

Justin Kan's celebrity career began on March 19 at 2 AM, when he woke up and strapped a videocam to his head. Since then, he's provided a live Web feed to his fans every day, all day long, letting them observe life from his perspective. Kan's allure is unrelated to talent or physical appearance (he rarely turns the camera on himself). Watching his streaming video and sending him IMs with comments and suggestions, his audience gets to experience his rise to fame from the inside out.

Kan is no Justin Timberlake—or even a gossip magnet like Paris Hilton. But he is taking advantage of the same underlying forces that gave them star power: As media have gone interactive, stardom has become participatory. Celebrity has gone open source. Forget Hollywood, Big Music, and Broadway. The unruly crowd now auditions its own stars, wiki-style, helping to decide who will enter the world stage and how long they'll stay in the public eye. As a result, celebrities are performing their essential role in society—binding us together through gossip, inspiration, and slander—more efficiently than ever.

Of course, we've always been invested in the lives of the famous. That's their primary value to us. While the legitimately accomplished contribute to society regardless of what we think of them personally—it made no difference that Charles Lindbergh was photogenic when he was flying over the Atlantic—celebrities matter most when their extracurricular affairs and binges resonate culturally. With society endlessly subdividing into narrower niches, we're much less likely to collectively experience the same books, TV shows, or songs. Celebrities provide vital common reference points. We know when Lindsay Lohan is in rehab. And for an instant, we could all recognize the father of Anna Nicole Smith's baby.

The new wiki celebrity is exquisitely tuned to the culture's anxieties, needs, and desires. The Grammy-winning success of *American Idol*'s Carrie Underwood stands for our belief in the American dream; the staying power of Sanjaya Malakar, voted into round after round in part at the irony-laden urging of radio host Howard Stern, shows that stardom has nothing to do with talent. And Lauren Conrad's onscreen metamorphosis in the first season of MTV's *Laguna Beach: The Real Orange County* demonstrates our potential for reinvention.

Wiki celebrity works because of the blogosphere, which has given us an unprecedented conduit for direct involvement in celebrity lives. Sites such as AOL's TMZ.com provide a constant feed of personal information—conveniently sorted into categories such as Break-Ups and Train Wrecks—with a submissions page promising that "all hot tips are immediately forwarded to TMZ staff." On Gawker.com, readers contribute to a Stalker page, where a map of New York City is continuously annotated with celebrity sightings. On a recent afternoon, actor Alec Baldwin was spotted talking on a cell phone at Broadway and West 65th Street. "He is goin' nuts," reported a citizen gossip monger. "Totally unreal."

Celebrities can also contribute to their wiki image. Many have chosen to blog in self-defense. On her MySpace page, the formerly full-figured porn star Jenna Jameson addresses gossip about her weight loss. "People are hateful and accuse me of being a drug addict or an anorexic," she writes. "Does anyone remember the fact that I am going through a nasty divorce?" And in the Huffington Post, Mia Farrow presents a photo diary of her travels in Darfur, signaling her transformation from actress to activist.

Obviously, there's a distinction between Jameson's self-serving jottings and Farrow's authentic activism. Like Bono and Angelina Jolie, Farrow is leveraging her celebrity for the benefit of society. The 24/7 availability of today's wiki celebrities, their total negotiability as conversational pawns, probably makes it easier for people with something to say to be taken seriously. The wiki celebs so flawlessly deliver grade-A gossip that Farrow, Bono, and Jolie are freed to promote worthy causes and appear in photo ops with world leaders. But the greater significance is for the thinkers and innovators—those deserving of long-term fame—who may now be able to totally circumvent the papparazzi treatment. Perhaps with less attention from everyone, Lindbergh would have made commercial aircraft as efficient as *The Spirit of St. Louis*. But he died nine years before Justin Kan was born.

Mirror, Mirror On the Web

By Lakshmi Chaudhry
The Nation, January 29, 2007

"Everyone, in the back of his mind, wants to be a star," says You-Tube co-founder Chad Hurley, explaining the dizzying success of the online mecca of amateur video in *Wired* magazine. And thanks to MySpace, YouTube, Facebook, LiveJournal and other bastions of the retooled Web 2.0, every Jane, Joe or Jamila can indeed be a star, be it as wannabe comics, citizen journalists, lip-syncing geeks, military bloggers, aspiring porn stars or even rodent-eating freaks.

We now live in the era of micro-celebrity, which offers endless opportunities to celebrate that most special person in your life, i.e., you—who not coincidentally is also *Time* magazine's widely derided Person of the Year for 2006. An honor once reserved for world leaders, pop icons and high-profile CEOs now belongs to "you," the ordinary netizen with the time, energy and passion to "make a movie starring my pet iguana . . . mash up 50 Cent's vocals with Queen's instrumentals . . . blog about my state of mind or the state of the nation or the *steak-frites* at the new bistro down the street."

The editors at *Time* tout this "revolution" in the headiest prose: "It's a story about community and collaboration on a scale never seen before. It's about the cosmic compendium of knowledge Wikipedia and the million-channel people's network YouTube and the online metropolis MySpace. It's about the many wresting power from the few and helping one another for nothing and how that will not only change the world, but also change the way the world changes."

This is the stuff of progressive fantasy: change, community, collaboration. And it echoes our cherished hope that a medium by, of and for the people will create a more democratic world. So it's easy to miss the editorial sleight of hand that slips from the "I" to the "we," substitutes individual self-expression for collective action and conflates popular attention with social consciousness.

For all the talk about coming together, Web 2.0's greatest successes have capitalized on our need to feel significant and admired and, above all, to be seen. The latest iteration of digital democracy has indeed brought with it a new democracy of fame, but in doing so it has left us ever more in the thrall of celebrity, except now we have a better shot at being worshiped ourselves. As MySpace luminary Christine Dolce told the *New York Post*, "My favorite comment is when people say that I'm their idol. That girls look up to me."

So we upload our wackiest videos to YouTube, blog every sordid detail of our personal lives so as to insure at least fifty inbound links, add 200 new "friends" a day to our MySpace page with the help of friendflood.com, all the time hoping that one day all our efforts at self-promotion will merit—at the very least—our very own Wikipedia entry.

In *The Frenzy of Renown*, written in 1986, Leo Braudy documented the long and intimate relationship between mass media and fame. The more plentiful, accessible and immediate the ways of gathering and distributing information have become, he wrote, the more ways there are to be known: "In the past that medium was usually literature, theater, or public monuments. With the Renaissance came painting and engraved portraits, and the modern age has added photography, radio, movies, and television. As each new medium of fame appears, the human image it conveys is intensified and the number of individuals celebrated expands." It's no surprise then that the Internet, which offers vastly greater immediacy and accessibility than its top-down predecessors, should further flatten the landscape of celebrity.

The democratization of fame, however, comes at a significant price. "Through the technology of image reproduction and information reproduction, our relation to the increasing number of faces we see every day becomes more and more transitory, and 'famous' seems as devalued a term as 'tragic,'" Braudy wrote. And the easier it is to become known, the less we have to do to earn that honor. In ancient Greece, when fame was inextricably linked to posterity, an Alexander had to make his mark on history to insure that his praises would be sung by generations to come. The invention of the camera in the nineteenth century introduced the modern notion of fame linked inextricably to a new type of professional: the journalist. Aspiring celebrities turned increasingly to achievements that would bring them immediate acclaim, preferably in the next day's newspaper, and with the rise of television, on the evening news.

The broadcast media's voracious appetite for spectacle insured that notoriety and fame soon became subsumed by an all-encompassing notion of celebrity, where simply being on TV became the ultimate stamp of recognition. At the same time, advertisers sought to redefine fame in terms of buying rather than doing, fusing the American Dream of material success with the public's hunger for stars in programs such as *Lifestyles of the Rich and Famous*.

But the advent of cyber-fame is remarkable in that it is divorced from any significant achievement—farting to the tune of "Jingle Bells," for example, can get you on VH1. While a number of online celebrities are rightly known for doing something (a blogger like Markos Moulitsas, say), and still others have leveraged their virtual success to build lucrative careers (as with the punk-rock group Fall Out Boy), it is no longer necessary to do either in order to be "famous."

Fame is now reduced to its most basic ingredient: public attention. And the attention doesn't have to be positive either, as in the case of the man in Belfast who bit the head off a mouse for a YouTube video. "In our own time merely being looked at carries all the necessary ennoblement," Braudy wrote twenty years ago, words that ring truer than ever today.

Celebrity has become a commodity in itself, detached from and more valuable than wealth or achievement. Even rich New York socialites feel the need for their own blog, socialiterank.com, to get in on the action. The advice for aspiring celebutantes may be tongue-in-cheek—"To become a relevant socialite, you are virtually required to have your name in the press"—but no less true in this age of Paris Hilton wannabes.

> Celebrity has become a commodity in itself, detached from and more valuable than wealth or achievement.

Fame is no longer a perk of success but a necessary ingredient, whether as a socialite, chef, scholar or skateboarder. "For a great many people it is no longer enough to be very good at what you do. One also has to be a public figure, noticed and celebrated, and preferably televised," writes Hal Niedzviecki in his book *Hello, I'm Special*. When it is more important to be seen than to be talented, it is hardly surprising that the less gifted among us are willing to fart our way into the spotlight.

The fantasy of fame is not new, but what is unprecedented is the primacy of the desire, especially among young people. "I wanna be famous because I would love it more than anything. . . . Sometimes I'll cry at night wishing and praying for a better life to be famous . . . To be like the others someday too! Because i know that I can do it!" declares Britney Jo, writing on iWannaBeFamous.com.

She is hardly unusual. A 2000 Interprise poll revealed that 50 percent of kids under 12 believe that becoming famous is part of the American Dream. It's a dream increasingly shared by the rest of the world, as revealed in a recent survey of British children between 5 and 10, who most frequently picked being famous as the "very best thing in the world." The views of these young children are no different from American college freshmen, who, according to a 2004 survey, most want to be an "actor or entertainer."

Our preoccupation with fame is at least partly explained by our immersion in a media-saturated world that constantly tells us, as Braudy described it, "we should [be famous] if we possibly can, because it is the best, perhaps the only, way to be." Less obvious, however, is how our celebrity culture has fueled, and been fueled by, a significant generational shift in levels of narcissism in the United States.

In the 1950s, only 12 percent of teenagers between 12 and 14 agreed with the statement, "I am an important person." By the late 1980s, the number had reached an astounding 80 percent, an upward trajectory that shows no sign of reversing. Preliminary findings from a joint study conducted by Jean Twenge, Keith Campbell and three other researchers revealed that an average college student in 2006 scored higher than 65 percent of the students in 1987 on the standard Narcissism Personality Inventory test, which includes statements such as "I am a special person," "I find it easy to manipulate people" and "If I were on the *Titanic*, I would deserve to be on the *first* lifeboat." In her recent book *Generation Me*, Twenge applies that overarching label to everyone born between 1970 and 2000.

According to Twenge and her colleagues, the spike in narcissism is linked to an overall increase in individualism, which has been fostered by a number of factors, including greater geographical mobility, breakdown of traditional communities and, more important, "the self-focus that blossomed in the 1970s [and] became mundane and commonplace over the next two decades." In schools, at home and in popular culture, children over the past thirty-odd years have been inculcated with the same set of messages: You're special; love yourself; follow your dreams; you can be anything you want to be.

These mantras, in turn, have been woven into an all-pervasive commercial narrative used to hawk everything from movie tickets to sneakers. Just do it, baby, but make sure you buy that pair of Nikes first. The idea that every self is important has been redefined to suit the needs of a cultural marketplace that devalues genuine community and selfhood in favor of "success." In this context, "feeling good about myself" becomes the best possible reason to staple one's stomach, buy that shiny new car, or strip for a Girls Gone Wild video. The corollary of individualism becomes narcissism, an inflated evaluation of self-worth devoid of any real sense of "self" or "worth."

Since a key component of narcissism is the need to be admired and to be the center of attention, Generation Me's attraction to fame is inevitable. "You teach kids they're special. And then they watch TV, the impression they get is that everyone should be rich and famous. Then they hear, 'You can be anything you want.' So they're like, 'Well, I want to be rich and famous,'" says Twenge. Or if not rich and famous, at least to be "seen"—something the rest of us plebeians can now aspire to in the brave new media world. "To be noticed, to be wanted, to be loved, to walk into a place and have others care about what you're doing, even what you had for lunch that day: that's what people want, in my opinion," *Big Brother* contestant Kaysar Ridha told the *New York Times*, thus affirming a recent finding by Drew Pinsky and Mark Young that reality TV stars are far more narcissistic than actors, comedians or musicians—perhaps because they reflect more closely the reason the rest of us are obsessed more than ever with "making it."

Not only do Americans increasingly want to be famous, but they also believe they *will* be famous, more so than any previous generation. A Harris poll conducted in 2000 found that 44 percent of those between the ages of 18 and 24 believed it was at least somewhat likely that they would be famous for a short period. Those in their late twenties were even more optimistic: Six in ten expected that they would be well-known, if only briefly, sometime in their lives. The rosy predictions of our destiny, however, contain within them the darker conviction that a life led outside the spotlight would be without value. "People want the kind of attention that celebrities receive more than anything else," says Niedzviecki. "People want the recognition, the validation, the sense of having a place in the culture [because] we no longer know where we belong, what we're about or what we should be about."

Without any meaningful standard by which to measure our worth, we turn to the public eye for affirmation. "It's really the sense that Hey, I exist in this world, and that is important. That I matter," Niedzviecki says. Our "normal" lives therefore seem impoverished and less significant compared with the media world, which increasingly represents all that is grand and worthwhile, and therefore more "real."

No wonder then that 16-year-old Rachel, Britney Jo's fellow aspirant to fame on iWannaBeFamous.com, rambles in desperation, "I figured out that I am tired of just dreaming about doing something, I am sick of looking for a 'regular' job . . . I feel life slipping by, and that 'something is missing' feeling begins to dominate me all day and night, I can't even watch the Academy Awards ceremony without crying . . . that is how I know . . . that is me. . . . I have to be . . . in the movies!!!"

The evolution of the Internet has both mirrored and shaped the intense focus on self that is the hallmark of the post-boomer generation. "If you aren't posting, you don't exist. People say, 'I post, therefore I am,'" Rishad Tobaccowala, CEO of Denuo, a new media consultancy, told *Wired*, inadvertently capturing the essence of Web 2.0, which is driven by our hunger for self-expression. Blogs, amateur videos, personal profiles, even interactive features such as Amazon.com's reviews offer ways to satisfy our need to be in the public eye.

But the virtual persona we project online is a carefully edited version of ourselves, as "authentic" as a character on reality TV. People on reality TV "are ultra-self-aware versions of the ordinary, überfacsimiles of themselves in the same way that online personals are *recreations* of self constantly tweaked for maximum response and effect," writes Niedzviecki in his book.

Self-expression glides effortlessly into self-promotion as we shape our online selves—be it on a MySpace profile, LiveJournal blog or a YouTube video—to insure the greatest attention. Nothing beats good old-fashioned publicity even in the brave new world of digital media. So it should come as no shock that the oh-so-authentic

LonelyGirl15 should turn out to be a PR stunt or that the most popular person on MySpace is the mostly naked Tila Tequila, the proud purveyor of "skank-pop" who can boast of 1,626,097 friends, a clothing line, a record deal and making the cover of *Maxim UK* and *Stuff* magazines. YouTube has become the virtual equivalent of Los Angeles, the destination de rigueur for millions of celebrity aspirants, all hoping they will be the next Amanda Congdon, the videoblogger now with a gig on ABCNews.com, or the Spiridellis brothers, who landed venture capital funding because of their wildly popular video "This Land."

Beginning with the dot-com boom in the 1990s through to its present iteration as Web 2.0, the cultural power of the Internet has been fueled by the modern-day Cinderella fantasy of "making it." With their obsessive focus on A-list bloggers, upstart twentysomething CEOs and an assortment of weirdos and creeps, the media continually reframe the Internet as yet another shot at the glittering prize of celebrity. "We see the same slow channeling of the idea that your main goal in life is to reach as many people as possible all over the world with your product. And your product is you," says Niedzviecki. "As long as that's true, it's very hard to see how the Internet is going to change that." As long as more democratic media merely signify a greater democracy of fame—e.g., look how that indie musician landed a contract with that major label—we will remain enslaved by the same narrative of success that sustains corporate America.

In our eagerness to embrace the web as a panacea for various political ills, progressives often forget that the Internet is merely a medium like any other, and the social impact of its various features—interactivity, real-time publishing, easy access, cheap mass distribution—will be determined by the people who use them. There is no doubt that these technologies have facilitated greater activism, and new forms of it, both on- and offline. But we confuse the web's promise of increased visibility with real change. Political actions often enter the ether of the media world only to be incorporated into narratives of individual achievement. And the more successful among us end up as bold-faced names, leached dry of the ideas and values they represent—yet another face in the cluttered landscape of celebrity, with fortunes that follow the usual trajectory of media attention: First you're hot, and then you're not.

"It's all about you. Me. And all the various forms of the First Person Singular," writes cranky media veteran Brian Williams in his contribution to *Time*'s year-end package. "Americans have decided the most important person in their lives is . . . them, and our culture is now built upon that idea." So, have we turned into a nation of egoists, uninterested in anything that falls outside our narrow frame of self-reference?

As Jean Twenge points out, individualism doesn't necessarily preclude a social conscience or desire to do good. "But [Generation Me] articulates it as 'I want to make a difference,'" she says. "The outcome is still good, but it does put the self in the center." Stephen Duncombe, on the other hand, author of the new book *Dream: Reimagining Progressive Politics in an Age of Fantasy*, argues that rather than dismiss our yearning for individual recognition, progressives need to create real-world alternatives that offer such validation. For example, in place of vast anonymous rallies that aim to declare strength in numbers, he suggests that liberal activism should be built around small groups. "The size of these groups is critical. They are intimate affairs, small enough for each participant to have an active role in shaping the group's direction and voice," he writes. "In these 'affinity groups,' as they are called, every person is recognized: in short, they exist."

Such efforts, however, would have to contend with GenMe's aversion to collective action. "The baby boomers were self-focused in a different way. Whether it was self-examination like EST or social protest, they did everything in groups. This new generation is allergic to groups," Twenge says. And as Duncombe admits, activism is a tough sell for a nation weaned on the I-driven fantasy of celebrity that serves as "an escape from democracy with its attendant demands for responsibility and participation."

There is a happier alternative. If these corporate technologies of self-promotion work as well as promised, they may finally render fame meaningless. If everyone is onstage, there will be no one left in the audience. And maybe then we rock stars can finally turn our attention to life down here on earth. Or it may be life on earth that finally jolts us out of our admiring reverie in the mirrored hall of fame. We forget that this growing self-involvement is a luxury afforded to a generation that has not experienced a wide-scale war or economic depression. If and when the good times come to an end, so may our obsession with fame. "There are a lot of things on the horizon that could shake us out of the way we are now. And some of them are pretty ugly," Niedzviecki says. "You won't be able to say that my MySpace page is more important than my real life. . . . When you're a corpse, it doesn't matter how many virtual friends you have." Think global war, widespread unemployment, climate change. But then again, how cool would it be to bog your life in the new Ice Age—kind of like starring in your very own *Day After Tomorrow*. LOL.

She's Famous (and So Can You)

BY GUY TREBAY
THE NEW YORK TIMES, OCTOBER 28, 2007

Tila Tequila turned 26 on Wednesday, and the reader is advised to do whatever is necessary to forget that useless fact. Wipe it, as the metaphor goes, from the hard drive. Try also to obliterate the knowledge that Tequila is not, oddly enough, her real name (Nguyen is); that she is what Wikipedia—in an entry only slightly less extensive than that on Sigrid Undset, the Norwegian novelist and 1928 Nobel laureate for literature—refers to as an "American glamour model"; that she is a former performer on the Fuse cable TV show called "Pants-Off Dance-Off"; that she is the centerpiece of a hit MTV television series "A Shot at Love With Tila Tequila," which made its debut early on Oct. 9 and was immediately, as the Hollywood Reporter noted, No. 1 in its time period in the network's target demographic of people 18 to 34; and that the signal reason for this breakout success may also be the basis for Ms. Tequila's unconventional fame, her boast that she has 1,771,920 MySpace friends.

Dispose of the information. You won't need it for long.

How, one may ask, is it possible for a personality who great hunks of the citizenry never imagined existed to build up a social network more populous than Dallas? How can Tila Tequila have become enormously famous having done little of note beyond appearing as Playboy's Cyber Girl of the Week? When exactly in the Warholian arc of fame did we arrive at a point where we create celebrities of people so little accomplished that they make Paris Hilton look like Marie Curie?

It's routine to dismiss these people, to sniff from the sideline about the depths to which the culture has sunk. Misses Hilton and Tequila may represent, respectively, leisure-class and working-class variants of the same feminine caricature, a real-time Betty Boop. And yet each, in her own way, has divined truths about the marketplace that academics and industry are still laboring fully to comprehend. Each has understood the wacko populism of the cybersphere and pitched her ambitions to capitalize on what Joshua Gamson, the author of "Claims to Fame: Celebrity in Contemporary America" calls "a shift from top-down manufactured celebrity to a kind of lateral, hyper-democratic celebrity."

"Because of new technologies, we get to see now what happens when people have the option of making up their own celebrity," Mr. Gamson said. "We've gone from 'Oh, my God, they're so much better than I am,' to 'Oh, my God, they're so good at making themselves up.'"

We've gone from dazed idolatry to another and more familiar form of identification. Fame, when not concocted by Hollywood and available to only the genetically gifted few, takes on softer contours. It becomes less an exalted state than a permeable one, available to those from classes and cohorts that, in the days of the studio monoliths, the gatekeepers of the star-making machine kept at bay.

By the standards of the new "Jackass" landscape, traditional stardom, with its career building stations-of-the-cross, its rigid talent requirements, its "Entourage" shtick, seems clunky and out of step with a culture so much more fluid now that a hit record—like the recent Internet sensation "I'll Kill Her," by Soko—could emerge from a young French woman's bedroom and MySpace page.

Who says any longer that one must be able to sing or dance or emote in order to attract an audience or, anyway, a batch of new friends in the ether? Who says that only winners win? As reality TV, with its durable affection for flame-outs, car wrecks and actual losers, has made abundantly clear, even after the tribal council has voted you off their tropical island, you're still welcome in our homes.

When Jake Halpern set out to write "Fame Junkies," his book about what is now a universal obsession with celebrity, he was surprised to uncover studies demonstrating that 31 percent of American teenagers had the honest expectation that they would one day be famous and that 80 percent thought of themselves as truly important. (The figure from the same study conducted in the 1950s was 12 percent.)

"Obviously people have been having delusions of grandeur since the beginning of time, but the chances of becoming well known were much slimmer" even five years ago than they are today, Mr. Halpern said. "There are an incredibly large number of venues for becoming known. Talent is not a prerequisite."

The easiest thing to say about Ms. Tequila is that she lacks talent. In a review of "A Shot at Love with Tila Tequila"—whose flimsy premise offers 16 straight men and 16 lesbians the usual chance to swill alcohol, hang around in board shorts and bikinis (and, let's not forget, heels) and compete for her affections—a New York Times critic said she would rather watch a dating show starring Danny DeVito than endure another second of psychodrama with Ms. Tequila's sad-sack entourage.

Yet if Ms. Tequila is no Julie Harris, if she is not stereotypically stellar, she is still a hypnotic presence on the screen. Perhaps it is how her large head sits atop a pert pneumatic torso. Perhaps it is the way her wide-set eyes give her the look of a figure from an anime cartoon. Perhaps it is the steeliness of her will to succeed on whatever terms and the insistent sincerity she brings to the task.

With Ms. Tequila's hardscrabble upbringing, her story certainly contains elements of the classic show-business redemption narrative. Her family emigrated from postwar Vietnam to Singapore and later moved to Houston, where they lived in public housing and where, as she once said in an interview with Import Tuner, a car magazine, she became deeply disoriented about her identity: "I was really confused then, because at first I thought I was black, then I thought I was Hispanic and joined a cholo gang."

To judge from myriad Internet snapshots with captions like "Tila in Red Bikini," though, it is not the Emma Lazarus dimension of her tale that made Tila Tequila a social-network-magnet on MySpace or, for that matter, impossible to look away from on even the tiniest of hand-held screens.

It has been said many times of the Internet that it radically subverts the traditional relationship between high and low, in terms both of culture and class. Yet Meg Whitman, the chief executive of eBay, did not get her career start posing for the video game "Street Racing Syndicate" and, absent a miracle, Tila Tequila's chances of taking the helm of eBay are nil. Some structures remain rigid, and so it's worth pointing out that the primary purpose of trash entertainment may not be to provide critics with opportunities to take potshots, but to hold a mirror up to a constituency for whom Tila Tequila is more home-girl than pole-dancing oddity.

People watch her show and mob her on MySpace because, in some sense, they already know someone like her and are looking to participate in a trajectory that has vaulted her out of the projects, away from gangs and into an echelon of the "entertainment industry" that, while it will never include invitations to the Vanity Fair Oscar party or drinks at the Ivy with Demi Moore, still manages to give her recognition, limousine service and a shot at "love" with 32 brand new friends.

"Whether you think Tila Tequila is corny or not, she already has a certain legitimacy to her name," said Roger Gastman, the editor of Swindle magazine, an indie journal and Web site. Its most recent issue has Death and Fame as its theme. Tila Tequila may have "started out very niche, but she has crossed over to the mainstream," said Mr. Gastman, citing what he termed "a body of work" including a Maxim cover, a hit show, a MySpace page that now links to a site offering guidance on how to become like her. "Tila could probably do signings at comic book conventions forever if she wanted to," Mr. Gastman said.

And this would undoubtedly suit Ms. Tequila, for whom fame, she said, was never actually so much the goal as was fulfilling her love for acting and dancing and stripping and modeling and singing and, not incidentally, escaping the limited career growth available to someone who not long ago was posing half-naked on car hoods.

"The press and the media have glorified the celebrity thing and brainwashed people to live in that world," Ms. Tequila said. "People try to stand out for nothing and they end up getting quote-unquote famous. I'm not into that at all. If you're just into fame for fame, I'm like, 'O.K., but what are you good at? What can you actually do?'"

BIBLIOGRAPHY

Books

Boorstin, Daniel. *The Image: A Guide to Pseudo-Events in America*. New York: Atheneum, 1971.

Braudy, Leo. *The Frenzy of Renown: Fame and Its History*. New York: Vintage, 1997.

Cashmore, Ellis. *Celebrity Culture*. New York: Routledge, 2006.

De Zengotita, Thomas. *Mediated: How the Media Shapes Your World and the Way You Live in It*. New York: Bloomsbury, 2005.

Dyer, Richard. *Heavenly Bodies: Film Stars and Society, 2nd Edition*. New York: Routledge, 2004.

Evans, Andrew, and Glenn D. Wilson. *Fame: The Psychology of Stardom*. London: VISION, 1999.

Gamson, Joshua. *Claims to Fame: Celebrity in Contemporary America*. Berkeley: University of California Press, 1994.

Giles, David. *Illusions of Immortality: A Psychology of Fame and Celebrity*. New York: St. Martin's Press, 2000.

Guinn, Jeff. *The Sixteenth Minute: Life in the Aftermath of Fame*. New York: Jeremy P. Tarcher/Penguin, 2005.

Holmes, Su, and Sean Redmond, eds. *Framing Celebrity: New Directions in Celebrity Culture*. New York: Routledge, 2006.

Kroeber, Alfred. *The Nature of Culture*. Chicago: University of Chicago Press, 1952.

Lasch, Christopher. *The Culture of Narcissism: American Life in an Age of Diminishing Expectations*. New York: Norton, 1991.

Marshall, P. David. *Celebrity and Power: Fame in Contemporary Culture*. Minneapolis: University of Minnesota Press, 1997.

————, ed. *The Celebrity Culture Reader*. New York: Routledge, 2006.

Mills, Robert Lockwood. *The Lindbergh Syndrome: Heroes and Celebrities in a New Gilded Age*. Tucson, Ariz.: Fenestra Books, 2005.

Orth, Maureen. *The Importance of Being Famous: Behind the Scenes of the Celebrity-Industrial Complex*. New York: Owl Books, 2005.

Postman, Neil. *Amusing Ourselves to Death: Public Discourse in the Age of Show Business*. New York: Viking, 1985.

Rojek, Chris. *Celebrity*. London: Reaktion Books, 2004.

Schickel, Richard. *Intimate Strangers: The Culture of Celebrity*. New York: Ivan R. Dee, 2000.

Schroeder, Alan. *Celebrity-in-Chief: How Show Business Took Over the White House*. Boulder, Colo.: Westview Press, 2004.

Turner, Graeme. *Understanding Celebrity*. Thousand Oaks, Calif.: Sage Publications, 2004.

West, Darrell M., and John M. Orman. *Celebrity Politics*. Upper Saddle River, N.J.: Prentice Hall, 2002

Wilson, Cintra. *A Massive Swelling: Celebrity Re-examined as a Grotesque, Crippling Disease and Other Cultural Revolutions*. New York: Viking, 2000.

Additional Periodical Articles with Abstracts

More information about international perspectives on education and related subjects can be found in the following articles. Readers who require a more comprehensive selection are advised to consult the *Readers' Guide Abstracts* and other H.W. Wilson publications.

Becoming Extra-Textual: Celebrity Discourse and Paul Robeson's Political Transformation. Erika Spohrer. *Critical Studies in Media Communication* v. 24 pp151–68 June 2007.

The writer explores how Paul Robeson challenged the essentialism of celebrity discourse in the 1930s. At this time, news media presented celebrities as individuals whose public lives naturally reflected their private lives. Paul Robeson, however, provided a challenge to such seamlessness and in so doing foreshadowed contemporary evocations of celebrity that highlight the fabricated nature of public personas. During the 1930s, the discourse of scandal and movie stardom questioned celebrity seamlessness by constructing Paul Robeson as a site of extra-textuality: Paul Robeson "the artist" became separated from Paul Robeson "the man." Even if still caught up in essentialism, Robeson's extra-textuality was key to his activism, creating the space from which he voiced his most impassioned political polemics. Thus, the regressive discourses of scandal and movie stardom were liberatory for Robeson, helping him to move from spiritual-singing aesthete to outspoken political activist.

24-Hour Party People. Benjamin Svetkey. *Entertainment Weekly* pp9–10 June 15, 2007.

In the 2008 presidential campaign, Hollywood is a crucial battleground for candidates from both parties, according to Svetkey. This year, California's primary schedule moved forward to February 5, joining many other states to create a Super-Duper Tuesday early in the campaign cycle. With voter approval up for grabs, California is currently inundated with White House candidates from both sides. The battle has been savage even by Hollywood's ruthless standards, with death matches between Hillary Clinton and Barack Obama over David Geffen's support—which went to the Illinois senator—and for Steven Spielberg's endorsement, which remains undecided.

War of Words. Benjamin Svetkey. *Entertainment Weekly* pp12–13 February 28, 2003.

Actor Sean Penn is claiming that there is a new Hollywood blacklist against those protesting against war with Iraq, Svetkey reports. On February 11, the 42-year-old actor filed a $10 milion legal action in a California civil court alleging that "the dark era of Hollywood blacklisting" has returned. Penn claims that he and producer Steve Bing had an oral contract to make a comedy entitled *Why Men Shouldn't Marry* but that Bing backed out because of the actor's visit to Baghdad and his outspoken opposition to war with Iraq. Bing denies Penn's charges, however. Indeed, a close look reveals that none of the celebrities who have run into trouble in the delicate cultural climate of post-9/11 Hollywood appear to have suffered any long-term damage. For better or worse, it is difficult to unearth any celebrity who does not feel free to express an opinion about the potential war.

Angelina Jolie Dies for Our Sins. Tom Junod. *Esquire* vol. 148 pp78-85+ June 2007.

According to Junod, celebrity plays a bigger role in the strange story of how celebrities and their perceived power featured in America's response to the September 11, 2001, attacks. After 9/11, the culture's obsession with celebrity intensified, and the celebrities themselves seized on virtue as if it were one of fame's perquisites, with Jolie becoming exceptionally virtuous. In post-9/11 America, Jolie is the best woman alive in terms of her generosity, dedication, and bravery because she is the most famous woman alive. After 9/11, she became a good-will ambassador for the UN's High Commissioner for Refugees, going to some 30 refugee camps in the world's most isolated, inhospitable, and war-torn regions and becoming what she calls a "citizen of the world."

Using Your Star Power. Rob Long. *Foreign Policy* pp74–78 May/June 2006.

The writer offers advice to Hollywood celebrities on how to exert their influence on foreign-policy issues. He suggests that they select their foreign-policy issues carefully, avoid the World Economic Forum, and keep their activism separate from celebrity gossip.

Famous and Fabulous? Candace Bushnell. *Harper's Bazaar* pp196+ February 2000.

The writer, who was responsible for the book upon which the HBO television series *Sex in the City* is based, discusses what it is like to be semifamous.

Garibaldi: The First Celebrity. Lucy Riall. *History Today* v. 57 pp41–47 August 2007.

On the bicentenary of the birth of the Italian nationalist and soldier Giuseppe Garibaldi, the writer discusses his life and career and the circumstances by which he became the first celebrity of the modern political age: Garibaldi represents an alternative, democratic, tradition of political heroism, frequently overlooked by historians more interested in the origins of the authoritarian cults of the 20th century. His fame was a media creation made possible by the expansion in print culture and the increase in mass literacy, as well as the fit between the genres of romantic popular fiction and the spread of radical ideas. His popularity tells us much about the hopes and fears of a nascent mass society, and his military successes help explain the long reach of romanticism and the rapid regime changes of mid-19th-century Europe.

Celebrities Counter the War. Erika Waak. *The Humanist* v. pp20–23 July/August 2003.

The few celebrities who have bravely spoken out against the American war on Iraq are functioning as the only voice of the Democratic Party, Waak contends, even as Congressional Democrats have been broadly silent during the war. Although the media has attempted to portray these celebrities as losing support and even being the subject of ridicule, media exposure has kept them in the public eye and stimulated curiosity in the issues surrounding the war. Furthermore, sales of compact disks, books, and films of these dissenters have increased and boosted careers for the better. These "unpatriotic" celebrities—including Natalie Maines of the Dixie Chicks, rock singer Bruce Springsteen, film director and writer Michael Moore, and actors Susan Sarandon and Tim Robbins—are fulfilling a civic duty by representing those Americans who are too frightened to make their own opposition known but who are speaking out with their dollars.

Visualizing "The Sound of Genius": Glenn Gould and the Culture of Celebrity in the 1950s. Graham Carr. *Journal of Canadian Studies* v. 40 pp5–42 Autumn 2006.

This essay examines the role of photography, film, and television in constructing Glenn Gould's identities as an artist and celebrity in the late 1950s. It combines close readings of visual texts with analyses of published and unpublished primary documents. Gould's sudden rise to fame occurred in a period when technological and corporate changes were profoundly transforming North American music culture. Almost overnight, Gould became highly visible as a mass-mediated figure in the public domain. Beyond the breadth of his exposure, his burgeoning iconography was significant for its style and semiotic contents, which reflected both conventions of traditional portraiture and the influence of contemporary aesthetics. Drawing on media and communications theory, history, and political economy, this article explores the ways in which the visualization of Gould derived from, and contributed to, larger social discourses about music and the body, gender and masculinity, technology and work, privacy and fame. While Gould's exceptional musical talents were obviously crucial to his success, his stardom was equally a function of aggressive marketing strategies that successfully transformed him from a subject of critical adulation to an object of popular consumption.

"Elizabeth Hurley Is More Than a Model": Stars and Career Diversification in Contemporary Media. Lee Barron. *Journal of Popular Culture* v. 39 523–45 August 2006.

Elizabeth Hurley is a prime example of an individual who is a Hollywood "star" in the sense that her status is not dependent on any specific talent but rather is often based on her image and on her public and private activities, reports Barron. As such, she represents a good example of what seems to be a culturally significant trend emerging within the media industry, namely the increasing tendency of "stars" to diversify into a number of roles across the media. Hurley is an actress/model/producer who has used her "brand" name and image to diversify into several mutually reinforcing career strands.

In Defense of Liberal Hollywood. John Powers. *Los Angeles Magazine* v. 52 pp30, 32 September 2007.

The fact that nobody likes being preached at by people in a limo makes Hollywood liberals an irresistible target for mockery, but that does not mean that what they say is wrong, Powers writes. A great deal of today's knee-jerk disdain for Hollywood politics is based on stereotypes, half-truths, and simple misunderstandings, not to mention endless propaganda from right-wing ideologues. With great skill, the Right has demonized Hollywood as a smug, hypocritical elite that has lost touch with ordinary Americans, a charge that can be easily illustrated. Although it is tempting to accuse movie stars promoting liberal causes of hogging the limelight, a large part of the blame lies with the media's addiction to celebrity. The wider problem, however, is the seismic shift in U.S. political culture. If film star activists are more visible than ever, that is not because they are so heroically radical but because the Left has degenerated and there is no reigning idea, unless winning the presidency in 2008 can pass as an idea.

Star-Stricken. Jonathan Durbin. *Maclean's*, v. 117 pp56–57 June 21, 2004.

The writer discusses the public's insatiable appetite for celebrities—and their high-profile meltdowns.

The African Queen. Leon Wieseltier. *The New Republic*, v. 233 p34 October 24, 2005.

Not since the 1960s have so many celebrities been convinced that they can save the world, Wieseltier contends. Recently, the *New York Times* contained an editorial in which it was stated that Angelina Jolie was correct to suggest that investing in village-level programs could do much to reduce poverty in Africa. The same newspaper has highlighted the energetic peace activism of Michael Douglas, whose efforts seem to have been inconsequential. Famous people are also citizens, and they have the right and obligation to act on their convictions, raising money and consciousness. There is, however, the possibility that they corrupt the consciousnesses they raise because they confirm them in their belief in the moral authority of fame.

Celebrity Death. Kurt Andersen. *New York* v. 39 pp20, 22 April 3, 2006.

There are signs that the U.S. obsession with celebrity is waning, Andersen reports. The Nielsen ratings for this year's Oscars were down by 8 percent, and the Grammys ratings dipped by 11 percent. During the last half of 2005, the *Enquirer*'s newsstand sales fell by a quarter and *Entertainment Weekly*'s by 30 percent. The American *OK!* is said to be struggling, the magazine *Inside*

TV was launched and killed last year, and a magazine called *Star Shop* was killed before it began publication. After several decades of rising, the fascination with celebrities is perhaps now ebbing.

The Near-Fame Experience. Jennifer Senior. *New York*, v. 40 pp20–25+ August 13, 2007.

Shows such as *Project Runway* and *Top Chef* allow the Bravo cable channel to cleverly package the fantasy that talented amateurs can achieve overnight success, Senior argues. Contestants have an opportunity to demonstrate what they can do and in the aftermath pursue flourishing careers, but the shows prove to be the easy part. Although the shows promise the contestants, implicitly, that they can compress the savage urban mechanics of success—the political maneuvering, the wearying incremental labor—from a period of years to mere months, reality-show success can not match real-world experience. As with other trashier reality programs, the participants are obliged to exist in freak isolation from the rest of the world and claustrophobic proximity to each other and, although the producers claim this isolation maintains the contests' integrity, the purpose of these extreme measures seems to be to force the competitors to breaking point. In excerpts from conversations, contestants in Bravo reality contests discuss their experiences.

No Frivolity: Davos Tries Fewer Stars. Andrew Ross Sorkin. *The New York Times* ppC1, C8 January 26, 2007.

Klaus Schwab, the founder of the annual World Economic Forum in Davos, Switzerland, has requested that Hollywood celebrities stay home this year as a means of restoring the event's seriousness and purpose, Sorkin reports. Celebrities who attracted the media spotlight in previous years include Sharon Stone and Angelina Jolie, who, while promoting their own pet causes, added an element of glitz to the event.

Death on the CNN Curve. Lisa Belkin. *The New York Times Magazine* pp18–23+ July 23, 1995.

Robert O'Donnell, the firefighter who freed 18-month-old Jessica McClure from an abandoned well eight years ago, committed suicide in April. Fame killed O'Donnell just as surely as the shotgun blast that technically caused his death, maintains Belkin. When O'Donnell rescued McClure, the whole world was watching. He and the other rescuers, attracted by competing offers from movie producers, formed two rival associations, turning on each other. Much of Midland, Texas, where the McClures lived, was also turning on the family. While others returned to their normal lives, O'Donnell couldn't let go of the experience and his brush with fame. He lost his marriage, his job, and finally his life.

Rehab Reality Check. Jerry Alder. *Newsweek* v. 149 pp44–46 February 19, 2007.

The eventual discovery of a pill to treat addiction may end the strange medical field of celebrity addiction, Alder predicts. The all-exonerating, career-reviving ritual of checking into rehab has been a cultural fixture since Elizabeth Taylor first checked into the Betty Ford Center in 1983. In the intervening years, the number of residential treatment programs has increased substantially, and there have been fervent disputes between supporters of differing models of treatment. The true breakthrough in treating alcoholism and other addictions will arrive with the availability of safe, dependable drug treatments. Such drugs could make a substantial difference for people trying to overcome addiction and will end one of modern celebrity's most defining rites of passage.

Stagecraft and Statecraft. Jonathan Alter. *Newsweek* v. 134 p43 October 11, 1999.

Part of a special section on the political aspirations of celebrities. The majority of celebrities have an indirect impact on political campaigns, Alter says, but the increasing mix of entertainment and politics has offered them a new cultural sound stage to air their views on. Celebrities, with the help of the media, tend to trivialize politics by transforming it into entertainment. Their presence further subordinates substance to performance and encourages the media to focus on how something plays rather than analyze what is being said. Celebrities' involvement in American politics from the mid-20th century on is discussed.

Girls Gone Bad? Kathleen Deveny and Raina Kelley. *Newsweek* v. 149 pp40–44+ February 12, 2007.

Like never before, children are being assaulted by images of oversexed, underdressed celebrities, Deveny and Kelley maintain. Children, born in the new-media atmosphere, are fully aware of celebrity antics, but although boys are willing to glance at anyone showing skin, they are bemused by the feuds, fashions, and faux pas of such stars as Britney Spears, Paris Hilton, and Lindsay Lohan. Girls, however, are their most ardent fans. The writers discuss the recent history of female misbehavior and consider whether parents are raising a generation of young girls who dress like sluts, live for designer purses, and can neither spell nor define such words as "adequate" or whether the rise of the bad girl indicates something more profound, a coarsening of the culture and a devaluation of sex, love, and enduring commitment.

The Gossip Minus Guilt. Anna Quindlen. *Newsweek* v. 149 p78 March 5, 2007.

In the current celebrity culture, Quindlen contends, gossip has been transformed into something that is massive in scope and devoid of responsibility. In the past, most of the people doing the gossiping would have had actual knowledge of the people involved and they would have to see them in person, and eye contact has always had a dampening effect on trash talk. Now, the paparazzi and the gutter press are the major purveyors of gossip and consumers are distanced from the subjects. It is easy to blame certain vacuous celebrities for their own fate since they play out so much of their lives through the mass media. Laying the blame entirely on their exhibitionism misses the point that in such an arrangement there are always two parties.

Did You Hear the Latest About Paris-Britney-Lindsay? Jennifer Krause. *O: The Oprah Magazine* v. 8 pp230, 32 October 2007.

The writer discusses the current obsession with celebrity gossip. In a tabloid-fixated, YouTubing, reality-show obsessed world, one has to wonder about the effects of ubiquitous gossip. It remains to be seen whether society is sating itself with empty culture, feeding mindlessly on celebrities' dramas and distresses, and undermining its sense of decency, or whether reveling in famous people's squalid affairs serves a purpose.

In Search of Fame. Joanna Powell. *Parents* v. 75 pp269–70 September 2000.

According to Ron Taffel, author of *Nurturing Good Children*, today's preteens are more absorbed with fame than any preceding generation. This is partly due to the fact that the cult of stardom has pervaded the entire society to an unprecedented degree, and preteens are at a stage in their development that makes them particularly susceptible to this obsession. Advice on dealing with such fantasies is provided, and a sidebar provides tips for parents who are eager for their children to become stars.

Death as a Career Move. Donald Hall. *The Paris Review* v. 45 pp 255–58 Fall 2003.

The writer reflects on the renewed media attention paid to the poetry of his wife, Jane Kenyon, following her death from leukemia at the age of 47.

A School for the Starry-Eyed. Jake Halpern. *Psychology Today* v. 39 pp84–88 November/December 2006.

Many U.S. teenagers are obsessed with recognition, fame, and adulation, Halpern reports. Many educators believe that programs designed in the 1970s to boost pupils' self-esteem may have fostered a culture of narcissism in U.S. youth. Psychologist David Elkind maintains that many teenagers believe they are destined to live exceptional, celebrity-like lives because by their very nature, adolescents cannot grasp what other people are thinking or feeling, so they exist in a sort of egocentric daze, assuming that everyone else is as obsessed with their lives as they are, forming their imaginary audience. Elkind's theory of the Personal Fable contends that many adolescents believe that their destiny is special so they think they do not have to follow conventional rules. Psychologist Daniel Lapsley argues that many teenagers cannot distinguish between daydreams and reality.

The Year of Charitainment. *Time* v. 166 pp93–94 December 26, 2005/January 2, 2006.

The year just ended will be remembered as the year of "charitainment," the writer predicts. For example, over the past 12 months, television networks broadcast celebrity telethons for tsunami and Hurricane Katrina aid and Bono and Bob Geldof organized the Live 8 antipoverty concerts with the assistance of screenwriter Richard Curtis. In addition, charitainment became a genuine TV genre: Joining the ABC do-gooder hit *Extreme Makeover: Home Edition* and Oprah's giveaways and crusades was *Three Wishes*, in which Christian-rock singer Amy Grant bestows largesse on needy people each week. The writer examines the appeal to American audiences of shows about celebrities doing charity work.

Magnificent Obsession. Cintra Wilson. *Utne Reader* no. 99 pp44–47 May/June 2000.

At some point in their lives, all Americans have wished to be famous, Wilson notes. If a person today has any talent at all, it is considered their sacred obligation to seek out fame. In the past, people who became celebrities showed great skill in an artistic pursuit, but talent is no longer the reason for fame, because, as many critics have remarked, people are no longer interested in art for its own sake. Fame is a fundamental destroyer of human values, Wilson concludes, and the only way to dominate it is to stop believing in it.

Bland Ambition. James Wolcott. *Vanity Fair* pp128+ August 2004.

Once upon a time it took talent, time, and originality to become famous, but mass culture is pumping out a stream of reality-TV stars with nothing but copycat beauty and a craving for the spotlight, Wolcott contends. Fame is being defined downward so quickly that it is creating a race of temporary dwarf stars who appeal to those who think small. Looks are vital in popular culture, and everyone is beginning to look alike. With appearance so important, talent becomes a potential handicap to celebrity. Talent takes time to ripen, and it takes time to learn and hone a craft, but these people have no time for time. Mass culture is condescending to, if not contemptuous of, any quest for artistic expression that requires discipline, difficulty, sacrifice, and an adherence to traditions larger than oneself.

Rebels with a Cause. Barbara Howar. *Variety* pp76–79 October/November 2004 supp VLife.

Since the 1970s, Warren Beatty, Robert Redford, and Paul Newman all have channeled their fame for political causes and helped define what it means to be a celebrity activist, Howar says.. Newman, Beatty, and Redford threw their support behind George McGovern's failed presidential bid in 1972. Moreover, Beatty's fund-raising prowess and political strategies were—and continue to be—eagerly sought by and distributed to all viable Democratic candidates. The political activities of Newman, Beatty, and Redford are discussed.

Remember Elvis. Martha Bayles. *Weekly Standard* v. 12 pp43–46 August 20–27, 2007.

The deathless image of Elvis Presley was his own eccentric creation, according to Bayles. Inspired partly by Hollywood movies and partly by the sartorial style of the black musicians who played blues and R&B in the nightclubs of Memphis, his outlandish persona attracted taunts and jeers in the main, but he persisted because he could not help himself. Presley was encouraged to live in a fantasy world where everything centered on his charms and his wishes, so he developed an introverted, shy personality, but he was also desperate to connect with other people. Between July 1954 and September 1956, he became postwar America's first mega-celebrity, but it is still difficult to explain why that happened.

Bam! Making Sense of America's Celebrity-Chef Culture. Victorino Matus. *Weekly Standard* pp17–23 August 20–27, 2007

The writer discusses the current obsession with food and chefs in America. The recent convergence of food culture and entertainment-media-leisure cultures dates back to November 23, 1993, when the Food Network first aired. Conceived by CNN cocreator Reese Schonfeld, the network began with an audience of just 6.5 million subscribers, but that figure has grown to more than 90 million since. Over the years, the Food Network has augmented its programming, talent, and markets, with a trade publication revealing that the network's revenue from ad sales and licensing fees alone amounted to more than $448 million last year. Given the ubiquity of such celebrity chefs as Rachael Ray and Emeril Lagasse, one might think today's celebrity chef culture resembles nothing that has ever existed before, but modern mass-market celebrity chefs can trace their origins to the 19th century.

Index

academic celebrities, 19–20
"Adcult", 60–61
advertising, 62, 125–127, 128–132
    See also branding
alcohol use. *See* substance abuse
Anastasio, Trey, 131
Anger, Kenneth, 140–142
Aniston, Jennifer, 37
Anna Karenina, 79–80
artistic integrity, 128–132
athletes, 41
attractiveness, 22, 36–37, 84–85
    See also glamour
authors, 23–25

Bailey, James, 36
Bakker, Anna Marie, 126
Baldwin, Alec, 121–122
Ballard, J. G., 139
Barnum, P. T., 5
Benjamin, Walter, 134
"bling bling", 6
Bono, 85, 91–92
Boorstin, Daniel, 6–7, 11, 13
branding, 89, 101, 125–127
    See also publicity
Braudy, Leo, 14, 23, 38, 158–159
Brody, Michael, 127
Bryant, Kobe, 101
Bush, George W., 75–77

Caldwell, Christopher, 93–94
Campbell, Keith, 160
Cargill, Oscar, 19
Carson, Johnny, 18, 40
Cashmore, Ellis, 30
celebrity culture
    change in, 5–11
    commodification of music and, 128–132
    consumerism and, 29–32
    in contemporary society, 12–19
    legendary figures, 40–41
    outcomes, 107–117
    scandals, 26–28, 99–103, 104–106, 118–120, 121–123, 124–127
celebrity *vs.* fame, 13–14
celebrity watching
    celebrity-fan relationship, 17–18, 51–52, 104–106, 121–123
    impact, 112, 115–116
    psychology of, 33–39
Celeste, Rene, 133–149
Chaplin, Charlie, 134
Chaudhry, Lakshmi, 157–163
communications revolution, 6–7
Conley, Ann, 54–72
consumerism, 29–32, 130–131
Courtesans, 28
Creedon, Jeremiah, 132
criminal behavior, 19

Davis, Gray, 73–75, 76
Davis, Judy, 110
Dean, Howard, 77
democratization of fame, 155–156, 157–163, 164–166
Derakhshani, Tirdad, 29–32
Dolce, Christine, 158
Downey Jr., Robert, 120
Drezner, Daniel, 87–94
drug use. *See* substance abuse
Dumenco, Simon, 99–103
Dunbar, Robin, 36
Duncombe, Stephen, 163

Eastwood, Alison, 113
Eliot, T. S., 23
Eminem, 146
entitlement, 99
Epstein, Jean, 137–138
Epstein, Joseph, 12–25
Etcoff, Nancy, 36
exposure effect, 36

fame *vs.* celebrity, 13–14
family life, 113–115

fans. *See* celebrity watching
Farrow, Mia, 156
Feyerabend, Paul, 59
Figley, Charles, 108–109, 111, 114
film industy, 9–10
Fisher, Helen, 39
Flora , Carlin, 33–39
Fowles, Jib, 111
Fox, Michael J., 111
Fuller, Bonnie, 35, 38, 102

Gamson, Joshua, 164–165
Gastman, Roger, 166
Gee, Sophie, 27–28
Geldof, Bob, 92
Generation Me, 160
Gere, Richard, 92
glamour, 9–10, 100, 102–103
        See also attractiveness
Goldsmith, Oliver, 14
Gore, Al, 88
Grant, Cary, 17
Grose, Jessica, 26–28

Halpern, Jake, 165
Hasselhoff, David, 121–122
Hatch, Orrin, 78
Henderson, Amy, 5–11
Hilton, Paris, 101, 124
Houran, James, 39
Hung, William, 37
Hurley, Chad, 157

immigration, 8–9
immunity, 99, 119
impostor phenomenon, 116
InStyle magazine, 102
Intini, John, 40–41

Jackson, Michael, 41, 99
James, Caryn, 104–106, 121–123
Jameson, Jenna, 156
Jennifer Lopez, 37
Jolie, Angelina, 85, 87–88

Kamons, Andrew, 84–86
Kan, Justin, 155
Kanazawa, Satoshi, 35
Keats, Jonathon, 155–156
Keillor, Garrison, 112
Kenrick, Douglas, 36
Kilbourne, Jean, 129
King, Larry, 105

Kniffin, Kevin, 37

Lasch, Christopher, 107, 116
Leibowitz, Ed, 81–83
Lewis, R. W. B., 6
Limbaugh, Rush, 101
Loftus, Mary, 107–117
Lohan, Lindsay, 118–120
Lunden, Joan, 115

Madonna, 37
marriage, 114–115
McAllister, Matthew, 65, 68
McCune, Arthur, 107
McGuane, Thomas, 18
media coverage, 115–116
Melting Pot (Zangwill), 8
Michael Jackson, 101
"Mixed Media Culture", 63
Monk, Katherine, 118–120
Monroe, Marilyn, 118
Moss, Kate, 124–127
music industry, 128–132

narcissism, 160
Niedzviecki, Hal, 159, 161–162

O'Donnell, Rosie, 101
Obama, Barack, 79–80
Oberlander, Bill, 126–127
Oldman, Gary, 109–110
Oprah effect, 79–80
Orman, John, 85

Parker, Sarah Jessica, 113
Perkins, Tony, 116
Petroskey, Dale, 83
Pfeiffer, Michelle, 112
Phoenix, River, 110
"politainment", 54–71
politics
        activism, 50–51, 81–83, 85, 87–89,
                93–94
        credibility and, 49–51
        emergence of celebrities in, 47–49,
                54–71, 73–78
        endorsements, 79–80
        impact of celebrities, 52–53, 54–71,
                84–86, 91–94, 156
        soft news and, 89–90
Pope, Alexander, 27

(Product) Red campaign, 91
Proust, Marcel, 15
public intellectuals, 21–22
publicity, 18, 20–21, 23, 89, 118
Puff Daddy, 130

Quaid, Dennis, 111
Quinn, Aidan, 114
Quinn, Marc, 126

radio, 10
Radner, Gilda, 109
Ramey, Jenn, 125
"Rape of the Lock, The" (Pope), 27
reality TV, 38, 51, 103, 160, 161
relationships, 35–36, 113–115
Robbins, Tim, 81–83
Roberts, Julia, 116
Robinson, Eugene, 79–80
Roosevelt, Franklin D., 10
Rorty, Richard, 58–59

Scandal of the Season, The (Gee), 27
scandals, 26–28, 99–103, 118–120, 124–
    127
Schmid, David, 30–31
Schultz, David, 54–72
Schwarzenegger, Arnold, 50, 73–78
self-approval, 116
"Sell Out", 130
Sennheiser ad, 128–130
Sevik, Greg, 128–132
sexual behavior, 36, 101
Shriver, Maria, 75
Sils, Jennnifer, 115
Simon, Roger, 73–78
Simpson, Bart, 41
Sipple, Don, 75–76, 77–78
Smith, Anna Nicole, 104–106
Solanis, Valerie, 142
Sontag, Susan, 21–22
Spectator, The, 27–28
Spielberg, Steven, 92
sports, 40
Star magazine, 102
Starr, Kevin, 77

Stewart, Martha, 101
Stone, Sharon, 112
stressors, 108–109
Stutzman, Rob, 76–77
substance abuse, 41, 101, 105, 109–111,
    118, 119–120, 121–122, 124–125
Sundheim, Duf, 77

Taylor, Elizabeth, 118
television, 11, 35
    See also reality TV
Tequila, Tila, 164–166
Tobaccowala, Rishad, 161
Trebay, Guy, 124–127, 164–166
Twenge, Jean, 160, 162
Twitchell, James, 57–58, 60–62, 126
Tyler, Liv, 113

Urbanski, Douglas, 109–110

vaudeville, 8
Ventura, Jesse, 54–72, 85

Warhol, Andy, 13, 135–137, 142–143,
    144–146
Weah, George, 85
Wellisch, David, 110–111, 114
Wenner, Jann, 100
West, Cornel, 20
West, Darrell M., 47–53, 85
White, William Allen, 8
Williams, Brian, 162
Williams, James "Diamond", 131
Williams, Robin, 120
Williams, Ted, 13–14
Wilson, David Sloan, 37
Wilson, Edmund, 23
Winfrey, Oprah, 79–80
World Wrestling Federation (WWF), 62
writers, 23–25

YouTube, 162

Zangwill, Israel, 8